Intersections

Intersections

Theory–Practice in the Writing Center

Edited by

Joan A. Mullin
University of Toledo, Ohio

Ray Wallace
Northwestern State University, Natchitoches, Louisiana

National Council of Teachers of English
1111 W. Kenyon Road, Urbana, Illinois 61801-1096

Manuscript Editor: William Tucker

Production Editor: Michelle Sanden Johlas

Cover Design: Barbara Yale-Read

Interior Book Design: Tom Kovacs for TGK Design

NCTE Stock Number: 23317-3050

It is the policy of NCTE and its journals and other publications to provide a
forum for open discussion of ideas concerning the content and the teaching of
English and the language arts. Publicity accorded to any particular point of
view does not imply endorsement by the Executive Committee, the Board of
Directors, or the membership at large, except in announcements of policy,
where such endorsement is clearly specified.

Library of Congress Cataloging-in-Publication Data

Intersections: theory–practice in the writing center / edited by Joan A. Mullin,
    Ray Wallace.
       p.   cm.
    Includes bibliographical references and index.
    ISBN 0-8141-2331-7 : $19.95
    1. English language—Rhetoric—Study and teaching. 2. Interdisciplinary
approach in education. 3. Writing centers.   I. Mullin, Joan A., 1949 –   .
II. Wallace, Ray.
PE1404.I53   1994
808′.042′0711—dc20   94-26357
                                                  CIP

Contents

Introduction: The Theory Behind the Centers

Joan A. Mullin
University of Toledo

In this collection, first- and second-generation writing center practitioners discuss different theoretical cornerstones important to the development and evaluation of effective pedagogy. What becomes evident to readers of these essays is that although authors speak from different perspectives, each writer examines how various forces in collaborative relationships determine texts: they all focus on the collaborative moment during a tutorial. By presenting some theoretical bases underlying practices in writing centers, these essays explore the development of our collaborative theory-research-practice cycles. The collection challenges all of us to again reflect on our images of learners, and on our deeply held assumptions about teaching, collaboration, and writing centers.

As a first book on writing center theory, this collection begins to make available to a broader audience what veteran writing center practitioners have learned through research and experience. There are three primary objectives for doing so: Some in our academic community have just begun to look at writing center work with interest; they want to know on what theoretical claims a new writing center could be based, or how to train tutors to meet their theoretical objectives. This collection will make available to them the theory we have found useful, the theory on which they will want to build.

In addition, all of us who have worked with writers know the value of re-visioning the theories that inform our practice. This collection may serve as a resource from which veteran practitioners can review, rework, and critique ideas that, through use, may have become so embedded as to be transparent. Reassessment will enable us to articulate our theories and to review practices that may not be engaging our changing student populations.

There is yet another reason for a book on theory in the writing center. Many in our academic community have not fully investigated writing centers as sites where they may find solutions to conflicts now widely discussed in conferences and position papers. At a recent WPA conference, "Composition in the Twenty-first Century: Crisis and Change" (October, 1993; Miami University;

Oxford, Ohio), participants questioned whether we should abandon composition instruction altogether. As Robert Connors pointed out, since composition,
as a discipline, began at Harvard in the nineteenth century it has been criticized for not producing competent writers for contexts other than composition
classes. Not surprisingly, at this conference small-group discussions dissolved
in frustration as participants addressed the pressure of recently legislated
assessments requiring teachers to produce "results" with students from many
backgrounds, at many levels of ability, and with many different kinds of
literacies. Questions about the effectiveness of process writing practices,
peer-group interaction, academic culture, and definitions of literacy raised
serious doubts about the continuation of composition classes as we know
them. Yet, at the same time there existed a positive sense that our research
about learning and writing continues to provide sound theoretical frames for
creating new practices. "OK," challenged one participant, "In our new Department of Writing we have been told to design as innovative a composition
program as we want—and produce results! Based on what we know about
writing and learning, what should that look like?"

A writing center practitioner would have had several suggestions, but they
would have all derived from one: work in a writing center for a quarter or
semester. This participant could then have understood students' confusion
over assignments from process-based composition classes; she would have
heard students' interpretations of cultural-critique-based writing textbooks;
she could have struggled, along with students, to understand what instructors'
marginal comments meant, and by forming a clear sense of what not to do,
she would have begun to understand what she might do.

The discussions in this collection do not provide a single answer to the
conference participant's question. To do that, each chapter would have to be
expanded to booksize, exploring how a particular theoretical strand applies to
our practice, and then shaping the outcomes of the resulting practice to a
particular classroom. However, our discussions here, our practices, and their
evolution may well surprise those in the composition community who have
failed to see writing centers as resources for resolving problems facing the
discipline and the academy. The collection should also encourage writing
center practitioners to continue their theorizing, research, and practice, and to
move that cycle out of the center in order to explore its wider applications not
just within our own contexts, but in those with which we intersect.

Though all of these articles speak to each other, we have chosen to arrange
them somewhat "chronologically." We start with an examination of writing
center theory to that of the discipline of composition, and then proceed to
examine some of our beginnings: writing center lore, Ken Bruffee's call for

collaboration, and the origins of peer critique in the creative writing workshop. The essays then proceed to both justify and question the collaboration we claim to practice: they call for an examination of who "we" are. As the collection continues, the notion of "we" becomes more complicated. The writers employ theory to examine the cultural assumptions that affect our collaborations. They look at what the students bring to writing center tables—their backgrounds and experiences, their interpretation of the academy and their place in it, their professors and assignments. Likewise, the authors factor in real tutors who bring to the common table their own backgrounds and experiences, their knowledge of the professors, the assignments, and of other students they have tutored—as well as the words of their directors.

Thus, at the outset, Eric Hobson provides an overview of how theory shapes our field and how we have shaped theory to "fit" what we perceive we do. Hobson claims that "no single theory can dictate writing center instruction." He notes that theory and practice have trouble keeping up with each other because "writing center theory, to a large extent, is not based on the same foundations as the practice it is most often called upon to justify." This essay challenges all writing collaborators to explore the gaps between what they theorize and what they practice.

Sallyanne Fitzgerald links whole language theory and the day-to-day operation of a writing center. Fitzgerald points out that "working with others in a collaborative setting allows the writer or tutee to process information using all language arts simultaneously, and it allows the tutor to experience this same benefit. Such a mutual benefit reflects the best of what we associate with collaborative learning."

Continuing the focus on using all language arts, Katherine Adams and John Adams promote holistic learning by turning to a consideration of the creative writing workshop. They point out that these groups always acknowledge the individual's authority in ways that one-to-one collaboration may not. They insist that "writing tutors need to view their clients as writers also, who know more about the course material and have their own strengths. Then the tutor can make suggestions, ask questions, work as a real peer, without the burden of teaching and correcting everything." Adams and Adams, therefore, promote "a return to the real center of collaborative or collective learning: the group."

The assumed influence of the group is also a concern of Christina Murphy. Drawing on several examinations of collaboration, Murphy questions some practitioners' wholesale use of social constructionist pedagogy. She warns us that to think "the individual is wholly constructed by his or her social experience and cultural moment is to obviate the very real presence of individual, subjective experience—the majority of which is highly symbolic and often not capable of full translation into linguistic codes or sets that are predetermined by one's culture or society." Murphy points out that social constructionism "provides us with a paradigm that explains a number of aspects of writing instruction; however, to argue that it provides all the answers . . . seems unwise."

Alice Gillam pushes Murphy's questions further by focusing on how our theories about "collaboration" intersect with our "peer" practices. Gillam's microcosmic examination vividly shows how "theoretical constructions of the tutorial process both illuminate practice and, in turn, are challenged by it." It is in the writing center, claims Gillam, that we can "utilize theory to understand and interrogate the rich complexity of writing center practice and the protean forms of writing center practice to interrogate and reinterpret theory."

Janice Neulieb and Maurice Scharton enlarge Gillam's methodology by urging practitioners to move from "linear analytic methods" to ethnographic research models. This study suggests that "other directors write such archaeological ethnographies [like Neulieb and Scharton's] . . . beginning first with the assumptions underlying the births of the centers and moving to triangulated descriptions." Their own case study serves as a model for such a combined effort; they envision providing "a rich testing ground for [their] own assumption that interpersonal warmth is second only to tutorial ability and knowledge of the field." Combined studies, they argue, "would also test what each director sees . . . in his or her own center."

In his essay, Ray Wallace suggests that we continue revising our own definitions of pedagogy by looking "outward for some new, better answers to our field's questions." He explains how tutors' frustration with moving competent writers towards more challenging analyses led them away from areas bound by composition studies to rhetorical linguistics' "text-centered standards of Intentionality, Acceptability, Informativity, Situationality, and Intertextuality." Wallace shows how the collaborative search for workable theory gave new insight into a recurring problem, opened up new personal and tutorial strategies, and changed practices within the writing center itself.

Murphy's and Wallace's evaluations of collaboration gain force in light of Julie Neff's essay. Neff reminds us that the tutor "may have to help the student call up detail in ways that would be inappropriate for the average learner . . . But, paradoxically . . . must, at the same time, help the student be independent through self-cuing." Such statements point to the conflict between our theory and our practice but they are especially meaningful when we consider both the large number of undiagnosed learning-disabled students who find their way to the writing center and the number of techniques used with learning-disabled students that will work with all populations. Neff challenges our "collaborative" practice as she merges theory with case studies to demonstrate how students' learning disabilities change the non-directive collaboration we claim to practice.

Such an analysis gains special import when considered with Muriel Harris's essay. Research on cross-cultural differences demonstrates "what it means to individualize" instruction and "work with multicultural differences," Harris shows how tutors can provide transitional pathways for students from other cultures so they can succeed in our academic environment. This chapter reinforces Harris's long-held philosophy that "writing center theory specifies that we do not 'teach' students anything; we help them learn by themselves, and bridging cross-cultural differences, then, is one more thing we help students learn by themselves."

Harris's and Neff's explorations naturally lead to an examination of the interpersonal context surrounding a tutorial. With her essay, Pamela Farrell-Childers links the multitude of writing center services to the recent emphasis on affective education. She reminds us how the writing center creates an educational environment that taps personal resources and encourages genuineness of behavior, empathy, and respect for self and others—conditions affecting students' abilities to learn at all, and, particularly, to write.

Continuing to focus on that affective domain, Tom MacLennan looks closely at the relationship between tutor and student. MacLennan encourages tutors to approach "a session with an open, supportive, helpful frame of mind." Using Martin Buber's concepts of I-It, I-Thou, and the Narrow Ridge at different points of the tutoring process, MacLennan demonstrates how a "reciprocal relationship can be instituted at every stage of the composing process by remaining open to another's viewpoint and altering your own position when it leads to more effective collaboration." MacLennan and the remaining authors suggest that, despite our training as tutors, our unexamined philosophical positions may undermine the most well-intentioned of our practices.

In the next essay, Jay Jacoby examines the controversy which MacLennan's article suggests: how much intervention should a tutor provide? Effectively using the research (rather than just the metaphors) of medical ethicists, Jacoby concludes with what most tutors fear: "In encouraging the substitution of our discourse for the students' we are potentially erasing at least part of that student's identity—some of his or her authority—in order to meet the demand of the institution." In comparing this to the paternalistic (and colonialistic) position of the physician, Jacoby draws on definitions of "informed consent," applies these to writing center case studies, and suggests that a working knowledge of other medical theories can "help lead to more ethically sensitive tutors and more informed decision making in the writing center."

Using feminist theory to focus on the ethical relationship between student and tutor, writing center director Phyllis Lassner and tutor Susan French point out that writing centers, like women's studies programs, promote "student-centered, active learning as a way of democratizing higher education and

encouraging students to see that they do not have to assume the role of 'other'
themselves." Framed by an examination of the concept of "difference," their
explanation of tutors' self-discovery processes challenges all of us. Lassner
concludes that "only if we accept irreconcilable differences can we truly
respect the integrity of students' identities and explore what kind of learning
takes place between 'peers.'"

However, like our conceptions about gender, our concepts about literacy
can determine whether our tutorials succeed or not. Joan Mullin warns that "if
tutors' deeply held ideas about literacy correspond to a concept of literacy as
technology, then the student does not learn strategies as much as perform
technique." This chapter asks readers to examine their own definitions of
literacy in order to examine the practices based upon them. Mullin concludes
that "students and tutors [must] understand the limitations of a literacy definition which privileges and separates, [so] they can begin to engage in a true
dialogue."

What involves a "true dialogue," and, therefore, what constitutes a collaborative relationship which respects "dialogue," forms the heart of Mary Abascal-Hildebrand's essay. Using interviews with tutors and faculty linked
together through writing-intensive classes, this chapter looks to the "ethical
dimension inherent in the human relationships that make up tutoring." Tutoring seen as a translative process, "tutoring that enables both tutors and students to leave the tutoring event thinking and acting differently as writers,
enables them to renew themselves as persons."

Despite this deliberate organization of chapters, these individual essays
remain true to what theory must do: renew practice and expand perspective
through continued dialogue. For example, Adams and Adams suggest our
creative traditions may hold the answer for renewing and expanding some of
our practices, while Wallace proposes a more structured examination of student writing by using text linguistics as a means of moving tutors towards
solutions for complex textual events. However, both of these theoretical
discussions take on new meaning when grounded in Murphy's and Fitzgerald's very different examinations of collaboration. Like Adams and Adams,
Fitzgerald positively equates collaboration with whole language practices, but
Murphy asks whether theories like these, which lead to social constructionism, ignore factors of individual choice. In light of these discussions, does
Wallace's text linguistics promote collaborative practice, or does his approach
support Murphy's position? Do the Adamses' workshop approach offer a
compromise between Fitzgerald's and Murphy's collaborative discussions?
Do new theories emerge when practices derived from these are combined?

In the day-to-day work of writing centers, some of which is reflected here,
we resist treating learners as objects, or offering templated versions of the
learning experience to cover every instance of collaboration, even as we seek

to compare our experiences. Writing center practitioners can be more respon-sive to the individual learner in ways our composition classroom environ-ments cannot. Centers provide spaces where the personal and public, the individual and other, struggle to honor the singular voice, to recognize differ-ent language communities, without evaluative consequences. Yet those in writing centers also represent an academic culture which excludes individual voices and privileges its own language. The theories represented here help us construct alternative pedagogy to negotiate the thin lines between the conflicts which prevent true collaborations. We invite you also to participate as reader/practitioner/theorist—to continue the conversation begun here, to rear-range, overlap, reflect on, and expand our beginning dialogue.

1 Writing Center Practice Often Counters Its Theory. So What?

Eric H. Hobson
St. Louis College of Pharmacy

Thom Hawkins writes in the introduction to *Writing Centers: Theory and Administration* (1984), "Writing centers are doing so much now with collaborative learning that often their practice outstrips their theoretical grasp of principles behind their work" (xii). If writing center use of collaborative learning, for instance, races far ahead of theoretical support for those practices, the implied disciplinary solution to the problem is to jump-start theory—in this case, theory about collaborative learning and its use. Hawkins calls for that action:

> If writing centers are to continue making the substantial contributions to classroom practices and curricula, if they are to reach a productive and long-lasting maturity, they must do more than patch together fragments of successful theory. (xiii)

To "patch together" carries predominately negative connotations within the seamless, Enlightenment-defined vision of theory. Because of this tradition, the picture of an educational community piecing together bits of theories on which to ground its instruction has not helped reinforce a sense of theoretical and, thus, methodological confidence within the writing center community. This insecurity blinds the writing center community to ways in which contradiction between writing center theory and practice does not represent a structural weakness in the writing center, despite our having been trained to believe that theory and practice must conform. Working from recent critiques of writing center theory and practice (see Clark 1990; Hobson 1992; Murphy, this volume), however, I forward an alternative interpretation of Hawkins's observation: the distance between theory and practice in writing centers that Hawkins notes results less from a lack of knowledge than from how we think about knowledge production.

I would like to examine this theory/practice disjunction via the following theses:

1. Writing center theory has problems keeping up with writing center practice because writing center theory, to a large extent, is not based on the same foundations as the practice it is most often called upon to justify.

2. Beyond this one explanation, however, lies a more deeply rooted problem that reflects the writing center community's insecurity about its allegiance to, and belief in, writing center "lore" as a valid (philosophically *and* methodologically) means of making knowledge: we feel guilty about being more interested in the practice of writing center work than in its theory.

Conventional wisdom—at least within the rationally bounded discourse of academe—reinforces the idea that theory leads to practice. However, as practitioner narratives in composition suggest, the inverse is more often true. Recent critiques of knowledge production in composition suggest that the theory/practice dyad is itself insufficient, especially when theory is understood to mean metatheory—a totalizing explanation of experience. Writing center practice itself is capable of providing an informed self-critique sufficient for validating the knowledge that results from its critical action.

But how has the situation of contradiction and inconsistency within writing center theory and practice happened? The answers to this question are many, and they lie in the developmental history of the writing center movement and its relationship to composition programs. To examine and to critique these inconsistencies we must examine the roots of both writing center theory and writing center practice.

The History of Writing Center Theory and Practice

There was no disjunction of theory and practice in the writing center while it operated under the influence of Current Traditional Rhetoric. Working within an objectivist epistemology, where truth was knowable, neutral, and prescribable, some writing labs had students work on grammar exercises designed to make them master rules. Betty McFarland (1975) writes,

> An objective common to each [composition] course is mechanical correctness. Usually time and/or philosophy does not permit the teaching of grammar in each course; further, the variety and irregularity of student errors would not justify doing so. The logical place for such supplemental instruction is in a laboratory. (153)

The primary responsibility of writing center staff was to spot offending errors in students' papers and to ensure that those errors were corrected.

Throughout the 1970s and well into the 1980s, many post-secondary schools were slow to alter the practice through which writing was taught, even in light of the composition research of James Britton et al., Janet Emig, Mina Shaughnessy, James Kinneavy, Linda Flower and John Hayes, and Nancy Sommers, among others, that challenged the prescribability of writing processes. At many colleges and universities, the writing lab's relationship with the composition curriculum was understood as functional and pragmatic: to ensure classroom teachers that students had learned the rules. Theory and practice were in harmony.

As the composition curriculum responded in the late 1970s and into the mid-1980s to issues raised by the process movement, especially in its later manifestations as epistemic rhetoric, the harmony between the writing center's theory and practice began to crumble. In the old curriculum, the writing lab had been expected to simply "fix" writing problems (Harris 1990, North 1994, Wallace 1991). The process movement, however, forced the writing center community into a new phase of theoretical justification. Where the relationship between the composition curriculum and the practices of the writing lab had been clear-cut, there now existed no absolute answers. Practices viable within a positivist epistemology were no longer (politically or economically) credible. Because writing had been demonstrated to be an activity controlled not as much by concrete rules as by the context in which the communicative event takes place, writing centers had to alter their instruction. Instead of having students do workbook exercises, writing centers now had students talk to and work with trained writing tutors in the understanding that together these writers could use the generative power of conversation to discover ways to improve their writing (Bruffee 1984, Harris 1986). When writing centers changed their focuses to the contexts in which writing occurs and the ways these contexts impinge on the creation of texts, positivist-influenced instructional methods (not abandoned wholesale) created disjunctions between writing center theory and writing center practice. This, in turn, precipitated a crisis of identity that caused writing center practitioners to reevaluate not only their practice, but also the foundations on which that practice stood and the aims that practice was instituted to achieve.

Writing center theory grew out of practice because no theory called Writing Center Theory existed. Later, the theory drew from other disciplines because even as isolated, decontextualized events, tutorials do not exist within the tightly defined, disciplinary structures of academe; rather, they work within a process and thus within the complex whole that is the person. Thus, educational, psychological, social, behavioral, and analytical theories as well as the means of investigating them had to be drawn into the writing center and then applied and reconstructed to fit what we do. Early writing centers' practitioners believed that to ensure the writing center community a respectable place within the culture of academe they needed to work within its dominant descriptive paradigm (of theory leading to practice), and so they had to cobble together theories which justified their practice.

Collaborative learning and a commitment to individualized instruction are the most frequently cited theories used since the middle of the last decade to create a theoretical justification for writing centers. And yet, "collaborative learning," Trimbur writes, "is not a theoretically unified position but a set of pedagogical principles and practices worked out experimentally" (1985, 91); collaborative learning theory did not predate collaborative practice, nor can it exist apart from that practice. As the perceived mainstay of writing center theory, collaborative learning reinforces Bruffee's contention that writing center theory's roots are to be found in practice.

The liberatory elements articulated in writing center theory, the attempts to help students understand the systems of power in which they function, have been synthesized from the work of such diverse thinkers and teachers as John Dewey and Paulo Freire, and were appropriated by writing center practitioners to help locate the writing center within the context of challenges to the educational status quo frequent during the last two decades of writing center theoretical activity. Dewey's work, especially as it is presented in *Experience and Education* (1938), demonstrates how traditional education operates through a rigid system of controls—on behavior, school organization, subject matter, evaluation—to create passive individuals, who, while they pose no threat to society, do not learn how to learn in natural settings. "For Dewey," Trimbur notes, "learning should be experiential and should occur through the interaction of the learners and the wider social environment, not through the teacher's imposition of subject matter from above and outside the experience of the learners" (1985, 91). The writing center seemed to be a location for such activity.

Like Dewey, Brazilian educator Paulo Freire critiques traditional education on the grounds that it "teaches students how to live passively within oppressive and alienating structures, to adapt to the world as it is, instead of developing their subjectivity as historical actors" (Trimbur 1985, 93). Describing traditional education through a "banking" model, Freire demonstrates how students are viewed as empty accounts waiting to be filled by teachers who own knowledge. The writing center tutorial, with its "equal" participation of tutor and writer, resembles what Stanley Aronowitz and Henry A. Giroux understand as the "dialogic" nature of Freire's critique of traditional education: "learning occurs within conversation, and not as top-to-down instruction between the teacher and student" (1985, 12). Drawing the connection between Dewey's and Freire's ideas (in a way that is certainly reminiscent of rhapsodic accounts of the writing center tutorial) Aronowitz and Giroux demonstrate how Freire's reflexive concept of knowledge is compatible with Dewey's notion that experience is not reactive, but a creative and meaningful relationship between individuals and their historical and contemporary situation where changed circumstances produce new and transformed knowledge (12). Dewey's and Freire's ideas about educational reforms have been paramount to the development of the theoretical unity within the writing center community, and much of the foundational work in this effort was accomplished by Bruffee.

Bruffee is a synthesizer—the synthesizer the writing center community needed at an historical moment in its development. His articulation of a theoretical base from which to justify writing center activity depends largely on the ideas presented him by many of the most influential thinkers of the twentieth century (e.g., Michael Oakeshott, Thomas Kuhn, Richard Rorty, and Lev Vygotsky). Coming, as did the bulk of his writing, on the heels of the "process movement," Bruffee demonstrated how knowledge is inherently mutable—it changes according to historical and situational factors. This concept allowed many writing center practitioners as well as teachers to understand the profound changes being proposed by advocates of this movement. His assertion that the "conversation of mankind" is the sole basis for arriving at truth, that agreement and consensus among groups of knowledgeable peers is the foundation on which all "knowledge" rests, are direct challenges to positivist epistemologies and practices.

The mid-1970s to early 1980s was a time of intense activity within the writing center community. By 1985, two book-length collections of essays, Harris's *Tutoring Writing* (1982) and Olson's *Writing Centers: Theory and Administration* (1984), as well as the *Writing Lab Newsletter* (1976) and *The Writing Center Journal* appeared. Each attempted to provide the community with a means for sorting out its practice within the theories shaping the composition programs to which most writing centers were connected. The problem was fundamental: with Current Traditional Rhetoric and the mechanistic practices writing centers employed to help students master the prescriptive writing instruction associated with Current Traditional Rhetoric discredited, was there now a specific/prescribable task for writing centers? North (1984) provided the comparatively vague axiom "Our job is to produce better writers, not better writing" (438).

The writing center community knew what the practice of writing centers was within an objectivist epistemology and knew the center's goal was to produce better writing. But, as writing lost its linear and prescribable mask and was revealed to be a recursive and socially dependent activity, the equation of what practices achieve the writing center's goals for the writers who come seeking help with their writing became rather ambiguous. Educational theory and Bruffee suggested that instructional methods linked to collaborative learning and individualized instruction were the best alternatives for writing center practice. Such methods as one-to-one instruction and group tutoring produced desirable results with writers, and the writing center community enthusiastically endorsed these practices. Following Bruffee's earliest discussions (such as "The Brooklyn Plan: Attaining Intellectual Growth through Peer-Group Tutoring" 1978) of the role collaboration plays within student cultures, the writing center community has connected its principle instructional method—the one-on-one tutorial—to the principles of collaborative learning. The community claimed that tutors "are the architects and partners of collaborative learning. They redesign the learning environment so that more of the responsibility and the activity of learning is shifted onto the learner" (Hawkins 1984, xii).

In the midst of the rapid change during the 1970s and early 80s, the writing center community did not have time to examine how, or whether, their instructional practices are compatible with the new theories to which writing centers claimed allegiance.

Practice as Theory

Writing center-based investigations into the compatibility of theory and practice have come in several forms. These critiques, however, all point to a less-than-seamless overlay of theory and practice within the writing center. In 1984 Harvey Kail listed what he perceived to be "major problems with a one-to-one approach as the primary and often the only pedagogical strategy for writing centers." The most interesting of his three concerns for this present discussion is his third: "one-to-one tutoring continues a tradition of isolating students from each other, exchanging one narrow sense of audience (the teacher) for another (the tutor)" (2). Likewise, John Trimbur, in "Peer Tutoring: A Contradiction in Terms" (1987), not only deals with the puzzle mentioned in his title, but critiques the extent to which training tutors to work with writers actually subverts the non-authoritarian atmosphere described as the arena for collaborative learning.

Greg Myers's (1986) critique of collaborative learning, "Reality, Consensus, and Reform in the Rhetoric of Composition Teaching," must also be mentioned in this overview. His critique brings to the discussion the role ideology plays in the creation and perpetuation of any educational theory and practice, an issue heretofore not addressed by proponents of collaborative learning. As such, Myers challenges Bruffee's advocacy of collaborative learning as the means of arriving at communal consensus: Bruffee's program is blind to the reality that consensus is not always desirable.

Frequently, commentators on writing center theory and practice—building on the theoretical positions outlined by Dewey and Freire, for example—herald the liberatory and empowering potential of collaborative learning as central to writing center pedagogy. Even such careful and insightful critics as Kail and Trimbur (1987) have argued likewise: "The power of collaborative learning, we believe, is that it offers students a way . . . to reinterpret the power of the faculty, and to see that their own autonomous co-learning constitutes the practical source of knowledge" (10). Myers's thesis strives to demonstrate that even such laudable intentions often serve to leave students still vulnerable to the caprice of a conservative ideology.

Tom Hemmeter (1990), among others, notes many attempts within the writing center community to create a metatheory and metapractice that finds its epistemological roots in the positivism of Enlightenment thought. Discussing the "fragmentary nature of writing center theory," Hemmeter takes to task those members of the community whose articulations of writing center theory and practice reveal "a desire for wholeness and completeness in a pedagogy which covers all pedagogical bases and which works with the whole student" (39). He demonstrates how continuing to ignore or to explain away the disjunctions that exist between writing center theory and practice "is to fall into the structuralist trap of dualities" (43). Such is the dualistic nature of Enlightenment thought that holds hegemonic sway over the academy and requires us to discount as invalid any theory or practice demonstrated to be contradictory—that is, if we try to play by the rules of conventional theory building.

But, as poststructuralist critiques of positivist epistemology have demonstrated, this trap is fictional; it can ensnare us and our theory and practice *only* when we consent to live by the disciplinary "rules" of non-contradiction. As Sosnoski notes, "Postmodern critiques of disciplinary discourse have shown the limitations of totalizing paradigms, metanarratives, metacommentaries, binary thinking, the logic of consistency, wholeness, integrity, centeredness, and unity" (1991, 201). Likewise, for most writing center personnel, contradiction between their understanding of the theory and practice they employ is not a pressing problem. Echoing Hemmeter, Harkin observes:

> That these notions of writing may be incompatible with each other is not a problem for most practitioners. The inconsistency goes unrecognized because the "law" of noncontradiction is simply not involved and because the teaching practice is successful at achieving its often disparate practical goals. (1991, 126)

We worry that we must be doing something wrong in our work with writers. But, when we consider our theory and practice closely, we can admit (if we choose to do so) that the contradictions between our theory and practice do not negate the value of the work we do in our centers.

The problem we face is this: we have been trapped by a belief that the knowledge-making paradigm of the writing center community is not methodologically or theoretically sufficient to provide valid knowledge for the community—it cannot articulate a theory and practice that conform perfectly to the contours of each other. What results from discounting "lore"—the primary knowledge-making system of the writing center community—is that we are easily trapped by what Stanley Fish calls "theory hope," what Harkin describes as "[t]he belief that we [can] produce a metatheory to resolve this contradiction" (133). Twenty years of trying to produce such a metatheory, however, have not brought us any nearer to the consistency which disciplinary thought makes us desire.

A Critical Writing Center Praxis

What is available to the writing center community is the radical idea (institutionally at least) of acknowledging and articulating the ways that writing center discourse, as pragmatic and as contextually aware as it is, creates knowledge that is valid. This understanding of knowledge can be used to replace the modernist/disciplinary, theory/practice dyads with a more flexible, pragmatic understanding of contradiction as acceptable and responsible. This act of rejecting as valid a strict compatibility between our theory and practice does not mean we abandon wholesale theoretical inquiry about the foundations of writing center activity. If that were the case, this book would not exist: in this collection, the authors demonstrate the point that theoretical exploration grounded in the messy experience of writing center practice is a potent way to resist the empty promises of an overarching writing center metatheory.

Instead, a pragmatic perspective toward writing center knowledge accepts contradiction between theory and practice; we reject the "logic" of dialectics. We recognize Sosnoski's point that "Theory—of whatever sort—is always domesticated to be of use in the classroom" (204). In that domestication it is impossible to maintain a one-to-one correspondence between theory and practice because, in the first place, theory and practice are different types of discourse—theory is propositional; lore is procedural (Phelps 1991, 869). Secondly, the unique circumstances of every instance of application require a unique appropriation and implementation of theory into practice. As the other authors in this collection (especially Christina Murphy) make extremely clear, no single theory can dictate writing center instruction. Instead, we must reshape theory to fit our particular needs in the particular historically located situations in which writing center practitioners find themselves.

We are concerned with enacting a practice that is reflective. To achieve such a self-critiquing practice based on the knowledge provided us by writing center lore, we must keep the following in mind:

> Lore, as the version of the theorem that works, counts as understanding for teachers of writing. It is not however, formed in the way disciplines paradigmatically produce knowledge. It is contradictory. It disobeys the law of noncontradiction. It is eclectic. It takes feelings and emotions into account. It is subjective and nonreplicable. It is not binary. It counts as knowing only in a postdiciplinary context. Whether it counts is a political issue with many consequences. (Sosnoski 1991, 204)

Whether we make writing center lore count is also a political issue with many consequences for how we continue to understand, value, and critique what we do when we work with writers in our centers. We need to recognize and advertise the credibility of the knowledge we can produce as reflective writing center practitioners located "primarily in the intermediate space where activity and reflection transact" (Phelps 1991, 873).

References

Aronowitz, Stanley, and Henry A. Giroux. 1985. *Education Under Siege: The Conservative, Liberal and Radical Debate over Schooling.* Westport, CT: Bergin & Garvey.

Bruffee, Kenneth A. 1978. "The Brooklyn Plan: Attaining Intellectual Growth through Peer-Group Tutoring." *Liberal Education* 64, 447–68.

———. 1984. "Peer Tutoring and the 'Conversation of Mankind.' " *Writing Centers: Theory and Administration.* Ed. Gary A. Olson. Urbana, IL: National Council of Teachers of English, 77–84.

Clark, Irene Lurkis. 1990. "Maintaining Chaos in the Writing Center: A Critical Perspective on Writing Center Dogma." *The Writing Center Journal* 11.1, 81–93.

Dewey, John. (1938). *Experience and Education.* New York: Collier, 1963.

Harkin, Patricia. 1991. "The Postdisciplinary Politics of Lore." *Contending With Words: Composition and Rhetoric in a Postmodern Age.* Eds. Patricia Harkin and John Schilb. New York: Modern Language Association, 124–38.

Harris, Muriel. 1982. *Tutoring Writing: A Sourcebook for Writing Labs.* Glenview, IL: Scott, Foresman.

———. ed. 1986. *Teaching One-to-One: The Writing Conference.* Urbana, IL: National Council of Teachers of English.

———. 1990. "What's Up and What's In: Trends and Traditions in Writing Centers." *The Writing Center Journal* 11.1, 15–25.

Hawkins, Thom. 1984. "Introduction." *Writing Centers: Theory and Administration.* Ed. Gary A. Olson. Urbana, IL: National Council of Teachers of English, xi–xiv.

Hemmeter, Thomas. 1990. "The 'Smack of Difference': The Language of Writing Center Discourse." *The Writing Center Journal* 11.1, 35–48.

Hobson, Eric. 1992. "Maintaining Our Balance: Walking the Tightrope of Competing Epistemologies." *The Writing Center Journal* 13.1, 65–75.

Kail, Harvey. 1984. "The Best of Both Worlds." *Writing Lab Newsletter* 9.4, 1–5.

Kail, Harvey, and John Trimbur. 1987. "The Politics of Peer Tutoring." *WPA: Writing Program Administration* 11.1–2, 5–12.

McFarland, Betty. 1975. "The Non-Credit Writing Laboratory." *Teaching English in the Two-Year College* 1.3, 153–54.

Murphy, Christina. 1991. "Writing Centers in Context: Responding to Current Education Theory." *The Writing Center: New Directions.* Eds. Ray Wallace and Jeanne Simpson. New York: Modern Language Association, 276–88.

Myers, Greg. 1986. "Reality, Consensus, and Reform in the Rhetoric of Composition Teaching." *College English* 48.2, 154–74.

North, Stephen M. 1984. "The Idea of a Writing Center." *College English* 46.5, 433–46.

Olson, Gary A., ed. 1984. *Writing Centers: Theory and Administration.* Urbana, IL: National Council of Teachers of English.

Phelps, Louise Whetherbee. 1991. "Practical Wisdom and the Geography of Knowledge in Composition." *College English* 53.8, 863–85.

Sosnoski, James J. 1991. "Postmodern Teachers in Their Postmodern Classrooms: Socrates Begone!" *Contending With Words: Composition and Rhetoric in a Postmodern Age.* Eds. Patricia Harkin and John Schilb, 198–219.

Trimbur, John. 1985. "Collaborative Learning and Teaching Writing." *Perspectives on Research and Scholarship in Composition.* Eds. Ben W. McClelland and Timothy R. Donovan. New York: Modern Language Association, 87–109.

———. 1987. "Peer Tutoring: A Contradiction in Terms?" *The Writing Center Journal* 7.2, 21–28.

Wallace, Ray. 1991. "Sharing the Benefits and the Expense of Expansion: Developing a Cross-Curricular Cash Flow for a Cross-Curricular Writing Center." *The Writing Center: New Directions.* Eds. Ray Wallace and Jeanne Simpson, New York: Garland, 82–101.

2 Collaborative Learning and Whole Language Theory

Sallyanne H. Fitzgerald
Chabot College, Hayward, California

As a special project for a junior-level writing course, an honors student who plans to teach high school volunteered to tutor several hours a week in the writing center, keep a journal of her experiences, and write a research-based paper about the semester-long, tutoring commitment. Her journal entries over the first few weeks were distinguished by her discoveries about her own knowledge and that of the tutees, but I was surprised to find that she seemed to dominate every tutoring session, even though I knew the tutor's supervisor had trained her to work more collaboratively. Finally, about halfway through the semester, she seemed to achieve what I viewed as a "break-through" when she realized that because she was doing all the work in the conferences students did not seem to be making much progress. From that point on, her journal entries began to center more on the student and on what together they could accomplish. Her journal offered me a unique window on a collaborative writing conference where speaking, listening, and reading all serve writing.

Collaborative Learning Theory

Collaborative theory, as exemplified in the tutor/tutee conference, rests on the belief that knowledge, as Bruffee (1984) contends, is socially constructed:

> If we accept the premise that knowledge is an artifact created by a community of knowledgeable peers and that learning is a social process not an individual one, then learning is not assimilating information and improving our mental eyesight. Learning is an activity in which people work collaboratively to create knowledge among themselves by socially justifying belief. (11–12)

Writing center tutoring sessions offer examples of collaborative learning where tutors and students, either in conferences or in groups, work together on a product to construct meaning. Richard Behm (1989) calls such conferences "a communal struggle to make meaning, to clarify, to communicate"

(6), and John Trimbur (1987) speaks of "co-learners [who] invest in each other as they forge a common language to solve the problems writers face" (26). Finally, Anne J. Herrington and Deborah Cadman (1991) illustrate the value of collaboration in a particular anthropology course, and they conclude, "Individual autonomy was encouraged in the context of collaboration. Indeed, the aim of collaboration with peers was not to reach group consensus on ideas or ways of writing. It was, instead, for individuals to consult with others and, in the social context of sharing ideas and drafts, fashion their own ways of proceeding" (196). Julie Neff, in a later chapter in this volume, illustrates this type of empowering by referring in particular to learning-disabled students. In her essay she explains that we can help learning-disabled students specifically in the writing center by helping them to process language rather than to use it only in one medium.

Yet not everyone accepts that collaborative learning as it relates to social construction is positive. In this volume, Christinia Murphy finds fault with collaboration as it relates to social constructionist theory. She particularly criticizes the aspects, such as affect, that are ignored by theorists who view knowledge as the result of social construction or collaboration. However, the assumption that collaboration results in a leveling effect that excludes individualism seems to me to ignore a major benefit of collaboration. Unlike an emphasis only on the individual, collaboration "frees" each writer to seek his or her own ideas with support from the community. Since language is a social skill, developing one's use of language should be enhanced through a social or collaborative act. The reason for using collaboration, however, lies in a broader theoretical base than simply group work or conferences: the whole language theory underpins the collaborative learning framework.

Whole Language Theory

It is not simply the working together which produces good writing in a writing center, but the practice such work gives the tutee in all the language arts (see Lunsford, Bruffee, and Elbow). In a truly collaborative tutoring session, the tutor helps the student develop listening, reading, speaking, and writing skills simultaneously, so that what occurs is closely related to the benefits of whole language instruction rather than to group work alone. Phyllis Lassner, with Susan French, exemplifies this approach elsewhere in this volume, and she quotes Bruffee's 1984 speech where he explains that "tutors create conditions" where student writers talk and write like writers.

Whole language theory asserts that reading, speaking, writing, and listening, when used simultaneously, will assist each other so that students will more readily achieve success in communication acts. When used in a class-room, whole language approaches include teaching all the language arts simultaneously rather than in separate reading, writing, listening, or speaking lessons. In the writing center, using whole language means combining all the language arts while working on a writer's product. This theory finds its support in learning process theory, which in turn encompasses ideas of map-ping and scheme theory.

Pre-1980 theorists frequently viewed the language arts as separate. This was especially true of the differences stressed between speaking and writing (Emig, Einhorn). But with the acceptance of cognitive psychology's theory of learning processes which is reflected in both the writing and the reading process theories, more and more of us began to see the language arts as a continuum rather than as separate activities (Carroll, Collins and Williamson, Dyson, Green, Reid, Tannen). Gilbert states the case against the separation especially well:

> While the conventional features of spoken and written genres vary, drawing as they do upon different sets of paralinguistic features required to 'read' them, in fact speech and writing are but different modes or channels of the *same* system and so both could be included with the general rubric of language. Spoken discourse carries within it the same traces of absence and deferral of meaning as does written discourse. They are part of the same language system. (1991, 197)

Using all the language arts—Gilbert's total language system— to develop one of them is consistent with learning process theory also. The 1970s saw one change in psychology from a strictly stimulus response approach to wide acceptance of the process theory. The processing theory of learning suggests that we remember because we have processed something so thoroughly that it becomes accessible at a later time. For example, in studying for a test, students who read over their notes aloud are likely to remember the informa-tion more readily than ones who silently read because they are using both the reading and listening skills to process the information and thus to embed it more thoroughly so that they can recall it easier. In a writing center confer-ence, hearing the tutor read aloud what the tutee has written, or the tutee's reading aloud his or her own work, may help the tutee "see" where change is needed so that when composing subsequent drafts, the tutee is better able to remember what may be needed.

Tied to this idea of processing is Jerome Bruner's (1973) concept. He explains that we learn new information by attaching it to information we have already gained or adjusting old information to fit the new. For example, summarizing a reading selection in a journal and then writing about how the selection either "fits" with what the reader already knows or contradicts previous knowledge will help the writer to remember the reading selection because the act of summarizing and of responding embeds the information and allows the writer to call upon that knowledge later. In discussing an assignment with a tutor, a tutee frequently remembers what he or she has studied elsewhere. Sometimes a tutor assists in this process by helping the tutee to remember previous assignments. Or the tutor may share similar experiences to help the tutee make connections. For example, a tutee who has been asked to write about Hamlet's motivation may find it helpful when a tutor asks what the tutee knows about recent news reports of suicide or children who have attempted to murder their step-parents.

Process theory suggests that part of the process of learning may require us to attach new information in a fashion similar to what composition teachers call "treeing" or "clustering." Reading theorists often suggest that students create trees in order to understand the organization of what they have read. Such "trees" relate to the concept maps used in tutorials. For example, a tutor might help a student brainstorm a paper on the changing roles of women by creating a cluster starting with *professional* and connecting to *lawyer* or *policewoman*. Thus, in both writing and reading we are using the approach Bruner (1973) indicates is typical of how we learn.

Reading and writing theorists have suggested that both language arts rely on the processing of information. Traditionally, reading was viewed as a receptive art that takes in information, while writing was considered a productive one which gives form to what is already known by the writer. More recently, we have come to see both reading and writing as simultaneously assimilating and creating meaning. This aspect is repeated in the other language arts as well. For example, listeners both hear what is said and process it to create their own meaning. Therefore, processing language using all the language arts is most likely to benefit students in using one of them.

Several years ago, I experienced the value of using all the language arts in one particular tutorial. The student was an undergraduate psychology major who was trying to write a case study incorporating current literature citations. She was having difficulty explaining the case in the light of the literature although she understood both the case she had followed and the literature she had researched. Finally, I asked her to tell me what she wanted to say while I wrote it down as Zoellner recommends in his talk-write article (1969). The student exclaimed in amazement as she read what I had written, "I said that! That is good!" By using listening, reading, speaking, and writing collaboratively, she was able to express what she thought about both the case and the literature. Working with others in a collaborative setting allows the writer or tutee to process information using all the language arts simultaneously, and it allows the tutor to experience this same benefit. Such a mutual benefit reflects the best of what we associate with collaborative learning.

Collaborative Examples Reflecting Whole Language

In our writing center, we have three types of possible collaborations: writing support groups, tutor-tutor activities, and tutor-tutee conferences. Each collaboration offers an example of how participants engage in using all the language arts, although usually they intend to work only on writing.

Several years ago, we expanded our services to graduate students through voluntary writing support groups (see Fitzgerald, 1991). Collaboration was particularly evident in the second language writing groups, where students shared so many of the same surface-level problems such as subject/verb agreement and inappropriate preposition choice. While they felt comfortable sharing their ideas and their writing because they understood that the group members were experiencing many similar problems, the underlying benefit was the use of all the language arts: by speaking together, reading their papers aloud, and sharing ideas about writing, all participants were able to develop not only their particular writing project but also their speaking, listening, and reading skills.

Of a different sort is the collaboration occurring among the tutors in our writing center and leading to the use of all the language arts. Of course, tutors collaborate on their own projects, turning to each other for assistance with any writing project from an upper level English literature paper to a resume. We encourage tutors to ask each other or the supervisor for assistance if they have questions during tutoring. For example, a tutor might ask another tutor who is more experienced with business proposals to comment on the introduction of a tutee's proposal or on the headings for its different sections. Or a tutor who has just begun to help a tutee with the assignment may ask advice of another tutor who has worked with a similar assignment previously. Of particular note is a collaborative story that tutors began first by writing on a small blackboard and then by adding to the story in a spiral notebook. Even some tutees were motivated to add to the story. This activity involved reading and writing, but it also generated tutor discussions and even arguments as story twists were added and then critiqued by all the participants in both written and oral form. While I doubt that tutors or tutees saw the connection between their story and their tutoring, I believe that this social activity of creating together a written product is a mirror of what happens in a conference and provides just one more opportunity to employ writing, reading, and occasionally speaking in a collaborative effort. In each of these writing center encounters, the tutors employ the various language arts to assist them in either formal tutoring or in their own writing.

Collaboration among tutors is particularly apparent in the computer writing lab that we have added to our center. There, student and professional tutors have created examples to help tutees use a hypertext program, and frequently turn to each other for advice on helping tutees work on-line with a variety of writing projects. I experienced this computer-related collaboration when using tutors to help my writing class as the students began learning how to use the computers. The tutors helped me create exercises and revised my ideas, offering suggestions of their own. The journal I was keeping at the time is filled with references to collaborative incidents we all experienced as we worked with a trial copy of hypertext software for the first time in a classroom setting. Together we found solutions by talking, reading what each had suggested, listening to each other and to students, and writing together on the screen. For example, I decided to create a hypertext example for my students. In the process, I created about 100 links and a confused maze of boxes and lines. Mike, our tutor, saw my struggling and offered to help. We talked about what I was trying to do, and then together we worked to eliminate unnecessary links. Subsequently, Mike was able to help my students as they worked through the exercise because he and I had collaborated on creating it.

It is, however, in tutor-tutee conferences that writing center people most often find examples of collaborative activities that bring together all the language arts to develop the writing. In one student's journal about tutoring in the writing center, she explains, "I think that tutoring goes more smoothly if the tutor lets the student talk enough. This session, I tried to be quiet and let the student express herself. In orally speaking their ideas and problems, the students can better understand their own thoughts. Asking interested questions makes the student feel good that the tutor is interested in his or her work." This same tutor mentioned that she often began a tutorial by reading aloud the student paper. Clearly, this tutor used reading, listening, and speaking in helping tutees achieve writing success.

Recently, I listened to taped conferences we use to evaluate our writing center tutors. One session began with the tutee stating what she had intended to do in her paper, and then the tutor read the paper to determine how successfully the tutee's goals had been accomplished. As they began to discuss the paper, I heard them first disagree and then gradually arrive at a consensus. Through reading, speaking, and listening, they collaborated on the tutee's essay. Collaboration is sometimes difficult to achieve because the tutee may push the tutor to take charge or to fix the paper. For example, the taped conference with our tutor included a comment, "You tell me how to do it!" A tutor may find this very easy to do, as did the student mentioned at the beginning of this essay. But such behavior does not empower students in the way that Mary Croft (1984) recommends, and conferences dominated by tutor "fixers" lack all the language arts.

Problems in Non-Collaborative Conferences

We know that once a tutor takes control away from the student, instead of sharing that control, the tutor limits the amount of reading, listening, speaking, and writing that the tutee accomplishes. For example, in a research project with college teachers who had conferences with their basic writers, I found that the only papers that showed improvement in the cognitive skill of moving from general to specific and back again were those papers written by students who received collaborative conferences. Students who experienced teacher-directed conferences where they were told what to do only did what they were instructed to do and the writing remained virtually the same in each draft. In writing centers, tutors who tell students what to "fix" have the same results while those who work with students to change a draft find that the writing improves. Collaboration allows students to practice the language arts, to process information.

Whether in group tutorials, tutor-tutor conferences, or tutor-tutee conferences, collaborative learning empowers students to become successful writers because the underlying theory is the whole language theory. In using all the language arts, each collaborative act frees the participants by helping them process information in such a way as to ensure that it is accessible.

References

Behm, Richard. 1989. "Ethical Issues in Peer Tutoring: A Defense of Collaborative Learning." *The Writing Center Journal* 10, 3–12.

Bruffee, Kenneth. 1973. "Collaborative Learning: Some Practical Models." *College English* 34, 634–43.

———. 1984. "Peer Tutoring and the 'Conversation of Mankind.' " *Writing Centers: Theory and Administration.* Ed. Gary A. Olson. Urbana, IL: National Council of Teachers of English, 3–15.

———. 1991. Letter in Comment and Response. *College English* 53, 950–52.

Bruner, Jerome. 1973. "Readiness for Learning." *Beyond the Information Given: Studies in the Psychology of Knowing.* Ed. J. Anglin. New York: W. W. Norton, 413–25.

Carroll, Joyce. 1981. "Talking Through the Writing Process." *English Journal* 70, 100–102.

Collins, James, and Michael Williamson. 1981. "Spoken Language and Semantic Abbreviation in Writing." *Research in the Teaching of English* 15, 23–25.

Croft, Mary K. 1984. "'I Would Prefer Not To': A Consideration of the Reluctant Student." *Writing Centers: Theory and Administration.* Ed. Gary A. Olson. Urbana, IL: National Council of Teachers of English, 170–81.

Dyson, Anne. 1983. "The Role of Oral Language in Early Writing Processes." *Research in the Teaching of English* 17, 1–30.

Einhorn, Lois. 1978. "Oral and Written Style: An Examination of Differences." *Southern Speech Communication Journal,* 302–11.

Elbow, Peter. 1985. "The Shifting Relationships Between Speech and Writing." *College Composition and Communication* 36: 283–303.

Emig, Janet. 1977. "Writing as a Mode of Learning." *College Composition and Communication* 28, 122–27.

Fitzgerald, Sallyanne. 1987. "Relationships between Conferencing and Movement between General and Specific in Basic Writers' Compositions." Unpublished doctoral dissertation, University of Missouri–St. Louis.

Fitzgerald, Sallyanne, Peggy Mulvihill, and Ruth Dobson. 1991. "Meeting the Needs of Graduate Students: Writing Support Groups in the Center." *The Writing Center: New Directions.* Ed. Ray Wallace and Jeanne Simpson. New York: Garland, 133–44.

Gilbert, Pam. 1991. "From Voice to Text: Reconsidering Writing and Reading in the English Classroom." *English Education* 23, 195–211.

Green, Michael. 1985. "Talk and Doubletalk: The Development of Metacognition Knowledge about Oral Language." *Research in the Teaching of English* 19, 9–24.

Herrington, Anne J., and Deborah Cadman. 1991. "Peer Review and Revising in an Anthropology Course: Lessons for Learning." *College Composition and Communication* 42, 184–99.

Lunsford, Andrea. 1986. "Assignments for Basic Writers: Unresolved Issues and Needed Research." *Journal of Basic Writing* 5, 87–99.

———. 1991. "Collaboration, Control, and the Idea of a Writing Center." *The Writing Center Journal* 12, 3–10.

Reid, Louann. 1983, April. "Talking: The Neglected Part of the Writing Process." National Council of Teachers of English Spring Conference, Seattle, WA. ERIC ED 229 762.

Tannen, Deborah. 1982. Introduction. *Advances in Discourse Processes.* Ed. Deborah Tannen. *Spoken and Written Language: Exploring Orality and Literacy 9.* Norwood, NJ: Ablex Publications, 1–16.

Trimbur, John. 1987. "Peer Tutoring: A Contradiction in Terms?" *The Writing Center Journal* 7.2, 21–28.

Zoellner, Robert. 1969. "Talk-Write: A Behavioral Pedagogy for Composition." *College English* 30, 267–320.

3 The Creative Writing Workshop and the Writing Center

Katherine H. Adams and John L. Adams
Loyola University

Writing labs have changed a great deal since they arrived on college campuses—along with open admissions programs and a new concern for student services—in the late 1960s. Since that time, these facilities have been influenced by various developments in rhetorical theory and practice. Research showing the limited benefit of isolated grammar instruction heightened interest in alternatives to the drills and workbook exercises prevalent in some of the earliest labs. The writing process movement of the 1970s created a concern for the student's entire writing process, for invention, drafting, and revision and not just for the surface errors of final copies. Research on social constructionism and discourse communities fostered an emphasis on peer response, first in writing classes and then in writing centers (see this volume: Hobson, Fitzgerald, and Murphy).

In addition to these relatively recent developments, another influence on current writing center pedagogy is the creative writing workshop, a tradition thriving long before Janet Emig's work on writing process or Kenneth Bruffee's discussion of discourse communities. In English departments since the late nineteenth century, writing students have worked in small groups with their peers, reviewing content, structure, word choice, and possibilities for publication. These workshops provide a hundred years of experience with teaching advanced students to improve form and content, not just to correct the surface errors that became the obsession of freshman composition and many early writing labs. Careful study of creative writing classes suggests how this tradition can further shape the writing center's peer tutoring methodology. Specifically, the centers should adopt the empowering pedagogy of writing workshops, changing the tutor's primary role from authority in one-on-one conferences to facilitator in informal group sessions.

The Creative Writing Workshop

In the 1880s, Barrett Wendell and A. S. Hill of Harvard developed advanced classes to rescue students from the large, passive lecture meetings and set-format approach of the new freshman composition. These smaller workshop classes identified each participant as an active expert or professional: the writer would set goals and construct a text to fulfill them, the other class members would read the text carefully and then draw from their own strengths to help him realize those goals. In 1898, John Gardiner of Harvard described this new advanced-group structure, a collective individualism, in his first-day handouts: "In general, the purpose of such a course as English 12 is analogous to that of an atelier—to turn out men with something like a professional command of the art in which they are to practice" (Gardiner, Outline of English 12, Harvard University Archives). In mentioning the artist's studio or atelier, Gardiner was referring to a French artistic tradition of the nineteenth century, of informal academies, *ateliers libres,* where avant-garde artists worked together, drawing on each other's insights to extend their artistic skills.

George Pierce Baker's courses on playwrighting, which began at Radcliffe in 1903 and at Harvard in 1905, also involved students as an active group. Since the best plays might be performed on campus or at professional theaters where Baker had connections, the class members attended to the real goals of performance and publication, helping each other to refine their characters, move the action along effectively, and hone the dialogue. Baker encouraged students to visualize each other's plays upon the stage, to apply what they were learning about lighting, scenery, and stage movement to each manuscript. This seriousness of group purpose was for some participants the most important feature of the class. Eugene O'Neill focused on this "intelligent encouragement" and "believe in our work" attitude in his *New York Times* obituary for Baker.

Similar group discussions dominated the workshops taught at Chicago, Michigan, Newcomb College, and other schools before 1910, the Iowa Writers' Workshop begun in 1932, and the undergraduate classes offered at most universities after World War II. At Florida State University, in Jerry Stern's fiction workshops, students read their classmates' stories on reserve in the library, write responses, and discuss their reactions in class. In poetry workshops with David Kirby and Van Brock, students read their works aloud and invite oral response. These teachers provide comments about each piece, but they rarely dominate the in-class sessions. Instead, class members are expected to provide feedback on matters ranging from word choice to theme to length to audience response.

To foster such group participation, teachers and students have made work-shops less formal than the typical college class. The first textbooks demonstrate the careful consideration given to the setting for active work. In his 1917 poetry-writing text, William Carruth suggests workshops convene during a single period of at least two hours, instead of separate periods of one hour, to allow time for reading and discussing the students' pieces. He recommends an informal class structure:

> A classroom with straight rows of seats does not afford in any case the most congenial conditions for the enjoyment of poetry. It is especially unfavorable to verse writing and mutual criticism. If possible a verse-writing course should meet out-of-doors, or at least in a private study and around a table. Stiffness and conventionality must be dispelled. So far as may be, the class should be like a club of friends gathered for common enjoyment and helpful suggestions and criticism. In such surroundings it is easier to draw out the real thought and the serious consideration of even the shy members. (54)

Every week in Baker's playwrighting workshops at Harvard, students sat around a large oak table in a seminar room. In 1915, Edwin Ford Piper of Iowa met with his students in his office, as his student (and later his colleague) John Frederick describes in his journal:

> Attendance is optional, but there are few of us who fail to find our way in the late afternoon to Mr. Piper's basement office, where we sit in nooks between bookcases or even share a table with heaps of papers and magazines, and read the stories and poems and essays we have written for the comments of one another and of our leader. (Wilbers 22)

Workshops at Florida State usually meet in a seminar room where ten to fifteen students gather around a table. Sometimes the classes convene at teachers' homes, where the entire group can discuss the piece or smaller groups can focus on specific genres—say, mystery writers in the hall and dark humorists by the snack table.

In this carefully created atmosphere has often come honest, blunt criticism of drafts. In *Of Time and the River,* Thomas Wolfe recounts a critique session in Baker's playwrighting class, where students were commenting on an over-written melodrama containing lines like these: "So—it has come to this! This is all your love amounts to—a little petty selfish thing. I had thought you were bigger than that, John" . . . "But-but, my God, Irene—what am I to think? I found you in bed with him—my best friend!" Wolfe humorously recalls the class's response, but his satire reveals the possible precision of student critiques:

> Eugene [Thomas Wolfe] would writhe in his seat, and clench his hands convulsively. Then he would turn almost prayerfully to the bitter,

mummified face of old Seth Flint for that barbed but cleansing vulgarity that always followed such a scene:

"Well?" Professor Hatcher [George Pierce Baker] would say, putting down the manuscript he had been reading, taking off his eye-glasses (which were attached to a ribbon of black silk) and looking around with a quizzical smile, an impassive expression on his fine, distinguished face. "Well?" he would say again urbanely, as no one answered. "Is there any comment?"

"What is she?" Seth would break the nervous silence with his rasping snarl. "Another of these society whores? You know," he continued, "you can find plenty of her kind for three dollars a throw without any of that fancy palaver."

Some of the class smiled faintly, painfully, and glanced at each other with slight shrugs of horror; others were grateful, felt pleasure well in them and said under their breath exultantly: "Good old Seth! Good old Seth!"

"Her love is big enough for all things, is it?" said Seth. "I know a truck driver out in Denver I'll match against her any day."

Eugene and Ed Horton, a large and robust aspirant from the Iowa corn lands, roared with happy laughter, poking each other sharply in the ribs.

"Do you think the play will act?" someone said. "It seems to me that it comes pretty close to closet drama."

"If you ask me," said Seth, "it comes pretty close to water-closet drama. . . . No," he said sourly. "What the boy needs is a little experience. He ought to go out and get him a woman and get all this stuff off his mind. After that, he might sit down and write a play."

For a moment there was a very awkward silence, and Professor Hatcher smiled a trifle palely. Then, taking his eyeglasses with a distinguished movement, he looked around and said: "Is there any other comment?" (174–75)

In a Florida State workshop, John Adams submitted a poem about newborn sea turtles getting lost on the beach because of their attraction to street lights. Typifying the poem were lines like this one: "O turtle, hath thy seaward bobbing been renewed?" After a few vague comments about the diction possibly being too strained, one student came closer to the point: "You can't be serious. No one really talks like this." Later, this same group praised the exactness of the imagery in a poem about state fairs, which John later submitted to a journal. In a fiction workshop, a student writing about racial conflicts in her hometown was criticized for "creating stick people." Because John's first draft of a story on migrant workers seemed "too Joan Baez-ish," he worked on later drafts to better represent the migrant workers' attitudes about leaving Mexico. In these classes, as in Baker's, students' responses were personal, at times enthusiastic and at times critical—the real and useful reactions of attentive readers.

Creative Writing and the Writing Center

The writing center has endorsed the concept that appealed to Hill and Wendell, of students working together to improve writing, pooling their resources to enrich each student's text. The center has also followed the creative writer's recommendation of a work setting: writing centers generally contain informal arrangements of chairs and tables like the seminar rooms and offices used for workshops.

But in the actual working out of this active teaching method, the writing center has lagged behind. Even though centers have flourished along with an interest in collaborative learning, of collective individualism, most seem to involve only one-on-one work. In the writing center, the client generally sits down with one tutor who assumes the authority role, a "junior-teacher" offering suggestions and instruction to a clearly less capable "student." As John Trimbur has noted, tutors can feel uncomfortable in this peer role since they are expected to know more about writing than their clients, but are somehow not to assert their superior status.

In the creative writing class, however, the assumption is that each student takes writing seriously, that they all plan to polish their work for publication, that they all can be authority figures. Thus the peer's response is valued because the peer attends carefully to the writing, but the writer must be the first authority: she has set her own goals, and she has her own knowledge and feelings to convey. Writing tutors need to view their clients as writers also, who know more about the course material and have their own strengths. Then the tutor can make suggestions, ask questions, work as a real peer, without the burden of teaching and correcting everything. Freed from being the sole authority, tutors can offer their own personal responses as well as suggestions on paragraphing and grammar, establishing a conversation in which they can at different times be blunt or satirical or excited, like students in creative writing workshops. They can be thus freed of that insipidly encouraging "junior-teacher" role, never an appropriate one for peers.

The best method for redefining the tutor's role is to return to the real center of collaborative or collective learning: the group. One-on-one tutorial sessions replay the teacher-student office conference; a larger group can more easily embark on equal collaboration. Writing tutors might meet with two or three other members also offering their responses to the writer. At the University of Missouri–St.Louis, the writing center sponsors graduate student groups with a faculty monitor, in which participants can discuss their thesis projects (Fitzgerald, Mulvihill, and Dobson). At Villanova University, biology majors work in small groups with an undergraduate tutor so that together they can critique the content and structure of their papers (Hollis). This model is successful, both essays claim, because it allows for more interaction, for the contribution of each member's skills. Here at Loyola University, law students meet in small groups with a tutor to review course material and write sample exam answers; small groups of psychology students prepare for oral class presentations with a tutor; basic writers and their tutor collaborate as grammar-checkers. In these groups—formed by the writing center director, a teacher, or a tutor, either as a voluntary, recommended activity or as a course requirement—students usually work together for at least a few days or weeks, often for an entire term. In this environment, they learn to respect their own skills and judgments as well as the expertise of others.

As the creative writing workshop reminds us, tutors do not have to be lone authorities, imitating teachers in an awkward and inappropriate way. They can be peers who establish a group of two or three students and participate in the discussion, bringing to it their knowledge of writing and their interest in learning. As we discuss the theory of collaboration and arrange our centers physically for informal exchanges, we must, most importantly, shape tutorial sessions so that our tutors can work effectively and so that the writing of all students will improve.

References

Bruffee, Kenneth. 1984. "Peer Tutoring and the 'Conversation of Mankind.'" *Writing Centers: Theory and Administration.* Ed. Gary A. Olson. Urbana, IL: National Council of Teachers of English, 3–15.

Carruth, William Herbert. 1917. *Verse Writing.* New York: Macmillan.

Emig, Janet. 1971. *The Composing Processes of Twelfth Graders.* Urbana, IL: National Council of Teachers of English.

Fitzgerald, Sallyanne, Peggy Mulvihill, and Ruth Dobson. 1991. "Meeting the Needs of Graduate Students: Writing Support Groups in the Center." *The Writing Center: New Directions.* Ed. Ray Wallace and Jeanne Simpson. New York: Garland, 133–44.

Gardiner, J. H. "Outline of English 12, 1898–99," ms. in Pusey Library, Harvard University.

Hollis, Karyn. 1991. "More Science in the Writing Center: Training Tutors to Lead Group Tutorials on Biology Lab Reports." *The Writing Center, New Directions.* Ed. Ray Wallace and Jeanne Simpson. New York: Garland, 247–62.

O'Neill, Eugene. 1935, Jan. "Professor G. P. Baker." *The New York Times* 13, sec. 9, i.

Trimbur, John. 1987. "Peer Tutoring: A Contradiction in Terms?" *Writing Center Journal* 7.2, 21–28.

Wilbers, Stephen. 1980. *The Iowa Writers' Workshop: Origins, Emergence, and Growth.* Iowa City: University of Iowa Press.

4 The Writing Center and Social Constructionist Theory

Christina Murphy
Texas Christian University

In the research surrounding rhetoric and composition, social constructionist theory has begun to challenge the writing-as-process model as the dominant paradigm defining writing instruction. The emergence of social constructionist theory and its rise to prominence within the last decade have significant implications for writing centers and for the theories of discourse, social interaction, and assessment that define our work.

Certainly the most significant influence of social constructionist theory upon writing centers has been its endorsement of collaborative learning and collaborative writing. With the writing-as-process model, in which writing is largely viewed as a highly personal process and experience to be shaped and guided by a broader understanding of cognitive theory, the influence of the writing center tutor often has been perceived as an unnecessary, perhaps even harmful, intrusion. Lisa Ede has skillfully discussed the influence of the Romantic idea of the writer as solitary individual, concluding that this perspective tends "to view both writing and thinking—the creation of knowledge—as inherently individual activities," thus minimizing the influence of "social and cultural contexts of teaching and learning" (1989, 6). As Ede states, "Think for a moment, for instance, of Flower and Hayes's cognitive-based research—research that has been particularly influential during the past decade. Where in the flow charts depicting task representation, audience analysis, and short-term and long-term memory is the box representing collaboration and conversation?" (7).

Ede argues that "the assumption that writing is inherently a solitary cognitive activity is so deeply ingrained in western culture that it has, until recently, largely gone unexamined" (7) and suggests that this view helps to explain what, for her, has been "a puzzling and frustrating mystery: the fact that those who most resist or misunderstand the kind of collaborative learning that occurs in writing centers are often our own colleagues in departments of English" (9). A corrective to this point of view, Ede suggests, is to broaden—

through research and scholarship—our profession's understanding of the writing center's role within collaborative learning (9–11).

Central to this task of broadening an understanding of the writing center's role within the paradigm of collaboration is an assessment of the philosophy of social constructionist theory and its practical implications for writing instruction. Andrea Lunsford addresses the issue in this fashion:

> We might begin by asking where the collaboration bandwagon got rolling. Why has it gathered such steam? Because, I believe, collaboration both in theory and practice reflects a broad-based epistemological shift, a shift in the way we view knowledge. The shift involves a move from viewing knowledge and reality as things exterior to or outside of us, as immediately accessible, individually knowable, measurable, and shareable, to viewing knowledge and reality as mediated by or constructed through language in social use, as socially constructed, contextualized, as, in short, the product of *collaboration.* (1991, 4)

Joseph Petraglia claims that, for the field of rhetoric and composition, social constructionism has come to mean that "knowledge is created, maintained, and altered through an individual's interaction with and within his or her 'discourse community' " and that "knowledge resides in consensus rather than in any transcendent or objective relationship between a knower and that which is to be known" (1991, 38). He suggests that the following premises—derived largely from the work of the two best-known advocates of social constructionism in rhetoric and composition, Kenneth Bruffee and James Berlin—form the basis of social constructionism in composition: (1) real entities (reality) include knowledge, beliefs, truths, and selves; (2) all reality is arrived at by consensus; (3) consensus, and thus knowledge, is "discovered" solely through discourse (rhetoric); and (4) reality changes as consensus/knowledge changes (39).

James A. Reither (1986) has suggested that, for writing teachers, a social constructionist point of view has meant an emphasis upon discourse communities—communities that share "values, objects of inquiry, research methodologies, evidential contexts, persuasion strategies and conventions, forms and formats, and conversational forms" (18). As a result of their emphasis upon discourse communities, Petraglia contends that

> [S]ocial constructionists in composition of all political persuasions have sought to promote access to knowledge-creating communities as a critical first step toward student empowerment. Compared to current- traditional and cognitive rhetorics which focus on the individual writer and how he or she can and/or should shape discourse to gain the audience's assent, one might say that constructionists focus on the ways in which the audience (that is, the community) shapes the discourse of its members. (1991, 40)

While many social constructionists in rhetoric and composition—like Bruffee, Berlin, Patricia Bizzell, Lester Faigley, and David Bartholomae—tend to see this process as equitable and empowering, Howard Ryan (1991) argues that the social constructionist paradigm encourages social elitism and accommodation to the existing world order:

> In the growing composition trends toward collaborative learning and collaborative writing, collaboration normally refers to more than simply having students meet in groups to respond to individual papers; rather, it entails group decision making and group projects. As with other trends, the collaborative literature emphasizes utilitarian ends—that working in groups leads to better ideas, that it teaches the cooperative skills needed for academic and career success. Yet we may also read the literature as implying a particular social vision, and occasionally we find explicit references to larger aspirations. The collaborative better world is one in which people have learned to get along, where we either accept our differences or strive to work them out through cooperative and peaceful means. Oppressive gender, race, or class structures need not lead to divisive political battles in the collaborative better world: cooperative conflict resolution is the key. This vision, which I will call social harmonist, is not limited to advocates of collaborative learning; in fact, we may see it implied in any pedagogy that encourages a strategy of adjustment or accommodation—rather than challenge or confrontation—with the existing world order. (14)

Ryan is also concerned that a pedagogical emphasis upon collaboration or social harmony stifles dissent and encourages illusory views of peership. As he explains:

> Social harmonist ideologies are traditional means of elite social control and are used to stifle dissent or to direct dissent into safe channels that leave elite power intact. Members of exploited groups are invited to trust or to accept a false sense of peership with their exploiters.
>
> Composition teachers whose work is inspired by visions of a cooperative world must conceive as clearly as possible the terms of that cooperation. Students encouraged to see academe and the workplace beyond as "communities of knowledgeable peers," where "status equals" engage in agreed-upon discourses (Bruffee 642) may be ill-prepared for their present and future struggles within hierarchical institutions. Perhaps, rather than teach a value of blanket cooperativeness, our classrooms could ask critical questions about collaboration. (14–15)

While Ryan finds social constructionism problematic on a global or social level, other critics object to the philosophy for its limited understanding of the learning strategies of individual students. Donald C. Stewart argues that the privileging of the group or the community over the individual in social constructionism is "unsound psychologically" since it is not sensitive to different personality types and therefore different learning and writing styles

(1988, 75–76). He bases his critique in the Myers-Briggs theory of personality types, which is largely Jungian in emphasis, and argues that collaborative learning privileges extroverts, those who work well in groups, who are intellectually stimulated by talking their ideas out with others before beginning a writing project, and who enjoy making writing sound like talking. Introverts, by contrast, tend to prefer to work alone and feel that they are at their most creative and productive when given time for inner, private reflection. Stewart argues that extroverts, who work well in collaborative learning situations, typically describe those who do not adapt well to these environments as "unmotivated . . . inflexible," "highly-suspicious," "stubborn," and "infantile" (78–79). Thus, as Paul Heilker contends, "in these judgments we can see clear manifestations of how collaborative learning both privileges the collective side of the collective/individual binary at the expense of the individual side and also imposes constraining forces upon students' thinking and actions" (1991, 7).

Social constructionism has provided an even more fertile ground for dissent within psychology, especially for cognitive and psychoanalytic theorists, many of whom find social constructionism's understanding of the self as a social construct—similar to all other cultural artifacts—to be too restrictive. Joseph H. Smith (1991) contends that to argue that an individual is wholly constructed by his or her social experience and cultural moment is to obviate the very real presence of individual, subjective experience—the majority of which is highly symbolic and often not capable of full translation into linguistic codes or sets that are predetermined and defined by one's culture and society. Smith's concern is that much of the early, imagistic, creative thinking involved in personal, reflective efforts to interpret and create meaning will be truncated by a philosophy that favors secondary process thought, or thought that is constructed to take on the contours of the society it addresses. Will the world of each person's innersubjectivity—the source of so much creative thinking and so many creative insights—be lessened and devalued as a result? (17–18).

Further, Alice Brand and Jan Zita Grover express concerns similar to Smith's in arguing that social constructionism valorizes collaboration and cooperation while deemphasizing the emotions. Grover states that "social constructionism has no theory of desire" (1990, 21), while Brand (1991) devotes an entire critique to social constructionism's failure to address the issue of the role the emotions play in an individual's writing processes and claims that "up to now, attempts at social-cognitive theories of writing mask the emotional experience of writing." She concludes that "despite the fact that social cognition provides substantial information about writers, it seems at the same time to give us more ammunition to avoid studying their emotional experience" (396). Richard Gregg endorses the psychoanalytic distinction between individual and social knowledge and asserts that in each individual "there is a constant interaction between individual systems of meanings and a system of socially shared meanings" (1981, 136). Gregg holds that it is our capacity to form idiosyncratic associations and our concomitant ability to generate personal knowledge that define our individuality. Thus, rigid separations between personal and social knowledge are artificial, arbitrary, and, finally, unproductive.

These theorists' comments address a number of the issues surrounding creativity, insight, and self expression. Clearly, all of us who teach writing in a classroom or in a writing center are concerned with these issues; therefore, it is important to consider whether social constructionist theory—with its valorization of collaborative vs. individual learning strategies, its limited understanding of the role the emotions play in the writing process, and its emphasis upon only those aspects of knowledge that can be socially constructed—gives us a broad enough understanding of the meaning-making activities of individual writers to assist us in providing the most effective instruction we can.

Lunsford (1991) believes that social constructionism will have a radical, if not revolutionary, effect upon writing centers, turning them from "Storehouse Centers" and "Garret Centers" into "Burkean Parlor Centers" (4–7). A "Storehouse Center," she explains, is a writing center that holds to an earlier view of knowledge "as exterior to us and as directly accessible."

> The Center as Storehouse operates as information stations or storehouses, prescribing and handing out skills and strategies to individual learners. They often use "modules" or other kinds of individualized learning materials. They tend to view knowledge as individually derived and held, and they are not particularly amenable to collaboration, sometimes actively hostile to it. (4)

In contrast, "Garret Centers" are "informed by a deep-seated belief in individual 'genius,' in the Romantic sense of the term" and also by a "deep-seated attachment to the American brand of individualism." Specifically, "Garret Centers"

> don't view knowledge as exterior, as information to be sought out or passed on mechanically. Rather, they see knowledge as interior, as inside the student, and the writing center job as helping students get in touch with this knowledge, as a way to find their unique voices, their individual and unique powers. This idea has been articulated by many, including Ken Macrorie, Peter Elbow, and Don Murray, and the idea usually gets acted out in Murray-like conferences, those in which the tutor or teacher listens, voices encouragement, and essentially serves as a validation of the students' "I-search." Obviously, collaboration problematizes Garret Centers as well, for they also view knowledge as interiorized, solitary, individually derived, individually held. (5)

For Lunsford, the ideal toward which writing centers should strive under the social constructionist paradigm is the "Burkean Parlor Center." Lunsford then presents her idea of how the "Burkean Parlor Center" would be constituted:

> [I]ts theory of knowledge is based not on positivistic principles (that's The Storehouse again), not on Platonic or absolutist ideals (that's The Garret), but on the notion of knowledge as always contextually bound, as always socially constructed. Such a center might well have as its motto [Hannah] Arendt's statement: "For excellence, the presence of others is always required." Such a center would place control, power, and authority not in the tutor or staff, not in the individual student, but in the negotiating group. It would engage students not only in solving problems set by teachers but in identifying problems for themselves; not only in working as a group but in monitoring, evaluating, and building a theory of how groups work; not only in understanding and valuing collaboration but in confronting squarely the issues of control that successful collaboration inevitably raises not only in reaching consensus but in valuing dissensus and diversity. (8–9)

Lunsford's essay is worth quoting at length because it is indicative of many of the concepts and beliefs—both stated and implied—that surround the philosophy of social constructionism. For one, despite all of Lunsford's praise for the transfer of control from teacher/tutor/student to the group, Lunsford, like other theorists, never makes quite clear exactly how this transfer of power is to occur and exactly *how* it will be mediated within the constructs of American education. To say that this process will be difficult and that it *should* occur are far different issues from explaining how it can, or will be, carried out. These theorists never explain, for example, why hegemony of groups— with all the inequities and marginalization hegemony involves—is no less likely to occur than hegemony of individuals. Lunsford, for example, while advocating collaboration, is concerned that it may lead to a type of "homogeneity that squelches diversity, that waters down ideas to the lowest common denominator, that erases rather than values differences" (7). "This tendency is particularly troubling," she states, "given our growing awareness of the roles gender and ethnicity play in all learning" (7). Yet, beyond acknowledging this problem, she provides no sense of how to deal with these issues should they occur. In fact, she does state, " . . . as the latest pedagogical bandwagon, collaboration often masquerades as democracy when it in fact practices the same old authoritarian control. It thus stands open to abuse and can, in fact, lead to poor teaching and poor learning" (3–4).

However, while these are valid precautionary points, they do not explain how issues of hegemony and counterhegemony within groups will be dealt with. In some ways, they seem, in fact, to echo a principle of the Jeffersonian ideal of democracy that truth will win out if all groups are allowed their say and will reason together toward a consensus. Whether, in actuality, this principle of the Jeffersonian ideal will work in educational settings, social constructionism has yet to prove to many theorists' satisfaction. Some, like Hugh Tomlinson (1989), do not feel that consensus within a group is necessarily the equivalent of truth, only of agreement. Tomlinson argues that one can agree, in principle, with what is false, harmful, ineffective, and the like. Consensus alone is no guarantee of the merit or validity of one's ideas or beliefs (53–55).

Second, as Stanley Aronowitz and Henry A. Giroux (1985) have argued, philosophies of education generally reflect political philosophies or assumptions, and, with social constructionism, the predominant concept of education seems to be preparation of the individual for the workplace. Even Lunsford, for example, buttresses her argument for the "Burkean Parlor Center" with concepts from the workforce. She mentions, for example, that collaboration is the norm for most professions and cites an impressive list to support her case. In emphasizing that "collaborative environments and tasks must *demand* collaboration," she notes that "studies of collaboration in the workplace identify three kinds of tasks that seem to call consistently for collaboration: high-order problem defining and solving division of labor tasks, in which the job is simply too big for any one person; and division of expertise tasks" (6). Are we to assume from this example that educational settings based on collaboration will prepare individuals more adequately for situations they will encounter in the workforce, or are we to assume that what works well in the workforce will also work well in educational settings?

Lunsford is not alone in her emphasis on concepts taken from the workplace and applied to theories of education. Thomas Trzyna and Margaret Batschelet (1990) emphasize how often collaborative writing assignments are "designed to emulate 'real workplace' situations" (23) and note the encroachment of "management techniques" into the structuring of collaborative learning (28). Harvey Wiener (1986) describes the successful teacher as a classroom manager, while Udai Pareek (1981) discusses the relevance of management strategies to effective teaching (168). And Bruffee, in advocating collaboration, states:

> In business and industry . . . and in professions such as medicine, law, engineering, and architecture . . . collaboration is the norm. All that is new in collaborative learning, it seems, is the systematic application of collaborative principles to that last bastion of hierarchy and individualism, the American college classroom. (1984, 647)

Aronowitz and Giroux call this philosophy "technocratic rationality" (15) and identify it with the conservative view of education in which educational systems are the "mechanism through which the [middle class] reproduces itself culturally" (5). Preparing students to take their place and function well within the workforce has long been an ideal of the conservative philosophy. Perhaps Bruffee is pleased that collaborative learning will remove individual-ism from the American college classroom, but many theorists find this idea more disturbing than encouraging. Further, Greg Myers (1986) and John McKinley (1980) emphasize that the requirements and aims of collaboration in the classroom are more complex than those of collaboration in the work-force. Collaboration in the workforce, McKinley notes, is "product oriented," while collaboration in the classroom is "inquiry oriented" and "decision oriented" as well.

Identification of social constructionism with methods and ideologies drawn from the workforce creates particular problems for writing center theory. If education is a microcosm of the power relations and oppositional politics that exist in any society and any historical era, embracing the ideas of social constructionism means for writing centers an endorsement of the view that writing centers are effective when they advance a student's mastery of social skills—in this case, skills drawn from the values of consensus, collabo-ration, group work, and knowledge that is socially constructed. Even Luns-ford's choice of the name "Burkean Parlor Centers" suggests an emphasis upon consensus and cooperation, for Kenneth Burke, in *A Rhetoric of Motives*, defines rhetoric as "the use of language as a symbolic means inducing coop-eration in beings that by nature respond to symbols" (43).

As Lunsford has indicated, writing centers that endorse this philosophy and become "Burkean Parlor Centers" seek to challenge and supplant "Garret Centers" based upon Romantic notions of individualism, in which knowledge is seen as "interior, as inside the student, and the writing center's job as helping students get in touch with this knowledge, as a way to find their unique voices, their individual and unique powers" (5). The difficulty with "Garret Centers," to Lunsford, is that they "view knowledge as interiorized, solitary, individually derived, individually held" (5), while the superior ap-proach, one must assume, is to believe that knowledge resides in the power of groups to negotiate and adjudicate what shall and shall not be viewed as knowledge. The implications of this shift are significant: the least effective writing center tutors will be those who operate from a Romantic perspective, while the most effective will be those best adept at inspiring in students a capacity for group work; the mastery of social skills—especially those most adapted to the workforce—will replace a concern for developing the individ-ual's unique voice and unique powers; and consensus will become the greatest measure of truth—even though, as Hugh Tomlinson and Carole Blair point out, consensus is no guarantee of ethics or morality.

Advocates tend to view social constructionism as a liberatory philosophy in emphasizing the decentralization of power within education—moving power away from the control of any one individual—teacher/student/tutor—

and giving it to the group. Yet even this particular liberatory view of social constructionism is not sufficient to answer Lunsford's question about "where the collaboration bandwagon got rolling" and "why has it gathered such steam?" (4).

Part of the answer must reside in the fact that social constructionism is a response to the times. The educational community has continued to grow more diverse culturally, and multicultural voices and values have begun to emerge as challenges to monocultural classrooms and writing centers. In addition, major philosophical challenges to conventional education in the postmodern era have made us more aware of a diversity of perspectives. Feminism, for example, has questioned male hegemony in education and the valorization of male ways of knowing that are reflected in our teaching and scholarship. Marxist critics have made us sensitive to "an economic interpretation of the function of schools, including their role as reproducers of prevailing social relations" and have forced us to take seriously Marx's belief that "the ruling ideas of any society are the ideas of the ruling class" (Aronowitz and Giroux 6). Deconstructionist philosophers like Michel Foucault and Paulo Freire have critiqued the lack of empowerment within education and have proposed viewing education as both a struggle for meaning and a struggle over power relations. In *Power and Knowledge*, for example, Foucault emphasizes how power works on the nature of learning itself by determining what shall be included in mainstream explanations and what shall be excluded. Obviously, social constructionism's belief that knowledge is constructed (and deconstructed) by groups resonates with the challenges to current educational practices expressed by these philosophies.

Within rhetoric and composition, social constructionism reflects an additional trend, one that finds its origins in nineteenth-century discussions of hermeneutics and the nature of language within discourse communities. Many of the issues that define social constructionism reflect the communication-based social theories of Wilhelm Dilthey, Sigmund Freud, Karl Marx, and Friedrich Nietzsche in the nineteenth century, and of Jürgen Habermas, Paul Ricoeur, Jacques Derrida, and Jacques Lacan in the twentieth century. Philosophically, these writers ground their views in an "architectonic view of communication" and emphasize the "complex relationships among thought, discourse, and action." All foreground "communication, not philosophy, in their theories." Their social theories are, in many respects, themselves "responses to perceived flaws in the explanatory scope and heuristic value of philosophy's concerns. They are geared, in other words, toward replacing the issues of being and knowledge with views of communication" (Blair 21–22).

Perhaps the most representative of these philosophers is Habermas (1973), who argues that institutionalized forms of thought are based on what he terms "cognitive interests." The three primary cognitive interests or "knowledge-constitutive" interests, he writes, are the technical, the practical, and the emancipatory. Habermas also envisions a tripartite typology of knowledge with three disciplinary categories, each corresponding to one of those cognitive interests. The empirical-analytic disciplines of the natural sciences are underpinned by a technical interest directed toward control over natural phenomena. The historical-hermeneutic disciplines of the social sciences serve to elucidate the conditions that underlie communication and social interaction. Thus, they function to promote intersubjective understanding, those shared cultural meanings that are the prerequisites for social consensus on the practical dimensions of life. The empirical-critical sciences are guided by an emancipatory interest and are distinguished by their capacity to reflect critically upon their own ideological foundations. Empirical-critical sciences represent, to Habermas, forms of a depth hermeneutic since they incorporate "in their consciousness an interest which directs knowledge, an interest in emancipation going beyond the technical and practical interest of knowledge" (1973, 9).

Within the choices provided by Habermas, social constructionism is best understood as a historical-hermeneutic philosophy with a "cognitive interest" grounded in cultural critique and an understanding of how language operates for social consensus in daily life. In contrast, the opposite of social constructionism—what Ede and Lunsford have termed the Romantic perspective—is less concerned with social consensus and more focused on the development and enrichment of the individual. In this philosophy, social and cultural contexts are deemphasized in favor of an exploration of the individual's consciousness and innersubjectivity. From this perspective, the Romantic philosophy is best understood as an empirical-critical philosophy with an interest in "emancipation." Lunsford comes close to Habermas's understanding of "emancipation" in her statement that "Garret Centers," representative of the Romantic position, "see knowledge as interior, as inside the student, and the writing center's job as helping students get in touch with this knowledge, as a way to find their unique voices, their individual and unique powers" (5). Specifically, "emancipation" is concerned with exploring "the inner states" of communicants (Rapoport 1954, 199). Given social constructionism's emphasis upon social consensus, it is clear why "emancipation" would tend to be undervalued and collaboration highly valued as a standard for inquiry, evaluation, and action.

The history of rhetoric and composition makes it clear that the oppositions between social constructionism and the Romantic perspective are more than differing viewpoints on how knowledge shall be constructed and evaluated. In the fullest sense, these oppositions represent the history of our discipline and its current struggles in the contemporary era. The discipline of rhetoric and composition has emerged from the humanities and the humanistic tradition—a

philosophical perspective that exemplifies Habermas's concept of an empirical-critical tradition of inquiry. Yet, the discipline of rhetoric and composition
in the second half of the twentieth century has moved increasingly toward
taking on the ethos and methodology of the social sciences. Robert Connors
(1983) has documented the desire for scientific status within rhetoric and
composition. Social constructionism, with its emphasis upon social consensus
and its interpretive frameworks for understanding cultural mediation and
societal interaction, thus seems a natural methodological concomitant for an
era concerned less with individualism—and all that the term implies—and
more with defining the shaping forces of societal structures and giving them
a type of quasi-scientific validity and significance.

Louise Wetherbee Phelps (1988) would have us believe that our discipline's progression toward social science status has been tempered by an
affiliation with humanistic concerns, thus making the discipline a "human
science." Even if the broadest allowances are made to associate the term
"human science" with Wilhelm Dilthey's concept of *Geisteswissenschaften,*
or the study of human conduct with a focus on "understanding" *(Verstehen)*
versus the causal explanation *(Erklaren)* of the social sciences, it is clear that
Dilthey's views emerge from the positivism of the nineteenth century and
have largely found a more receptive climate and philosophically congruent
application in the social sciences, especially psychology, than in the humanities. When composition is looked upon as an art form, in the sense of a
creation of a set of symbols, composition as a "human science" becomes
tenuous, if not erroneous, for even Phelps admits that "sciences differ [from
the humanities, especially philosophy] in the use of measurements, logic,
techniques of observation, experiment, narration, and other aspects of
method" (24).

Further, Anthony Giddens (1977) points out via a critique of Habermas's
Toward a Rational Society that a "knowledge-constitutive interest" in the
historical-hermeneutic perspective the social sciences embody "has to be seen
as complemented by an interest in prediction and control"—both of which are
issues much more characteristic of the social sciences than of the humanities
or of a humanistic tradition (12–13). Perhaps Louis A. Sass (1988) best
articulates the differences in the humanistic versus the social science epistemologies in stating:

> [B]oth humanists and hermeneuticists are heirs to the intellectual tradi-
> tion of Romanticism, itself largely a reaction against the Enlightenment
> tradition of objectivism. . . . Indeed, both these groups can be called
> *humanistic* in a broad sense—if by this we mean committed to develop-
> ing an approach respectful of the special characteristics of human expe-
> rience and action, and free of the positivism, mechanism, and

reductionism of 19th-century physical sciences and the social sciences
modeled on them. (222)

If W. Ross Winterowd is correct in asserting that "defining literacy is not
idle semantic debate or academic hair-splitting but is almost always a conse-
quential political act" (1989, 4), the ongoing debate between the social constructionist and Romantic or humanistic points of view has significant
implications for writing center theory and practice. Lunsford has stated that
"Burkean Parlor Centers" have revolutionary implications for writing centers
and their interactions with the broader academic community. As Lunsford
indicates, "This alternative, this third idea of a writing center, poses a threat
as well as a challenge to the status quo in higher education" (1991, 9). Part of
the status quo in higher education, of course, involves the Romantic or
humanistic tradition and its respect for the individual learner. Social constructionism would have us believe that, in the classroom or the writing center,
students learn more through collaboration and group work than they do as
individual learners. For many theorists, this is a dubious proposition and one
that requires further investigation before wholesale acceptance and application within curricula emphasizing critical thinking skills (Mishler 1979,
Roderick 1986).

Certainly, the greatest challenge facing rhetoric and composition involves
the construction of a maximally inclusive and relevant theory to help those of
us teaching in writing classrooms and writing centers be the most effective
and beneficial instructors we can be. Social constructionism provides us with
a paradigm that explains a number of aspects of writing instruction; however,
to argue that it provides all the answers, or even answers sufficient to warrant
the devaluing of other theories and philosophies of education—especially the
Romantic or humanistic—seems unwise. For one, it is largely still an untested
philosophy in educational settings. Even Lunsford describes collaboration as
"the latest pedagogical bandwagon" and concedes that the term "collaboration" did not appear in titles for CCCC presentations until 1985 (3). Second,
the history of education—and our own experience with students—makes it
clear that different students require different pedagogical approaches. While
group work and collaboration might be highly beneficial for some, it can also
be stifling, intimidating, or silencing for others, and the best teachers and
tutors will be aware of this dynamic.

Blair states that social constructionism is the latest in our discipline's
searches for a "meta-ideology" (1989, 21). If so, perhaps the greatest value of
a "meta-ideology" should reside in its capacity to respect philosophical differences and to find merit in both "Garret Centers" and "Burkean Parlor Centers." As James Phillips points out, "the consequence of a multiplicity of
models is not chaos and capriciousness" but "a dialectical process" in which,

no matter what theory we espouse, we must be sure not to use it "to foreclose rather than to continue inquiry" (1991, 377). For tutors in "Garret Centers," "Burkean Parlor Centers," or centers representing a range of philosophical perspectives, Phillips's admonition offers wise and beneficial advice.

References

Aronowitz, Stanley, and Henry A. Giroux. 1985. *Education Under Siege: The Conservative, Liberal and Radical Debate over Schooling.* Westport, CT: Bergin & Garvey.

Blair, Carole. 1989. "'Meta-Ideology,' Rhetoric and Social Theory: Reenactment of The Wisdom-Eloquence Tension after the Linguistic Turn." *Rhetoric and Ideology: Compositions and Criticisms of Power.* Ed. Charles W. Kneupper. Arlington: Rhetoric Society of America, 21–29.

Brand, Alice. 1991. "Social Cognition, Emotions, and the Psychology of Writing." *Journal of Advanced Composition* 11, 395–407.

Bruffee, Kenneth A. 1984. "Collaborative Learning and the 'Conversation of Mankind.'" *College English* 46, 635–52.

Burke, Kenneth. 1967. *A Rhetoric of Motives.* Berkeley: University of California Press.

Connors, Robert J. 1983. "Composition Studies and Science." *College English* 45, 1–20.

Dilthey, Wilhelm. 1961. *Meaning in History: Wilhelm Dilthey's Thoughts on History and Society.* Ed. H. P. Hickman. London: Allen and Unwin.

Ede, Lisa. 1989. "Writing as a Social Process: A Theoretical Foundation for Writing Centers?" *The Writing Center Journal* 9.2, 3–13.

Foucault, Michel. 1980. *Power/Knowledge: Selected Interviews and Other Writings.* Ed. C. Gordon. New York: Pantheon.

Giddens, Anthony. 1977. *Studies in Social and Political Theory.* New York: Basic Books.

Gregg, Richard B. 1981. "Rhetoric and Knowing: The Search for Perspective." *Central States Speech Journal* 32, 133–44.

Grover, Jan Zita. 1990. "Words to Lust By." *The Women's Review of Books* 8.2, 21–23.

Habermas, Jürgen. 1973. *Theory and Practice.* Boston: Beacon.

Heilker, Paul. 1991. "The Bi-Polar Mind and the Inadequacy of Oppositional Pedagogies (Or the Dead Poets Society Revisited)." *Freshman English News* 19.3, 5–8.

Lawson, Hilary. 1989. "Stories about Stories." *Dismantling Truth: Reality in the Post-Modern World.* Ed. Hilary Lawson and Lisa Appignanesi. New York: St. Martin's, xi–xxviii.

Lunsford, Andrea. 1991. "Collaboration, Control, and the Idea of a Writing Center." *The Writing Center Journal* 12.1, 3–10.

McKinley, John. 1980. *Group Development Through Participation Training.* New York: Paulist.

Mishler, Elliot G. 1979. "Meaning in Context: Is There Any Other Kind?" *Harvard Educational Review* 49.1, 1–19.

Myers, Greg. 1986. "Reality, Consensus, and Reform in the Rhetoric of Composition Teaching." *College English* 48, 154–71.

Pareek, Udai. 1981. "Developing Collaboration in Organizations." *The 1981 Annual Handbook for Group Facilitators*. New York: University Associates, 165–82.

Petraglia, Joseph. 1991. "Interrupting the Conversation: The Constructionist Dialogue in Composition." *Journal of Advanced Composition* 11, 37–55.

Phelps, Louise Wetherbee. 1988. *Composition as a Human Science: Contributions to the Self-Understanding of a Discipline*. New York: Oxford University Press.

Phillips, James. 1991. "Hermeneutics in Psychoanalysis: Review and Reconsideration." *Psychoanalysis and Contemporary Thought* 14, 371–424.

Rapoport, Anatol. 1954. *Operational Philosophy: Integrating Knowledge and Action*. New York: Harper.

Reither, James A. 1986. "Academic Discourse Communities, Invention, and Learning to Write." ERIC, ED 270 815.

Roderick, Rick. 1986. *Habermas and the Foundations of Critical Theory*. New York: St. Martin's.

Ryan, Howard. 1991. "The Whys of Teaching Composition: Social Visions." *Freshman English News* 19.3, 9–17.

Sass, Louis A. 1988. "Humanism, Hermeneutics, and the Concept of the Human Subject." *Hermeneutics and Psychological Theory: Interpretive Perspectives on Personality, Psychotherapy, and Psychopathology*. Eds. Stanley B. Messer, Louis A. Sass, and Robert L. Woolfolk. New Brunswick: Rutgers University Press, 222–71.

Smith, Joseph H. 1991. *Arguing with Lacan: Ego Psychology and Language*. New Haven: Yale University Press.

Stewart, Donald C. 1988. "Collaborative Learning and Composition: Boon or Bane?" *Rhetoric Review* 7, 58–83.

Tomlinson, Hugh. 1989. "After Truth: Post-Modernism and the Rhetoric of Science." *Dismantling Truth: Reality in the Post-Modern World*. Eds. Hilary Lawson and Lisa Appignanesi. New York: St. Martin's, 43–57.

Trzyna, Thomas, and Margaret Batschelet. 1990. "The Ethical Complexity of Collaboration." *Writing on the Edge* 2.1, 23–33.

Wiener, Harvey S. 1986. "Collaborative Learning in the Classroom: A Guide to Evaluation." *College English* 48, 52–61.

Winterowd, W. Ross. 1989. *The Culture and Politics of Literacy*. New York: Oxford University Press.

5 Collaborative Learning Theory and Peer Tutoring Practice

Alice M. Gillam
University of Wisconsin–Milwaukee

Theory galvanizes and disrupts the system, changing its very questions, undermining long-held beliefs, introducing ambiguities, revealing complexities, setting new tasks, forcing risks (1991, 883).
                                                            —Louise Wetherbee Phelps

Simultaneous with the emergence of contemporary peer tutoring programs in the late 1960s and early 1970s was the emergence of the collaborative learning movement, a movement with which peer tutoring has long been associated through the work of Kenneth Bruffee. Over the years, it has been Bruffee's project to transform collaborative learning from a collection of loosely related pedagogical principles and practices which aim to decentralize classroom authority and actively involve students in their own learning into a coherent conceptual framework grounded in social constructionist theories of language and knowledge (1984, 635–52; 1986, 773–90). In accomplishing the above goal, Bruffee has used theory in two ways: first, to "disrupt" and critique traditional teacher-centered practices; and second, to consolidate and validate collaborative learning practices.

Thus, in Bruffee's work, the critical or subversive operations of theory move in only one direction—outward toward the pedagogical practices which Bruffee wishes to displace. By contrast, Bruffee's use of theory in relation to collaborative learning practices is uncritically justificatory; theory, specifically social constructionist theory, acts as a warrant or rationale for practices to which he is already committed. In other words, Bruffee's theoretical work is an *ex post facto* "attempt to rationalize theoretically the methods he earlier developed" (Myers 1986, 168). As a result, Bruffee's theoretical formulations of practice tend to be idealized, unproblematic, and acontextual. This is not to dismiss Bruffee's valuable contributions to both theory and practice. In a sense, he has accomplished both aspects of his reformist agenda—that is, his critique of "traditional," teacher-centered pedagogies is widely accepted in theory, if not always in practice, and his advocacy of collaborative learning

39

pedagogies has contributed in no small part to their widespread popularity. Testifying to Bruffee's contributions, John Trimbur writes:

> Bruffee's work has been important because it teaches us to read the classroom and the culture of teaching and learning as a social text . . . What before had seemed commonsensical became in Bruffee's reading of the classroom as a social text a set of historically derived practices. (1989, 605)

Nevertheless, the time has come to turn the critical operations of theory inward and to interrogate collaborative learning theories and practices. Many have already taken up this task, "introducing ambiguities" and "revealing complexities" within collaborative learning theory and noting disjunctures between theory and practice.

The Critical Debate Over Collaborative Learning

In recent years, those who oppose collaborative learning suggest that its emphasis on group process and consensus-building enforces conformity, lowers standards, and denies the importance of the individual mind (Johnson 1986, 76; Foster 1987, 711; Stewart 1983, 66–80). Further, Stewart darkly warns of *collaboration's* equivocal nature: "Those of us who lived during that period [World War II] and were old enough to be interested in what was going on remember what *ugly* connotations attended the word *collaborator*" (66). Yet other objections are raised by David Smit (1989), who challenges what he considers to be the three central arguments for collaborative learning (1) its claim to teach students "a critical stance toward authority and the ability to cooperate and to solve problems of social concern"; (2) its claim to enact the "social nature of language and writing"; and (3) its claim to empirically-demonstrated success (46). According to Smit, the first two claims are faulty in that other pedagogies accomplish the same goals and the third is faulty in that the evidence is still not in on whether or not collaborative learning pedagogies are effective in improving student writing (46–55).

Alternatively, collaborative learning advocates critique Bruffee for his failure to acknowledge the role of ideology in knowledge construction and for his theoretical inconsistencies. Greg Myers (1986), for example, takes Bruffee to task for his failure to acknowledge the unequal power relationships which affect the social construction of knowledge and the process of coming to consensus among collaborative learners (166–67). Similarly, Trimbur faults Bruffee for his failure to "develop a critical version of collaborative learning" which distinguishes between collaborations which reproduce the status quo and collaborations which challenge "the prevailing conditions of [knowledge] production" (1989, 612). Finally, Zavarzadeh and Morton (1991), drawing on postmodern critical theory, launch an even stronger attack on Bruffee's work both for its apolitical nature and for its "reification of the subject":

> There is in Bruffee no sense of the politics of cognition that organizes this socially constructed knowledge. . . . [I]n Bruffee, the subject is presented as an uncontested category . . . and is characterized by coherence, unitariness, and rationality. Bruffee's "collaborative learning/teaching" is, in other words, the latest reproduction of the "management" of the subject and the latest effort to save it through "collaborative learning and the *'conversation of Mankind.' "* (16–17)

My purpose in this paper, however, is not to address the general debates about collaborative learning, but rather to address those that focus on the relationship between collaborative learning theory and peer tutoring practice. For within writing center discourse, as within the larger field of composition studies, there has been a parallel critical turn. Former assumptions about the nature of peer tutoring and other writing center collaborations are being called into question, and contradictions and ambiguities are being acknowledged. In "Collaboration Is Not Collaboration Is Not Collaboration," for example, Muriel Harris discusses the misunderstandings which have arisen from the conflation of various collaborative practices, specifically peer tutoring and peer group work in the classroom. Others, like Thomas Hemmeter (1990) and Christina Murphy (in this volume), note the disjunctures between collaborative learning theory, with its emphasis on socially constructed knowledge, and writing center practice, with its historical commitment to individually constructed knowledge. While Hemmeter noncommittally points out the contradiction in "using social constructionist theory to support a highly individualist pedagogy in which students *own* [my emphasis] their own writing" (41), Murphy directly questions the sufficiency and desirability of using social constructionist theory as the dominant paradigm for writing center practice. Even strong advocates of collaborative learning like Andrea Lunsford warn that "as the latest pedagogical bandwagon, collaboration often masquerades as democracy when it in fact practices the same old authoritarian control" (1991, 1).

Seldom, however, are theory and practice considered together, that is, in terms of one another. Seldom do we ask what does theory offer practice and what *does* practice offer theory? What's missing from these discussions are particular, "contextualized" illustrations of the relationship between theory and practice. In the remainder of this essay, I review several versions of peer tutoring practice based on collaborative learning theory; then I consider a particular case of peer tutoring in terms of these theoretical constructions.

Collaborative Learning Theory and Peer Tutoring Practice

If, as John Trimbur says, collaborative learning is "a method of conducting the business at hand" (1989, 87), then we might begin our discussion of peer tutoring by reviewing collaborative learning's theoretical constructions of the three primary aspects of this "method": the *relationship* between the participants; the *process* itself; and the desired *goals* or outcomes. Since the general goal of collaborative learning is to replace the alienating, teacher-dominated methods of traditional instruction, it is not surprising to find that the relationship, process, and goals of peer tutoring are often figured in oppositional terms.

Unlike the traditional learning context in which the primary transaction occurs between status unequals, the student and the teacher, the peer tutorial involves a transaction between status equals, two students. According to Bruffee, the participants in the peer tutorial not only share student status but also bring separate but equal knowledge: "The tutee brings to the conversation knowledge of the subject to be written about and knowledge of the assignment. The tutor brings to the conversation knowledge of the conventions of discourse and knowledge of standard written English" (1984, 10). Although Thom Hawkins (1932), like Bruffee, uses shared institutional status as the starting point for his notion of equality, his emphasis differs from Bruffee's. Rather than focusing on participants' "separate but equal" knowledge, Hawkins emphasizes the emotional bond or "intimacy" which results from shared status, what social psychologists call *identification:* "A peer tutor, unlike a teacher, is still living the undergraduate experience. . . . [B]oth know that the tutor is not so far along as to have forgotten what learning how to cope with the system is like. . . . When working together they comprise a social structure that enables both to rehearse being insiders" (30).

John Trimbur, however, reminds us that the notion of equality based on shared institutional status is problematic in that institutional hierarchies make "the words 'peer' and 'tutor' appear to be a contradiction in terms" (1987, 23). Though participants may technically share institutional status, the institution itself creates an inequality or asymmetry between tutor and writer which in turn causes a conflict of loyalties for peer tutors who "feel pulled, on the one hand, by their loyalty to their fellow students and, on the other hand, by their loyalty to the academic system that has rewarded them and whose values they have internalized" (23). For Trimbur, then, the notion of equality between tutor and writer must be constituted on grounds other than shared institutional status; it must be constituted on participants' perception of themselves as "co-learners." However, such a perception requires a "resocialization" of tutors and tutees in which both come to "redefin[e] learning as an event produced by the social interaction of the learners—and not a body of information passed down from an expert to a novice" (23).

However determined, the reconstituted relationship between the principal participants in the learning transaction enables, according to collaborative theorists, a reconstituted process of learning, one which is based on social constructionist epistemology rather than on traditional, positivistic epistemology. In the past, many writing centers reflected traditional ideas of teaching and learning in which a knowledgeable tutor, or teacher surrogate, "hand[ed] out skills and strategies to individual learners" (Lunsford 4). By contrast, the collaborative center or "Burkean Parlor" views learning as a process of constructing meaning through the social interaction of peers who are equally "knowledge-able" (Lunsford 4). As Bruffee puts it, "What peer tutor and tutee do together is not write or edit, or least of all proofread. What they do together is converse" (1984, 10). Because peer tutors do not have grade-giving power over the writers they tutor and because they presumably have many experiences in common and "speak the same language," they offer more suitable conversational partners than do classroom teachers. In other words, the peer tutorial relationship changes the social context for learning, enabling tutor and writer to "experience and practice the kinds of conversation academics most value" (7).

The key term in this reconstituted notion of learning is *conversation,* "a social constructionist code word to talk about knowledge and teaching and learning" as interactive, as created through social activity rather than as cognitively perceived by an individual mind (Trimbur, 1989, 605).[1] According to Bruffee, the peer tutorial conversation mirrors the process of knowledge construction which occurs among knowledgeable peers in the real world, where people

> socially justify belief . . . by cancelling each other's biases and presuppositions; by negotiating collectively toward new paradigms of perception, thought, feeling, and expression; and by joining larger, more experienced communities of knowledgeable peers through assenting to those communities' interests, values, language, and paradigms of perception and thought. (1984, 12)

Ideally, this sort of conversation and consensus building not only simulates the general process of knowledge construction, but also reproduces the very dialogic process of writing, which is "temporally and functionally related to conversation" (7). In short, the peer tutorial process involves both the short-term goal of offering practice in the kind of talk that the writer can then translate into academic writing and the long-term goal of offering practice in the kind of talk that will enable both students to join the larger discourse community of college-educated men and women.

Not all agree with Bruffee's idealized version of the peer tutorial conversation which seems to conflate peer tutoring collaborations with other forms of collaborative learning and to ignore the particular expectations and goals involved in peer tutorials. Muriel Harris (1992), for example, argues for a view of writing center collaboration which recognizes that the two participants have different investments and roles in the conversation: "The focus of the effort and attention of both people is solely on the writer" (6). According to Harris's version of the process, the dialogue ought to be constrained by the tutor's mandate to help the writer "find her own answers," to guide the writer "by questioning rather than by telling or explaining" (10).

Yet another, more politicized version of the peer tutorial process is offered by Harvey Kail and John Trimbur (1987) who foreground the idea of co-learning rather than the idea of conversation. According to Kail and Trimbur, the "semi-autonomous space" of the writing center, in which traditional authorities are absent and tutors refuse to act in their stead, precipitates a "crisis of authority" (10–11). This crisis of authority in which students "unlearn" their habituated reliance on teacher authority, argue Kail and Trimbur, is preliminary to co-learning. Borrowing their terms from Richard Sennett, Kail and Trimbur describe this crisis as occurring in three stages: detachment, reflection, and reentrance (10–11). If the writing center environment is sufficiently separate from the student's required curriculum, it "detaches" students from the traditional, familiar situation of learning. Further, the shared student status sets the stage for tutor and writer to reflect on their common subordination within the educational system and their struggles to compete and survive in this system. Finally, this reflection can lead to a questioning and demystifying of traditional authority and ultimately to a reengagement with authority, albeit on reformulated terms.

Understandably, these different versions of the peer tutorial process—the Bruffee model, the Harris model, and the Kail/Trimbur model—entail differing goals. In the Bruffee model, the long-range social goal seems to supersede the immediate educational goal—that is, the goal of the tutorial conversation is to enable students to join both specific and general discourse communities in which they will converse with others to create knowledge, justify and challenge belief. However, Bruffee's theoretical model also gives a nod to the short-term educational goal which is to enable student writers to write successfully in the academic discourse community. Muriel Harris's discussions, however, focus on the latter, more immediate goal: "to help the writer improve her own abilities and produce her own text—though, of course, her final product is influenced by the collaboration with others" (1992, 2).

In the Kail/Trimbur model, the goal of the tutorial is twofold: (1) to produce a new critical consciousness in which both tutor and writer realize that "power ascribed to the faculty depends on the students' own sense of powerlessness and their need for omnipotent authority"; and (2) to encourage students to be "active agents [in constructing knowledge] rather than as passive objects of transmission" (12). Although the goal of Kail and Trimbur's model is cast in terms which refer specifically to education, this model implicitly suggests the larger social goal of a critically conscious and politically active citizenry. Notably, neither Bruffee's nor Kail and Trimbur's model focuses primarily on explicit writing goals. But rather both models view writing as an epistemological and ideological activity and therefore regard its teaching as inextricable from wider institutional and social/political contexts and purposes.

To illustrate both the explanatory power as well as the limitations of these theoretical conceptualizations, I offer an example. While this peer tutorial session is not typical in any of its particulars—in my experience, there is no such thing as a "typical" session—it is typical in its complexity and resistance to easy assessment.

Collaboration in Context: The Case of Kari and Suzanne

What follows is a reconstruction of a tutorial session between Kari, a freshman pre-med student in an introductory composition course, and Suzanne, her peer tutor, a junior English major, who was enrolled in my 400-level tutor preparation class at the time. The session described here, their second of the semester, was audio-taped, as were all their sessions that semester; in addition, both Kari and Suzanne were interviewed at the beginning and end of the semester, and both submitted their journals and course papers to our research team.[2]

Although this was only their second session of the semester, Kari and Suzanne had already established a congenial relationship, in large part on their personal and academic backgrounds. Both are from white middle-class backgrounds; both are "good" students. Their conversation during the first session seems almost like a textbook illustration of Bruffee and Hawkins's claims about the "intimacy" and parity possible in peer tutorial relationships. As Kari describes it in her journal: "It was a break from the usual teacher-student relationship. It wasn't all just her talking or just me talking." Although Kari clearly regards Suzanne as the senior partner in the relationship—after all, Suzanne is already a successful student writer—Kari is actively involved in the tutorial from the beginning, asking questions of Suzanne, stating her opinion, and directing the focus of the conference toward her concerns.

To this second session, Kari has brought a draft of a paper based on Anna Quindlen's essay, "Death Penalty's False Promise: Eye for an Eye" (1988). The task is to write a critical response to Quindlen's argument against the death penalty. Suzanne begins by asking Kari about the assignment and her work so far. Kari responds, "What I did was I analyzed her opinion and then what I feel. . . . I've never had any experience thinking about it, so I just wrote how I feel about capital punishment." Feelings, Kari implies, are distinct from thoughts and insufficient for academic discourse, no substitute for knowledge and experience. A student herself, Suzanne identifies and sympathizes, "That's kinda hard to do. I mean I haven't seen a lot of shows or anything on capital punishment. It's not really fair." Despite the warnings issued in her tutor preparation class against directly criticizing the teacher's assignment, Suzanne exhibits what Trimbur (1987) describes as students' automatic impulse to "unionize" (23). Like Kari, Suzanne has undoubtedly had to write about subjects about which she has little prior knowledge or interest, and capital punishment is a subject about which even she, the experienced partner in the collaboration, has little information. Whatever the cause, Suzanne clearly allies herself with Kari and against the teacher authority, whose assignment she calls "unfair."

What we also begin to see in this passage is that Suzanne and Kari's collaboration is not atomistic, but rather part of a larger network of collaborations. In fact, what we expect to be the primary collaboration, the tutorial conversation between Kari and Suzanne, is subordinated by two other "collaborations" set in motion before Kari arrives for her tutoring appointment: first, her literal collaboration with her teacher, and second, her figurative collaboration with the Anna Quindlen text. Not surprisingly, Kari's collaborations with these authorities—her teacher and the published text—shape the tutorial collaboration between Suzanne and Kari.

Kari's relationship with her teacher is simultaneously friendly and adversarial. On the one hand, Kari wishes to please her teacher and to comply with the demands of the task he has set, partly to prove to herself that she can write acceptable college-level essays, but mostly to earn a good grade on her paper and thereby move toward her overriding goal, the *A* she believes she needs to get into medical school. On the other hand, she resents this assigned topic which involves a subject she knows nothing about and discourse conventions which are a mystery to her.

Kari's comments to Suzanne regarding her meeting with her teacher the previous evening offer further insight into this relationship:

> I asked him last night [about how to go about the assignment]. I go, "When should you do it [add your own opinion]? Should you go her argument, your argument, her argument, your argument? Or should you go all hers and then yours?" He said, "If you're against hers, you could do her argument and then base . . . [trails off]." I don't know what it is officially, but he said like if you agree with every one of her arguments then you should do her/you, her/you, her/you.

Besides illustrating Kari's willingness to ask for help and her teacher's accessibility, this exchange, or at least Kari's report of it, is noteworthy for its focus on form versus content and for its illustration of Kari's translation of her teacher's advice. In recounting the conversation to Suzanne, she briefly quotes her teacher, then shifts quickly to paraphrase, translating his comments into formulaic terms—"her/you, her/you, her/you"—the same terms used in her initial question. In effect she appropriates the teacher's advice and interprets it as approval for the strategy she already has in mind. Although her teacher frames his advice on form in terms of content—"If you're against her [position], you could . . ."—Kari's comments refer only to form. Significantly, Kari chooses not to discuss content, or more specifically her lack of knowledge about the subject, with her teacher. Perhaps she feels that such an admission would be embarrassing, or fears that it would affect his opinion of her abilities. Or maybe she believes that it is acceptable to seek procedural advice from a teacher but not acceptable to reveal ignorance about a topic or frustration with the assignment.

With Suzanne, however, Kari feels no such reluctance, and she candidly admits her frustration, disinterest, and resignation: "None of this [Quindlen's argument concerning capital punishment] struck me. I just do the assignment. . . . I was doing it because he told us to do it." Although Kari likes her teacher as an individual, she resents the teacherly authority he represents and the helplessness such authority evokes in her. Suzanne, by contrast, has no authority over Kari and has identified herself as an ally in her willingness to judge the assignment "unfair." As a result, Kari feels free to voice her resentment and sense of inadequacy in meeting the assignment's demands. This intersection of collaborations between Kari and her teacher and Kari and her tutor shape the agenda for their session. Since Kari has already come up with a procedural plan based on her discussion with her teacher, she looks to Suzanne for practical help with the content of her essay.

Here, however, Kari and Suzanne encounter the problems entailed in Kari's prior "collaboration" with Quindlen's text. Both agree that the content of Kari's draft is weak. As Suzanne rather bluntly puts it, "What you're doing is just sort of regurgitating her ideas." For her part, Kari realizes that the task requires that she distinguish her position from that of Quindlen even though she would prefer simply to defer to the authority of Quindlen's text. Early in this segment of their conversation, Kari makes a telling comment: "It was just the exact way I felt. So she just . . . In a way she just repeated what I was thinking." Although she has given little prior thought to the subject, it is as though Quindlen "repeats" what was in her head. In other words, Quindlen articulates for her what was already there in inchoate form. And since Quindlen says so well what Kari would have said had she thought to say it, there is really nothing left to say. Quindlen's text has taken her voice away by speaking for her. Perhaps, she reasons in this same passage, she can solve her problem by substituting another voice for her own: "So I can just find an article and read it and write about that as my experience."

This sense of having her thoughts inscribed by the power and authority of the Quindlen text is evident everywhere in Kari's draft. She begins by announcing herself as "an Anna Quindlen follower," who agrees with "every one of her contentions," then proceeds to paraphrase Quindlen's argument:

> In the beginning Anna provides us with background to her relationship to the subject of capital punishment, with where actually her position started on the matter. . . . As a reporter, Anna learns of Ted Bundy, a man who has murdered dozens of girls. She realizes that she is like any other girl who [might] succumb to the handsome looks of a young gentleman. If Ted would have showed up at the right time, she could have been his next victim.

Even more interesting is the self or persona that Kari constructs in her text. This self openly identifies with Quindlen: Kari refers to Quindlen familiarly as "Anna"; asserts their solidarity—"Both of us believe that the death penalty doesn't live up to most people's expectations of severest revenge"; and speaks knowingly about her collaborator's experiences and writing motive—"Without these strong lessons she obviously would have never written the essay."

Plainly, helping Kari revise the content of her essay is a daunting task. It is one thing simply to hear out and emotionally support a fellow student; it is another to help that writer generate ideas and establish a sense of authority in relation to a subject about which she has little knowledge or interest. Ever the resourceful one, however, Kari announces a plan for feigning interest and establishing writerly authority: "So what I was thinking about doing was rereading each paragraph [of Quindlen's essay] then thinking about each paragraph and how I feel about it." Since Quindlen begins by explaining how she came to be interested in the topic of capital punishment, Kari also plans to begin with an explanation of her interest in the topic: "I could say that 'I wasn't affected by it [the issue of capital punishment] until . . .' Then I was gonna make up a lie there. 'I wasn't affected until I started reading articles in school and doing assignments and that's how I got affected.'" Laughing, Suzanne noncommittally replies, "That's one way to do it."

Although she is neither shocked or judgmental about Kari's plan, Suzanne is not entirely comfortable in simply encouraging this lie; therefore, she tries to steer Kari away from simply counterfeiting ideas. First, she tries to probe Kari's memory for possible connections with the subject—"Have you ever seen any shows? Read any newspaper articles? Seen TV newscasts?" When this doesn't work, Suzanne tries to elicit an emotional reaction by creating an imaginary scenario: "OK. Like there's a big murder, but you don't know what the guy's sentence is gonna be. Don't you ever think about 'Is this guy gonna get off scot free?' " Although Kari is able to dredge up some recollected "knowledge" about various murder cases—the TV movie about the murder of Adam Walsh, local lore about Wisconsin mass-murderer Ed Geine—the revision which follows this tutorial session exposes the "lie" that Kari has something to say and an interest in saying it in every awkward phrase:

> I did not have a standing position on capital punishment until I became aware of such insane criminals as Charles Manson and Ed Geine. After reading books on these killers, I realized that not even death as a punishment could equate to their grotesque crimes. Like Anna, I saw the TV program about the little boy, Adam Walsh, who was abducted from his mother and then brutally murdered . . . It was through such horrifying stories as the ones of Manson, Geine, and Adam that sparked my opinionated view against capital punishment.

Although Kari and Suzanne's conversation may seem a far cry from Bruffee's notion of the peer tutorial as the "conversation of mankind" writ small, Suzanne's persistent questions about Kari's views of the subject yield one important departure from Quindlen's position. In this same revision, which was her final draft of this paper, Kari distinguishes her position from Quindlen's by refashioning Quindlen's central argument into her own argument against the death penalty. For Quindlen, the death penalty falsely promises cathartic revenge to an outraged public. For Kari, the death penalty falsely promises to be the severest punishment possible: "I am not in favor of the death penalty. I feel that it is the easy way out for the criminal. In prison the criminal has to live a long boring life excluded from the rest of the world." In other words, she goes Quindlen one better, arguing that life without parole, unlike the death penalty, delivers the retribution that it promises and that the public seeks. Thus, Suzanne's probe-and-prompt conversational strategy eventually lead Kari to a "standing position" which is distinct from Quindlen's.

Theorizing Practice/Practicing Theory

So what does theory offer us in relation to this particular case of practice? Does theory help us to understand and interpret the case? Does it "galvanize" or "disrupt" our notions of practice? Alternatively, what does this instance of practice offer theory? Does this case "disrupt" our notions of theory? Does it confirm or disconfirm various collaborative learning conceptualizations of peer tutoring practice?

Judged in terms of the quality of Kari's final written product, the "success" of Kari and Suzanne's collaboration is questionable. The writing style in Kari's revision is stiff; the diction awkward and unidiomatic; and the "realization" unconvincing. Moreover, we might interpret the session as a collaboration in the sense suggested by collaborative learning critic Donald Stewart, a conspiracy in which Suzanne aids and abets Kari's "lie" and colludes with her in responding perfunctorily to an "unfair" assignment.

Yet judged in light of the collaborative learning theories mentioned earlier, this session appears differently. The "intimate" social context of their peer relationship offers Kari an opportunity to express a side of herself that resists the passivity that she felt was required of her as a student. Without the opportunity to admit her resentment about the assignment and to confess her "guilty" strategy, perhaps she would have been even more silenced by the authority of Quindlen's published text. In other words, I would argue that it was Suzanne's role as confidante and confederate which enabled Kari to construct a "standing position," wobbly though that stand may have been.

At the same time, this case raises questions about the various idealizations of peer tutoring forwarded by collaborative learning theorists. For example, is Suzanne and Kari's "intimacy" and rapport a result of their "status equality" or a product of chance factors—their shared gender, ethnicity, class background, and investment in academic success? If the latter is the case, and I suspect it is, then is it not naive to assume that student status alone will enable students to establish a trusting, reciprocal relationship? Further, the collaboration between Suzanne and Kari reveals that the peer tutorial relationship ought not be considered in terms which ignore the multiple other collaborations which intersect in the peer tutorial encounter. As Harvey Kail suggests, peer tutorials entail "a maze of influences and a tangle of conversations about writing" (1983, 597).

Similarly, theoretical constructions of the tutorial process both illuminate practice and, in turn, are challenged by it. Although Suzanne attempts to engage Kari in conversation about the subject, their conversation does not resemble the ideal intellectual conversation that Bruffee seems to have in mind in which the participants contribute equally to the construction of meaning. Rather, Suzanne and Kari's conversation resembles the sort of exchange described by theorists like Muriel Harris, who urge the tutor to play a limited role in the conversation, specifically the role of interlocutor. To some extent, Suzanne's probe-and-prompt strategy is successful. After all, Kari eventually does "find her own answer." But I cannot help but wonder whether Kari would not have been better served by a conversational partner who actively engaged her in debating the issues involved in the capital punishment question. For does not the prohibition on tutor participation in the conversation reenact what Lunsford calls the "Garret Idea" of the writing center, where ideas are somehow private property?

Certainly, we see in this tutorial process a "crisis of authority" which is not unlike the process outlined by Kail and Trimbur. Suzanne and Kari do "detach" themselves from traditional teacher authority, tacitly agree on its arbitrariness, and thereby indirectly "reflect" on it in demystifying terms. One might even say, that their faintly seditious comments and Kari's elaborated "lie" are acts of resistance. But whether this shared resentment over various "oppressions" they have suffered as students leads them to a critical understanding of "the structures of authority they have internalized" and to a subsequent sense of empowerment is unclear (Kail and Trimbur 1987, 11).

Finally, what of the outcome? As with the issues of the tutorial relationship and process, theory does not so much offer explanations or criteria for assessment as new perspectives. In this case, one might interpret Kari's "lie," which Suzanne tacitly encouraged, and Suzanne and Kari's search for "content" variously. One could interpret Kari's "lie" as a cynical accommodation to an "unfair" assignment, and Kari and Suzanne's conversation as a mockery of Bruffee's "conversation of mankind," in which participants have real investment in the subject and a genuine interest in a deeper understanding of the issues and of one another's ideas. On the other hand, it is possible to argue that Kari's "lie" served a useful developmental function and that her struggles to construct an argumentative position for herself required her to simulate an authority she did not feel. Playing the role of someone who has knowledge of and opinions about public policy issues may have been legitimate practice for constructing authority and knowledge in future academic writing tasks. As David Bartholomae suggests in "Inventing the University" (1986), and the Summerfields conclude in *Texts and Contexts* (1986), role playing or impersonation "is a way of entering/taking on the conventions, the determining environmental constraints, of a particular task/function or discipline/tradition" (202).

However we interpret the meaning of this case, it is clear that the critical operations of theory can challenge and enlarge our understanding of practice. Similarly, as Phelps suggests, practice enriches theory by "humanizing" it and "undercut[ting] its totalizing tendencies" (1991, 884). Indeed, what Phelps says of theory could also be said of reflective practice which "galvanizes and disrupts the system, changing its very questions, undermining long-held beliefs, introducing ambiguities, revealing complexities, setting new tasks, forcing risks" (883).

Along with others in this volume, I would argue that the writing center offers a fertile site for engaging in reflective practice and for generating paradoxical, contingent knowledge. Given the fact that writing center collaborations come "in a dizzying variety of modes about which we know almost nothing" (Lunsford 1991, 7), it is time we utilize theory to understand and interrogate the rich complexity of writing center practice and the protean forms of writing center practice to interrogate and reinterpret theory.

Notes

1. See Gregory Clark (1990) for a fuller explanation of how the conversational model has been deployed in composition studies as a metaphor for writing and writing instruction.

2. This case is abstracted from a larger study in which my colleagues, Susan Callaway and Katherine Hennessey Wikoff, and I gathered data on four semester-long peer tutorial relationships. Conducted in 1987, this study was supported in part by a grant from the Graduate School at the University of Wisconsin–Milwaukee.

References

Bartholomae, David. 1986. "Inventing the University." *Journal of Basic Writing* 5.1, 4–23.

Bruffee, Kenneth. 1984. "Peer Tutoring and the 'Conversation of Mankind.' " *Writing Centers: Theory and Administration.* Ed. Gary A. Olson. Urbana, IL: National Council of Teachers of English, 3–15.

———. 1986. "Social Construction, Language, and the Authority of Knowledge: A Bibliographical Essay." *College English* 43, 773–90.

———. 1989. "Collaborative Learning and the 'Conversation of Mankind.' " *College English* 46, 635–52.

Clark, Gregory. 1990. *Dialogue, Dialectic, and Conversation.* Carbondale: Southern Illinois University Press.

Foster, David. 1987. "Comment and Response." *College English* 49.6, 709–11.

Harris, Muriel. 1992. "Collaboration Is Not Collaboration Is Not Collaboration: Writing Center Tutorials vs. Peer Response Groups." *College Composition and Communication* 43.3, 369–83.

Hawkins, Thom. 1982. "Intimacy and Audience: The Relationship Between Revision and the Social Dimension of Peer Tutoring." *Tutoring Writing.* Ed. Muriel Harris. Glenview, IL: Scott Foresman, 27–31.

Hemmeter, Thomas. 1990. "The 'Smack of Difference': The Language of Writing Center Discourse." *The Writing Center Journal* 11.1, 35–48.

Johnson, Thomas S. 1986. "Comment and Response." *College English* 48.1, 76.

Kail, Harvey. 1983. "Collaborative Learning in Context: The Problem with Peer Tutoring," *College English* 45.6, 594–99.

Kail, Harvey, and John Trimbur. 1987. "The Politics of Peer Tutoring." *WPA: Writing Program Administration* 11.1–2, 5–12.

Lunsford, Andrea A. 1991. "Collaboration, Control, and the Idea of a Writing Center." *The Writing Center Journal* 12.1, 4–10.

Myers, Greg. 1986. "Reality, Consensus, and Reform in the Rhetoric of Composition Teaching." *College English* 48, 154–74.

Phelps, Louise Wetherbee. 1991. "Practical Wisdom and the Geography of Knowledge in Composition." *College English* 53.8, 863–65.

Quindlen, Anna. 1987. "Death Penalty's False Promise: An Eye for an Eye." Rpt. in *Writing with a Purpose*. 9th ed. Joseph F. Trimmer and James P. McCrimmon. Boston: Houghton Mifflin, 153–54.

Smit, David W. 1989. "Some Difficulties with Collaborative Learning." *Journal of Advanced Composition* 9, 45–58.

Stewart, Donald. 1983. "Collaborative Learning and Composition: Boon or Bane?" *Rhetoric Review* 7, 58–83.

Summerfield, Judith, and Geoffrey Summerfield. 1986. *Texts and Contexts: A Contribution to the Theory and Practice of Teaching Composition*. New York, Random House.

Trimbur, John. 1985. "Collaborative Learning and Teaching Writing." *Perspectives on Research and Scholarship in Composition*. Eds. Ben McClelland and Timothy R. Donovan. New York: Modern Language Association, 87–109.

———. 1987. "Peer Tutoring: A Contradiction in Terms?" *The Writing Center Journal* 7.2, 21–28.

———. 1989. "Consensus and Difference in Collaborative Learning." *College English* 51.6, 602–16.

Zavarzadeh, Mas'ud, and Donald Morton. 1991. "Theory Pedagogy Politics: The Crisis of 'The Subject' in the Humanities." *Theory/Pedagogy/Politics*. Eds. Donald Morton and Mas'ud Zavarzadeh. Urbana, IL: University of Illinois Press, 1–32.

6 Writing Others, Writing Ourselves: Ethnography and the Writing Center

Janice Witherspoon Neuleib and Maurice A. Scharton
Illinois State University

In *Reading to Write, Exploring a Cognitive and Social Process,* Linda Flower gives an amusing picture of positivistic research as it might be imagined but as it never happens in writing research:

> In the mythos of experimental research one begins in the morning with a clear-cut hypothesis—a potential answer to a well-defined question. By noon that hypothesis is expressed in an experimental manipulation and set of pre-/post-tests. A large pool of subjects known only by number are 'run,' and once the results come in, the meaning of the study swiftly emerges, expressed as an Anova, or, better yet, a more powerful stepwise regression, in which a set of clear main effects can speak for themselves with little need for interpretation. . . . In contrast to that procedure, the process of much research in composition shows an alternative picture of how knowledge can be developed. (7–8)

Flower goes on to argue for "controlled empirical observation" as she introduces the lengthy study that is the subject of her book.

Positivistic research presents a variety of difficulties for our field. Theorists question the appropriateness of applying linear analytical methods to the complex interactions of factors in research that concerns human learning, composing, and decoding (Lauer and Asher 1988). Perhaps the most intractable difficulty with positivistic research is that, in educational contexts, we find it nearly impossible to select a truly random sample, unlike researchers in the less complex populations of the physical sciences or in some animal research based on generations of selective breeding. Writing center personnel have long known that differing traffic patterns, varied clientele, and assorted instructional practices make even less rigid research methodologies, like surveys and protocols, difficult to implement in writing centers. No survey catches all the types who use the center or asks the kinds of questions that can explain the nature of the interactions between tutors and their students. A reading or writing protocol must be taken in an artificial context outside the usual tutoring patterns and therefore may not reflect true behavior.

54

To do controlled research in group settings such as classrooms, we must accept the assumption that the group is an organism which functions in a coherent, purposeful way. For anyone who has spent much time tutoring, this assumption is strongly counter-intuitive. Student writers are not laboratory rats, with genetic and behavioral constants we can manipulate experimentally. Scientifically speaking, their origins are chaotic. As workers in a writing center, we know that we must proceed by guesses, luck, and intuition, since not even our clients are aware of all the factors affecting their learning. Instead of attempting to maintain the dispassionate distance of scientists, we habitually seek to immerse ourselves in the student's experience, trusting that our perceptions will lead us where a carefully organized lesson plan cannot hope to go. Our knowledge is heuristic, hypothesis-generating, even anecdotal. Positivistic research may in time begin where our observations leave off, but positivistic research cannot proceed at all without the intuitions of those who observe behavior in "natural" settings.

In doing research, we can draw on the observation and record-keeping techniques we have developed in this clinical setting, but in order to discipline our perceptions and communicate our understanding, we must adopt, as Flower suggests, controlled methods of observation. Given our insider's view of students, ethnographic methodology suggests itself as a technique which, appropriately modified, may offer potential as a method of observation to help writing centers become a primary hypothesis-generating mechanism for composition research. The most suitable methodology for us is some variation on an ethnographic model, so we need to understand both how that research can improve our centers and how the theoretical basis for the research may affect our everyday functioning as tutors and teachers of those who seek our help.

Ethnographic Methodology

A primary assumption of modern ethnomethodology is that the researcher and the native population affect each other. Clifford Geertz (1988) analyzes several famous anthropologists as scientists and writers. The conclusions he draws center around fluid definitions of author and authority. He posits the theory that ethnographers write not only about the cultures they study but about themselves as well. Using the writings of Levi-Strauss, Evans-Pritchard, Malinowski, and Benedict, he shows that each writer revealed his or her own personality and culture while at the same time the native culture absorbed and changed the writer.

The anthropologist always looks through the eyes of his or her own experience, but also must inevitably be changed by the culture being studied. Thus Evans-Pritchard both critiqued and became like the African natives he studied, and Benedict criticized her own culture while praising the Japanese way of life. Neither necessarily intended that the cultures would blend and comment on one another in the written work, but through the process of writing about the others, the authors lost the boundaries between themselves and those they studied. In a way reminiscent of physical science's Heisenberg principle (that we change what we observe by the act of observation), they changed the objects of scientific study by observing them, but also changed themselves while observing.

James Clifford (1988), in his analysis of modern ethnography, explains that the western view of culture became one of "cultures" only at the turn of the century, when scientists and scholars began to define the word as "plural, suggesting a world of separate, distinctive, and equally meaningful ways of life" (93). Geertz and Clifford speak of a world in which the admission of differences allows for a new approach to both authorship and authority. They rest their work on modern theorists who question the foundations of culture, especially Foucault's archeology of cultural assumptions. They ask questions about what we know in our own cultures and about how we can be changed by exposures to other cultures.

Anthropological field research has changed its basic assumptions since this new theoretical underpinning has emerged. Ethnographers become true participant observers, aware that their participation in the process of doing their research will make them a part of the culture. They will also share the authorship with those being observed; authority for any text or study no longer lies in the hands that play over the keys of the computer but also in the minds and actions of those who are observed. Clifford and Marcus summarize the perspective: "Once 'informants' begin to be considered as co-authors, and the ethnographer as scribe and archivist as well as interpreting observer, we can ask new, critical questions of all ethnographies" (1986, 17).

Karen LeFevre (1987) has extrapolated these ideas of group text to describe what she calls collective writing, that done by a group working together. Such collective work of authorship certainly describes any ethnographic study of a writing center, since all the tutors, students, and staff participate in the construction, collection, and interpretation of data. Writing center researchers should understand and be able to apply ethnographic approaches while understanding this new perspective on the authorial stance they are taking; thus, when they theorize the results both for the center being studied and for the profession at large, they will realize the problematic and yet pleasingly complex voice with which they speak.

When we abandon or seriously modify the researcher's stance as unmoved mover, credibility becomes a central problem in research. How can we trust the perceptions of someone who has gone native? People in writing centers are all too familiar with the attitudes of those who patrol the boundaries we help people cross. From our vantage point, we can see how unequal distributions of power afflict every interaction between the students and teachers of writing. We are privy to knowledge which, imparted to others, might cause anything from political conflict to litigation. An authentic ethnographic study may have to risk some of those consequences.

A key to surviving such peril is meticulous and comprehensive record keeping. The record-keeping system of a writing center constitutes the control of observation for which Flower called in her critique of positivistic research. In keeping records, writing centers have written a critical history of the contact between students and the professoriate. We have been taking notes on our center for years, not so much to understand it as to answer the feared attacks of budget cutters who someday might strike. These data provide one version of fieldnotes: notes that cover everything from tutor activities to the content of grammar hotline calls, student papers both in tutoring files and in writing assessment folders, recorded interviews with tutors, evaluation forms filled out by tutors and the students with whom they worked, and our own massive year-end reports based on a data-keeping system comparable only to the federal government's spy system back in the cold war days. These records are the key to beginning an ethnographic study, but before looking at the study itself, an ethnographer can profit by an effort to understand the assumptions underlying the culture being investigated.

Excavating Our Assumptions

Linda Brodkey (1987) warns that it is difficult to separate perceptions from assumptions in telling a story. We need to consider Foucault's archaeological approach when we begin to study our centers. Foucault (1973) asks what assumptions lie behind any theory, system, or institution. Where was the field born; what were the assumptions at the time of that beginning? We might well ask the same questions both about writing centers and about the masses of data and materials we have gathered and decide how they can best be used to study what we do. What happens when we look at ourselves through the eyes of the anthropologist and the archaeologist?

What political and social situations informed the design of our center at its beginning? How did that original political situation affect design choices? How does it continue to affect the operation of the center? What do our collections of data tell us about the center, and how do our own agendas affect what we see as we observe our center in operation (Brodkey)? How have we been changed by the experiences of working with and observing center operations? These questions can help a center director see the center through new eyes and define the nature of research outcomes. For example, to understand our present center at Illinois State we must return to the 1976 center. We must ask what political and social situations informed the design of our center at its beginning. To answer that question, we must be willing to ask ourselves what was not said explicitly at the time.

The political situation was volatile in the English department and in the College of Arts and Sciences. The first negative tenure decisions ever to be made in the department had been handed down the year before, and the college had supported the decisions. The English department chair was a woman, and so was the dean of the college. Both were feared and hated by those who had suffered or whose friends had suffered from the negative tenure decisions. The dean wanted a writing center because she had read about centers in current administrative newsletters. She suggested to the chair that the department establish such a center. Meantime, Neuleib had suggested to the chair that a materials and tutoring center would be a good addition to the department. The department chair suggested that Neuleib propose a writing center in her presentation for a tenure-line contract, the first such presentation attached to a national search in the department's history.

Not only were the department politics sensitive, the job situation nationally was at one of its bleakest points. The number of majors in English was down by the hundreds at our university, and more negative tenure decisions seemed likely. It was in this politically volatile situation that our center began. Given the economy today, new center directors may find themselves in equally tentative and vulnerable situations. With these unspoken political necessities always in mind, the center began with much self-protective behavior. Every record was kept meticulously: every hour of tutoring, every type of assistance, every planning period for tutors, every presentation to campus facilities like dorms and fraternity houses, every speech given at a convention or workshop, every computer program run, every moment of every day for everyone who worked in the center was recorded. Each student using the center was asked to evaluate the experience and to fill out a form documenting that experience. At the end of the first year, an elaborate report went out to every corner of the campus showing how busy the center had been and how effective the tutoring had been in the eyes of users. For years the reporting mechanism remained the same, producing a campus-wide perception of industry and effectiveness for the center.

In 1986 the administration decided to combine, under Neuleib's direction, the writing center with the less heavily used study/skills center. None of the initial conditions existed that had informed the beginning of the Writing Center. The directors (Neuleib and Scharton) had long since been tenured and were not in the vulnerable position of those early days of the center. Department and college politics had lost most of their volatility: a different chair and dean had been successful in their jobs for some years—both were relaxed and confident in their decision-making. Yet, as we noted above, cautious self-reporting and detailed data collection had become such a habit of operation and such a rule for administration that no one questioned whether it should continue. The "someday-they-will-check-up-on-us" attitude was still operating somewhere at the barely conscious level and was conveyed more by example than by precept to the two assistant directors. The original political context of the Writing Center's birth clearly has had more influence on practice in the much larger and politically more stable Center for Learning Assistance than any current example or model.

Another important factor in 1976 was the movement away from drills and programmed instruction in writing center design. Already theoretically opposed to the use of workbooks and grammar programs, Neuleib visited several writing centers in the Midwest, noting the difference between personal, interactive centers like those at Purdue and Iowa City and some of the programmed instruction-based centers in community colleges in the state of Illinois. After observing the difference in the centers' atmospheres, she was quite determined that no one would be wired to a tape recorder in the name of teaching writing.

This policy, like that of keeping careful records, carried over into Writing Center rules and regulations to create in the staff a distaste for the impersonal and dogged atmosphere of those centers where the human element did not come first. Coffee is available to every person who comes into the Center, despite our current president's distaste for food in the workplace. We initially screen tutors for academic and intellectual ability; then we train them in tutorial and interpersonal skills. We use personality type as a frame within which to teach tutors what personal tactics and nonverbal signals to use to make students comfortable in the Center (Jensen and DiTiberio 1989; Scharton and Neuleib 1990). Much of this stress on atmosphere was grounded in the arguments that Mina Shaughnessy, Muriel Harris, and many others made against impersonal, generalized algorithmic methods of dealing with writing instruction. All those powerful voices of the seventies have so influenced Illinois State University's Center that it would be hard to rethink the current activities with a nineties perspective.

Perhaps an ethnographer who was not a part of the writing center culture would be the best evaluator of the ways in which these assumptions have worked themselves out in the day-to-day operation of the Center. Since assistant directors, office manager, and tutors are all chosen with the center's tone and methods in mind, the inevitable effect is to reinforce the original assumptions and to avoid ideas and practices that would produce a contrary pattern. For instance, the need for a programmed chemistry tutorial has been noted by several center tutors, and everyone on the staff agrees that the program would be a wonderful idea. No one, however, has found the time and interest to look at the many chemistry tutorials that are available. Thus, the theory about not teaching writing through grammar workbook exercises, no doubt the best idea in its time and possibly still the best idea, has influenced other practices that might better be served by programmed instruction.

One sort of technology, however, enhances the interpersonal strengths of the center tutors. Since 1986, all writing tutors in the Center have had access to computers in order to work with students on their papers on-screen when necessary. The assumptions upon which we introduced the computers, of course, tie back to exactly the same theory that prohibited programmed grammar instruction. These assumptions are the same that underlie our insistence on extensive variety in the generation of papers, the need to revise after having appropriate readers look at the papers, and the need to continue looking at a text as a work in process through multiple revisions.

Thus, the personal computer became the tutoring tool of the well-trained tutor, though the tutor was never, of course, to use the computer for any programmed workbooks. We are being just a bit ironic about our own theoretical assumptions, but we give Foucault his due in admitting that we have been so thoroughly controlled by those assumptions that we find it difficult even to see that anyone else could work from any other perspective. What we have done in our Center seems so theoretically sound and so without question the best way to tutor writing that we find it difficult to imagine that other assumptions could have led to another sort of center.

That is exactly the point, though: another set of assumptions *could* have led to a far different type of center, as those original visits to other learning centers demonstrated. The centers that had silent rooms with programmed instructional booklets and tape recorders were informed by a different set of assumptions. Most of us, today, still would not call those learning laboratories writing centers or reading centers, but that refusal to even share our names with theirs only emphasizes the difference in controlling visions.

Triangulating Data

Having done some archeology on our early assumptions, we can begin to look at our centers as an ethnographer might. The central analytical approach of an ethnographer is a method called triangulation (Lauer and Asher 1988; Spradley 1980) through which an observer can look at the same world from several different perspectives. Ethnographers do not test hypotheses, but rather generate hypotheses from triangulated data and then measure those hypotheses against more data (Spradley). We have mentioned the masses of data we have collected. Combined with our observations, these data can be informative about the nature of tutoring and outcomes in our center and can provide a rich research base for generating hypotheses about tutoring in writing centers.

Studying a center's operation will illustrate this triangulation. Our readers are well aware of how to use records to document student progress, so we will turn our attention to the reflexive effects that center operations exert on those who are nominally the agents and instruments of change in students. We will use our records to assume the perspectives of the tutor, the administrator, and the teacher. From the triangulated viewpoint which emerges, we will generate hypotheses about the center.

Tutor's Perspective

An example of this rich cross-sectional study can begin in a writing-across-the-curriculum (WAC) tutor's file. The tutors in writing-across-the-curriculum are hired specifically to work for one faculty member in a department that is a part of the English department's WAC program. These tutors then spend six hours per week working for the teacher to whom they are assigned, marking papers and responding to journal entries and the like. They spend one hour per week in staff meetings on tutorial issues. The other three or more assigned hours per week are spent tutoring either students from the assigned WAC class or from other writing classes. Tutors write records of all tutoring sessions in their own personal files, recording their tutoring activities and future plans for working with students. Tutors also write records of their tutoring experiences in student files, recording tutorial information for their future session plans and to inform a succeeding tutor or an inquiring professor of the tutoring events.

One WAC tutor, Mark, works for a sociology professor who is one of the most energetic and devoted of the university faculty who emphasize writing in their content-area classes. From Mark's personal files, we can develop a picture of the writing center enterprise as Mark experiences it. He takes meticulous notes when he tutors, and he pays careful attention to advice both in the tutor handbook and in the weekly staff meetings.

Mark pays close attention to the needs of his students, worrying when they miss appointments and checking on their progress in the class for which he is a tutor. We note that Mark fits many of the ideal tutor patterns that we have urged on all our tutors and have selected for when interviewing each year. He listens more than he talks, checks on students when they miss sessions, keeps the pen or keyboard in the hands of the student he is helping, and tries to keep in mind the class expectations which the student must meet with the paper being written. His tutoring notes display a thoroughness and sympathy for each student with whom he works. He often comments when a student misses a session or does not give a paper the same enthusiasm that he would for one he himself was writing. All in all, he is the "ideal tutor." Generally, Mark represents the kind of tutor the center staff try to hire and train.

We also have staff notes, taken on Mark's tutoring methods and style. We assume that male and female tutors will react in certain culturally determined ways, males tending to be slightly more directive and dominant in tutoring sessions. We also assume, however, that tutors of various personality types will react to others in the patterns predisposed by those patterns. Mark is a type given to introspection, imagination, helping others, and keeping options open (Introverted, Intuitive, Feeling, Perceiving) in Myers-Briggs's terms, so we assume that he will not follow cultural stereotypes for men. Our observations seem to confirm those assumptions. Of course, our note-taking may be informed by our assumptions about what we expect of a male English major who has the extreme introverted personality indicated by his responses to the personality indicator.

Jenna is as nearly opposite Mark as possible, yet she too fits the pattern for a desirable tutor. She is lively, enthusiastic, eager to help everyone around her. Of course, she does share Mark's interest in others and shows that concern in her work with those whom she tutors. Her tutoring records indicate her more outgoing and vivacious personality: she sees more people per week, though she tutors the same number of hours, and writes less about each encounter. Her notes reveal a breathlessness, a need to move on to the next project or person. Everyone knows when she arrives in the Center with her cheerful and bright personality and her willingness to tell all about her most recent activity, whether that is writing a paper or making taffy apples for her whole apartment complex. Jenna, by the way, is the extraverted (Extraverted, Intuitive, Feeling, Judging) type in Myers-Briggs's terminology.

Administrator's Perspective

Our assumptions color our observations, since we come to both tutors with expectations and attitudes about what we expect them to do in any particular tutoring situation. But from watching Mark and Jenna and others like them, we are able to form some hypotheses about the nature of the tutoring expected, and performed, in our center. First, the candidate's personal concern and interest in the well-being of the students who will come for help are important considerations in our tutor choice and training. Our tutor handbook reinforces that hypothesis since it stresses interpersonal skills in nearly every one of its guidelines. Second, while tutors must be bright, they must also know how to communicate with those whom they tutor. Jenna and Mark, both Undergraduate Teaching Assistant tutors, are, by definition, excellent students since the university requires a B average or above for UTAs in all areas. Our tutor screening, which includes extensive group interviews, stresses picking those tutors who have skill in working with others in the group and in cooperating rather than competing.

Those who are acquainted with the personality-type assumptions that underlie our comments above may be amused to know that we seldom choose our own personality types as tutors since the particular caring qualities we stress in our tutors are not the first-line qualities of our own competitive natures. That observation leads to our major hypothesis: *Writing Centers must resist the dominant academic ethos of competition, replacing individual success with cooperation achievement for all.*

This hypothesis emerges after long consideration. From years of working with staff, tutors, and students, we have come to think of ourselves as more patient teachers, improved problem solvers, somewhat more humane administrators, and far better negotiators for academic improvement. We have learned to use our intellectual and social skills to improve the learning environment for others, and in learning that lesson, have become better scholars and teachers ourselves. We have learned to understand, even to value, ideas and practices which run counter to our own inclinations.

We have also observed that a writing center provides an opportunity for the field testing of teaching methods that can improve teaching across the curriculum. The tutorial methods in our own center find applications in the classes of our former tutors as well as in the classes of faculty who send students to the center. Collaboration and peer response come easily to our former tutors' classrooms, as does the easy relinquishing of authority to the writers and readers of student texts. Our center has been a prime testing ground for student-centered writing instruction and continues to be a place where innovation and creativity are encouraged and rewarded.

A familiar example of this change is Ken Bruffee's (1984) work with collaboration, work that is firmly based in observational research in writing centers. From the tutorial experience which he observed, he was able to extrapolate a theory that has informed the profession generally. That research served to formulate concepts that had broader application than to writing centers alone. We find that the center is often a place for greater understanding of ourselves as college professors and for our colleagues' increased understanding of their students. And that understanding inevitably leads to change of various kinds, change that extends beyond the walls of the center and the departments who use the center regularly. We find our administrators bringing dignitaries such as visiting college board members or administrators from other schools through the center, showing them that the university does care about students. When administrators stress the need to understand and aid students, they themselves become more concerned for student well-being.

Teacher's Perspective

Now that we have begun to formulate our hypothesis—that centers catalyze change in all those who become involved in their activities—we will use another perspective to attempt to deepen, qualify, or perhaps rebut and abandon our hypothesis. The teacher perspective will help us in that effort. We are able to assume that perspective legitimately because, not in spite of, our status as teachers in our department. Like many center administrators, we assume both roles, and thus we partake in the subjective experience of both the center and the department culture.

We are accustomed to the notion of the professor as unmoved mover. Some professors refer students to the center from a distance by way of a form or a phone call. A few others escort students, introduce them personally, and continue to monitor their progress. Whether the professors assume the role of a transcendent or an immanent deity, they are seldom asked to change. Students, tutors, and center administrators view their task as meeting the expectations of the professor.

But as teacher-administrators we find that our intuitions and our records suggest that professors do change when exposed to writing centers. We can generalize that observation to include many of the teachers who refer students to the center or who conduct composition research. The phrase "personality conflict," often used to dismiss disagreements between faculty and students, in fact describes two fundamental problems in composition research and instruction. The first problem is that professors and graduate students may be inclined to emphasize their research over student needs. Our early records show, for example, an instructor who used the Flower and Hayes problem-solving model mechanically, insisting that students follow a set pattern for all writing in order to facilitate a research study. Many students found this cybernetic model unintelligible or constraining, complaining to tutors that they just could not communicate with the instructor. The tutors were able to spot the difficulty and communicate to the professor the need to help them to help the students understand the research model informing the instruction. The professor altered the presentation of the model to suit the students' needs so that both the students in the class and the instructor profited from the change induced through the observations of the tutors.

The second problem is that graduate students can bring a senior professor's theories to the classroom with a zeal that blinds them to the limitations of their own beliefs. In writing centers, we see students struggling to find some personal meaning in a teacher's exhortation to empower themselves in the academic world, or to learn techniques for critical evaluation of the culture, or to accept the communal nature of knowledge. Tutors are often well-positioned to assist composition students to sift the instruction from the ideology, and classroom instructors often learn from tutors where the students have lost track of the connections between theory and practice. The center can provide a ground of communication between students and teachers that leads to changed perspectives on both their parts.

The View from Inside the Triangle

Thus, writing centers inevitably change those who interact in and with them. As observers of our own center, we have noted changes in ourselves as well. We have discussed at length our various tactics calculated to establish and maintain a center that could constantly prove its worth and at the same time provide sensitive and adaptable tutoring for all. Observing that center in action as it is now with tutors like Mark and Jenna has helped us to see how the center has changed us as well. Like the administrators and dignitaries we show through the center, we find that we have almost inadvertently committed ourselves to the well-being of students. It's a frightening observation that college professors do not make often enough: we really are changed by espousing goals that demand the improvement of the young.

Finally, we have observed that centers change the college or university community in which they exist, for the schools, by making a social and financial commitment to student assistance, become more than a gatekeeper and source of academic credentialing. Knoblauch argues that "the concept of literacy is embedded in the ideological disposition of those who use the concept, those who profit from it, and those who have standing and motivation to enforce it as a social requirement" (1990, 74). When a school provides a place where students can help one another and establish a network of concern and assistance, it redefines literacy as a skill to be shared and enhanced, not only as a talent to be measured and rewarded. A school that values the means of achievement as well as the ends gives back to its culture the support it has been given and finds in itself the potential for adjusting to an ever more diverse culture.

We have offered this triangulated ethnographic construction of a small locale, the Illinois State University Center for Learning Assistance, to show how varied pieces of data can give a picture of a center at work. We have asked questions about what is important to that center, whether we made the right choices in designing the center, and whether we should continue or alter current practices. We might propose the hypothesis that this design is a successful way to construct a center, either a writing center or a larger learning center. Our experience certainly confirms that hypothesis for us, but an outsider might argue that we have merely affirmed our own original intentions, formulated many years ago when observing centers before setting up the original writing center.

We would suggest that a research design to test this hypothesis might be to have other center directors write such archaeological ethnographies of their own centers, beginning first with the assumptions underlying the births of the centers and moving out to a triangulated description of the centers as they now present themselves through the notes of tutors, the evaluations of students tutored, the papers written by those students, and the center directors' own observations of the day-to-day working of the staff. These combined studies would provide a rich testing ground for our assumption that interpersonal warmth is second in importance only to tutorial ability and knowledge of the field. It would also test what each director discovers in becoming an ethnographer "other" in his or her own center.

We found that watching the University Center for Learning Assistance work through the eyes of observers rather than as persons-in-charge proved both instructive and enriching. Daily demands can so stress busy directors that they may forget to stop and observe what happens with tutors and staff. Are the original assumptions, if they were the best ones, still in operation? Mary Croft, author of the first article on writing centers in *Change* magazine in 1976, once observed that a director should not get too far away from the center, either in space or thought. It was good advice in 1976, and it is still good advice. The ethnographer can be both researcher and necessary participant. If we are changed by being in the culture, as Geertz observes, then we can be sustained by being in our own center cultures. We can stay in touch with the social discourse that keeps a center alive and active and continue to be sensitive to the subtle messages flowing from the people who tutor together, reinforcing one another's values and sustaining the qualities that make tutorial centers uniquely valuable for all who work in them.

References

Brodkey, Linda. 1987. "Writing Critical Ethnographic Narratives." *Anthropology and Education Quarterly.* 18, 67–76.

Bruffee, Kenneth A. 1984. "Peer Tutoring and the 'Conversation of Mankind.'" In *Writing Centers: Theory and Administration.* Ed. Gary A. Olson. Urbana, IL: National Council of Teachers of English, 3–15.

Clifford, James. 1988. *The Predicament of Culture: Twentieth-Century Ethnography, Literature, and Art.* Cambridge: Harvard University Press.

Clifford, James, and George E. Marcus. 1986. *Writing Culture: The Poetics and Politics of Ethnography.* Berkeley: University of California Press.

Croft, Mary K. 1976. "The Writing Lab: Serving Students and the Community." *Change* 8, 46–47.

Flower, Linda, et al. 1990. *Reading-to-Write: Exploring a Cognitive and Social Process.* New York: Oxford University Press.

Foucault, Michel. 1973. *The Archaeology of Knowledge and the Discourse on Language.* Trans. A. M. Sheridan Smith. New York: Pantheon-Random.

Geertz, Clifford. 1988. *Works and Lives, the Anthropologist as Author.* Stanford University Press.

Jensen, George, and John K. DiTiberio. 1989. *Personality and the Teaching of Composition.* Norwood, NJ: Ablex.

Knoblauch, C. H. 1990. "Literacy and the Politics of Education." *The Right to Literacy.* Eds. Andrea Lunsford, et al. New York: Modern Language Association, 74–80.

Lauer, Janice M., and J. William Asher. 1988. *Composition Research: Empirical Designs.* New York: Oxford University Press.

LeFevre, Karen Burke. 1987. *Invention as a Social Act.* Carbondale, IL: Southern Illinois University Press.

Marcus, George E., and Michael M. J. Fisher. 1986. *Anthropology as Cultural Critique: An Experimental Moment in the Human Sciences.* Chicago: University of Chicago Press.

Porter, James E. 1992. *Audience and Rhetoric.* Englewood Cliffs, NJ: Prentice-Hall.

Scharton, Maurice, and Janice Neuleib. 1990. "The Gift of Insight: Personality Type, Tutoring, and Learning." *Expanding and Changing in the Writing Center: New Directions.* Eds. Ray Wallace and Jeanne Simpson. New York: Garland, 134–204.

Spradley, James P. 1980. *Participant Observation.* New York: Holt, Rinehart, and Winston.

7 Text Linguistics: External Entries into "Our" Community

Ray Wallace
Northwestern State University

Introduction

While the main title of this essay suggests a discussion revolving around the practical application of several textual linguistic theoretical issues to the writing center environment, the more important purpose stems from the second half of the title. Therefore, this essay, like many in this collection, is not simply a discussion of a particular theory and an investigation into how this theory can be extensively applied to "our" environment. This essay serves as a case study of how writing center personnel come to realize the need for, search for, and then apply appropriate theory to "their" world. As such, then, this is not an essay about text linguistic theory, although those unfamiliar with this exciting area of linguistic study will be given sufficient sources with which to further consider possible applications; this essay describes one center's exploration of theretofore unexplored theoretical concerns. The discussion revolves around the perception of a difference between current composition theory and practice in the writing center, and what steps one writing center took to overcome this difference by searching for a more promising theoretical construct. This essay, then, offers a case study into how one writing center looked to theory emerging outside the traditional composition world for possible solutions to problems occurring inside the composition world. Obviously, the time and space permitted in such a collection does not allow a full-blown rationale for the introduction of text linguistic theory into the composition world; the use of a case-study approach is meant to show others in our community the possibilities such a journey outside our community can offer and promote, and to raise implications for further study.

Discussion

Although most would admit that it is "our" conference and the most prestigious/important one "we" own, each year the myriad of interest groups attend-

68

ing the Conference on College Composition and Communication usually come away with the feeling that they have not been well-served by this gathering and that the definitions of "we" and "our" are unclear, to say the least. Many feel that their suspicions of other groups of attendees have been proved once again, others feel that their so-called "colleagues" neither speak the same language nor have the same concerns as they do, and yet others feel that they are being left behind to wave adieu to former colleagues who have jumped on the latest and fastest-moving train pulling out of Bare Obscurity to fame, fortune, and political clout within our organization.

With so many diverse and contradictory views of "our" field being touted as "truth" or "knowledge," many in the field are unclear as to where the community of those interested in the teaching of writing begins and ends. One group, those defining themselves as composition teachers, feel that they are now members of something they had tried to escape: name-tag reading, theory mongering, "big-name" session attendees—a group more interested in flair than dialogue, more content with hype than help. The wordy, the unclear, and the politically correct, they feel, are rewarded at the expense of the practical, the applicable, and the real. This group feels cheated when presented treatises on Sophistry, Aristotelian Logic, Gorgias and the Neo-Platonists, Neo-Marxist Approaches to Discourse Studies, and a plethora of thinly disguised papers on the teaching of literature, at "their" composition conference. Of course, North's (1987) book has been of great help in classifying all these groups into methodological communities: the micro-communities of Practitioners, Historians, Philosophers, Critics, Experimentalists, Clinicians, Formalists, and Ethnographers form the macro-community of Composition. Yet, he gets to the crux of the problem when he points out two important political ramifications of our divisions:

> The first is that the new investigators have tended to trample roughshod over the claims of previous inquirers, especially the "indigenous" population that I will call the Practitioners. In other words, much of what especially teachers . . . have claimed to know about writing has been ignored, discounted, or ridiculed—so that, despite their overwhelming majority, they have been effectively disenfranchised as knowledge-makers in their own field. Second, the growth of methodological awareness has not kept pace with the struggle for the power and prestige that go with being able to say what constitutes knowledge. Investigators often seem unreflective about their own mode of inquiry, let alone anyone else's. The predictable result within methodological communities has been disorder: investigators are wont to claim more of their work than they can or should. Between communities, it has produced a kind of inflation: in the absence of a critical consciousness capable of discriminating more carefully, the various kinds of knowledge produced by these modes of inquiry have been piled up uncritically, helter-skelter, with little regard to incompatibilities. The result has been an accumulated knowl-

edge of a relatively impressive size, but one that lacks any clear coherence or methodological integrity. Composition's collective fund of
knowledge is a very fragile entity. (3)

Perhaps we cannot hope for a macro-community consisting of content, power
sharing, respectful, micro-communities just yet; we must wait until we each
have more carefully analyzed our own stances, philosophical cornerstones,
and the roles and places of theory in these communities.

Such a feeling of division is certainly alive and well in the writing center
movement. Indeed, it would not be too great an exaggeration to suggest that
there is an "us" against "them" feeling when those called Practitioners are
confronted by the theorists. In the writing center area, until recently, we were
seen by the other communities as primarily Practitioners—an appellation we
did not disagree with. Jeanette Harris points out that even our most recent
publications tend to show ourselves as "primarily pragmatists rather than
theorists—in Stephen North's terminology, practitioners rather than researchers or scholars" (1992, 209). Indeed, most of us got into this field
because we believed in the power of one-to-one tutoring as a result of our
having been tutors "in the trenches."

My academic career focused on teaching writing precisely because I was
influenced by a no-nonsense, down-to-earth, writing center director who
stressed that my main tutoring objective was to help writers meet their readers'
expectations. As a new tutor, there seemed to be nothing very "theoretical"
about this task—we achieved it without great deliberations as to the "power"
of the tutor, the student's Myers-Briggs type, classical or modern theories of
rhetoric, or of the marginalized voice we were forcing into a prestige dialect.
Our tutor-training sessions seemed very practical what-to-do-on-Monday-
morning affairs. We discussed problem cases, developed tutoring strategies to
deal with them, tried the strategies at the next tutoring session, modified them
on the spot if they were not working, and came back to report successes and
failures at the next tutor-training session. What I remember of this experience
was a real sense of experimentation and freedom, of not being shackled to one
guiding theoretical camp or community of scholars. What I did not realize at
the time, but do now, was that my writing center director was exposing me to
various theoretical/scholarly approaches without ever naming them as such.
Indeed, the single most instructive point in my graduate career was having a
writing center director who could (and would) quickly dispatch stand-alone
theory and name-dropping scholarship to the nether regions of hell! Instead,
without in-depth discussions of their theoretical underpinnings, she simply
helped tutors see which approaches worked well in the center and which did
not, and how such effectiveness might transfer to our classroom. We didn't
know Derrida from Donald Duck, we would scoff at anyone attempting to
sway us with "Foucault and the Freshman Writer" and, quite frankly, the idea

of sitting down with a student to explain the composing process in detail by drawing triangles and cylindrical models seemed a little off-topic to say the least. What I didn't realize at the time was that my first writing center director (herself writing one of the first, and finest, rhetorical defenses of writing centers) was instilling in me something much more than practitioner awareness. What I got instead was one person's view on how a writing center practitioner could reapply theoretical ideas from other communities into our own.

Left alone, and many writing center personnel have been surely left at this stage, the writing center tutor, as simple practitioner, stagnates. We all know the writing center practitioner. This is the person afraid of theory, this is the person unwilling to cross self-imposed boundaries to attempt application from historical, philosophical, critical, experimental, clinical, formalist, and ethnographic areas of scholarship in the composition community, and this is the person who feels out of place in what is now our truly cross-disciplinary field. The writing center profession cultivated by such practitioners will surely reap a bitter harvest. Many of our own sessions at the field's (note, not "our") national conferences have become closed-door, incestuous, complaint sessions. We complain about our budgets, about our low status in our departments, and about how even our own composition colleagues outside our centers don't understand us! We are becoming our own worst enemies in the profession—if all we can do is complain about how badly we are treated, how no one sees our worth in the composing process, and how we never are given enough resources to do our job, then we clearly are not doing enough to sell ourselves to the external forces who control much of our destiny. If all we can do is publish ourselves in our own closed journals, then we are preaching to the converted. We must reach out to other communities in our profession, and such outreach is done by reflection about our own claims and those of other communities. If at first our messages are not readily accepted in other communities, then we must write louder and stronger messages until they are heard and taken to heart.

It is time for the writing centers to move beyond the practitioner's goal of guiding students' writing instruction in a one-to-one tutorial situation. We must begin to show others in the field of composition that what the writing center has to offer is a great deal more than soft chairs, caring people, and free coffee. We must show these people, our colleagues, that we have strong theoretical underpinnings, we have a solid awareness of the theories we can and can't use in our tutoring situations, and that we can and do formulate our own theories after exposure to others', and as a result of the valuable practitioner-knowledge we gain on a daily basis in the writing center. We must promote our environment as a center for composition research, as well as the center for writing on our campuses.

Many in the writing center world are beginning to travel outside the confines of the Practitioner community and are beginning to see links with other communities' theories and practices, evidenced by this collection and others in the past few years (Olson 1984; Farrell 1990; Wallace and Simpson 1991). Many of the new generation of writing center directors are emerging from composition and rhetoric programs with broad educational experiences which enable them to show links between the various communities North has described, and are bringing the needed cross-disciplinary perspective with them. Writing center personnel are now being trained by those much more influenced by other camps and not afraid to discuss these areas. Hence, the difference between me as tutor and my tutors in this generation is that the current tutors are now much more open to seeing composition instruction as an amalgamation of theories and practices. The tutor-trainer now does not need to cover theory up; theory can be discussed in writing center tutor-training meetings much more openly.

It is safe to assume that we are looking for more varied theoretical and practical approaches to help define our place in the field of writing instruction. We have grown rapidly in the past ten years, and with this growth has come the need for theoretical/scholarly sophistication. We are now willing and able to question the tenets that formed our field only a decade ago. In order for a more varied theoretically based writing center to occur, the writing center director and writing center personnel must question what they have always taken for granted and grow outward from the experience. Such an event occurred in my center a few terms ago. Because the conclusion to this event has allowed me to look at the composing process in the writing center a little differently, has allowed me to examine a new theory more closely, has allowed me to share this theory with my tutors and other compositionists, and has, in turn, demonstrated this theory's interdisciplinariness, I feel writing center philosophy has advanced within the composition community in a way North calls for.

Theory-Building in the Writing Center: A Case Study

As each academic year draws to a close, writing center directors prepare their final reports, count the number of student visits, and plan their budget requests for the next year. Across the country, we busily prepare these statements to show what great jobs we did, how our students progressed as writers, and how, in general, our tutors helped students succeed in academic writing. For many years I had included statements on how my tutors helped students "understand their own composing processes" and successfully approach writing from a "less product-oriented approach." I talked about our "outreach to other discourse communities," our attempts at "computer-assisted composition," our movement toward "satellite writing centers," and our centers as "places where collaborative approaches to writing instruction and learning are stressed."

I include such statements because (A) I believe them, (B) I know my VPAA and Dean have heard of at least some of them, will not question their truthfulness, and like to see mention of them, (C) I have heard other writing center people talk about them at conferences and have read about them in the literature, and (D) these statements represent the *lingua franca* of my profession and its survival in the face of other communities' successes. Yet, as I was writing about how my writing center was changing the face of writing instruction as we know it at my institution, how the center has improved both writing and writer, how we have developed cooperative/collaborative skills in both writer and tutor, and how we have advanced effective writing skills across the campus, I thought of North's statement that we want to claim more for our work than we can or should. Each year I make the claim that our tutors help students learn how to compose in a more effective manner—we teach effective composing skills and we are there to help students at any stage of their composing process.

However, when I looked around my center (usually closed by the time finals were upon us), I noted my own tutors composing in ways I had tried all year to teach them to teach students not to do. Tutors were writing up to the very last minute before their own papers were due. Indeed, each term I saw them "pulling all-nighters" to finish their Dickens papers, cramming poorly selected (but long) quotes to pad their critical theory papers, struggling with length—"what else can I say to make this twenty pages long?" Do they revise as I have taught them good writers do and as I expected them to show tutees to do? No! I have seen experienced writing center tutors fail to proofread a hard copy of their graduate-level paper on the composing process! On countless occasions, I have witnessed my best tutors get the approximate length, throw in a few transitions, haphazardly proofread (on screen), print, stick a paper clip on one corner, and run to take the in-class final.

These tutors don't practice what we (and they) preach. They don't follow the guidelines we give to writers who come to us for help. They understand from tutor-training sessions how the composing process and the writing center tutorial combine in theory, having read the pertinent offprints we give them: Bruffee (1984), North (1984), Harris (1986), Meyer and Smith (1987), Kail and Trimbur (1987), and Trimbur (1989). They read and seem to understand the standard books and articles—Beach and Bridwell (1984), Faigley (1986), Flower (1988), etc.—we give them on composing; they understand how researchers tell them people compose: Fox (1990), and Selzer (1984); and they read and discuss, in Odell and Goswami (1985), and Brannon, Knight, and Neverow-Turk (1983), how important composing is in the lives of the professional and business writers, in careers many of them aspire to. More important than this tacit understanding is that, in the tutoring sessions, the tutors use the language presented in those books and essays and in my tutor-training workshops to explain the composing process to the first-year students who walk in our doors to receive the very help we advertise. They talk about the composing process in the terms we have given them, but they don't seem to practice what they preach as gospel. Why? After the conclusion of a recent term in which this phenomenon had again raised its mystifying head, after the tutors' papers had been written and graded, and after the writing center had closed for the term, I asked my tutors for one more tutor-training meeting (a collective groan was quelled with promise of free pizza afterwards).

I pointed out my observations to my tutors and they readily agreed—yes, in fact, they did not follow the advice they had given out to the students they tutored. Most seemed a little embarrassed that I should question their writing styles, but most seemed more embarrassed at my thinking that advanced writers such as they would ever practice theory obviously developed to explain the attempts at discourse freshmen produced. Indeed, the consensus was that the composing process as explained to them was all well and good for an introductory lesson on the beast, but they desired a much more theoretically advanced model to explain their own composing processes. Indignantly, they threw back at me the cliché that "the composing process is a highly individualized process" as evidence of the oversimplicity of the previous theories. If it is so highly individualized, why force-feed us essays by people trying to quantify and generalize about all first-year writers, they asked. Instead, these tutors demanded a more complex and individualized set of descriptions of their own composing processes and of those of advanced writers. And, frankly, since I had opened this can of worms, they looked to me to find the solution.

Searching Outside Composition

Having found the research on the composing process from inside the field wanting, I knew that I would have to look further afield. I turned to the work of Beaugrande and Dressler (1981) in text linguistics. I had first heard about this work from Maurice Scharton at Illinois State University, one of the first writing center practitioners spending time in the alien world of theory, and had run across it in a few papers by applied linguists at CCCC, linguists who, incidentally, seemed as marginalized as the writing center population at the conference.

After working through much of the literature being produced in the area, I offered a seminar in Text Linguistics and the Composing Process, and it was there that my tutors (many enrolled in the class) found the language which they could use to more effectively explain the composing process. It was through these theoretical discussions from an area outside the usual realm visited by writing center personnel that such a group of compositionists were able to apply theory to practice and, I believe, forward our understanding of composition. Since the course focused on the definition of boundaries of what a text is and when a text becomes a non-text, my students studied the various features of textuality as defined by several textual theorists and then how these theories might help explain the very individualized nature of advanced writers' composing processes.

A Brief Description of Text Linguistics

Briefly, text linguistics says a text is a communicative occurrence only when seven standards of textuality are met. The seven standards are thus seen as constitutive principles (defining textual communication) and can be broken down into the text-centered standards *Cohesion* and *Coherence;* and the user-centered standards of *Intentionality, Acceptability, Informativity, Situationality,* and *Intertextuality.* The degree to which these standards come into play is regulated by the principles of efficiency, effectiveness, and appropriateness. Beaugrande and Dressler (1980) claim that in their view of the textuality of a given document (we only dealt with written texts) all the standards of textuality must be present.

Cohesion deals with the ways in which grammatical dependencies form so that the words in a text (the surface text) depend (are mutually connected within a sequence) upon each other. Coherence, on the other hand, concerns the mutual accessibility and relevance of concepts and relations in the deep text. Intentionality refers to the text producer's attitude that the text fulfill his/her intentions for it. Acceptability concerns the text's relevance for a receiver. Informativity deals with the level of new knowledge as opposed to already known information presented in the text. Situationality concerns the factors which make a text relevant and easily accessible to the situation at hand. Finally, intertextuality concerns the genre under which like texts can be placed (3–11).

For the compositionists this was fairly new territory, and I worried that we would do the very thing that had alienated the practitioners from the rest of the composition community. I worried that we would get bogged down in theory with no practical application ever to result. However, while this new generation of writing center personnel found the theory to be exciting (and confusing), they never lost sight of their goal of developing a new method of describing how they compose. These compositionists were able to explore each one of these standards of textuality in isolation and then use their newfound knowledge to return to their own community to make it grow in a new direction.

In their work on cohesion, these pragmatic compositionists looked at the work of Keele (1973) and Loftus and Loftus (1976); at the field of Functional Sentence Perspective, especially Rummelhart's (1977) grammatical expectations and procedures; and at Winston's (1977) work in transition networks and the modeling of cognitive processes. In their work in Coherence, they looked at procedural semantics (Levesque and Mylopoulos 1979) and Tulving's (1972) episodic versus semantic memory studies, and they spent much of their time looking at Beaugrande's (1980) book dealing with primary and secondary control concept centers. While studying the textual standard of intentionality, they looked at the relatively early work in this area by philosophers Austin (1962), who focused much of his work on speech acts, and Searle (1969). In addition, the work of Grice (1978), especially his maxims, was important in this area of study. Moving into the area of acceptability, these students looked at levels of tolerance in texts, especially the differences between grammaticality and acceptability as discussed by Lakoff (1973), Dijk (1979), and Snow and Meijer (1977). When the students delved into informativity, Shannon and Weaver's (1949) information theory based on statistical probability was a good place to begin. However, they soon moved into other areas: Clark and Clark's (1977) levels of informativity, Colby's (1966) ethnographic semantics, and Givon's (1978) work on informativity and negation placement. In situationality, they quickly moved to explore the relevant research on situation monitoring and management as discussed by Osgood (1971), and Goffman (1974), and further elaborated on by Halliday and Hasan (1976). Finally, as the students concluded their research with intentionality, they focused on the characteristic text types, schemata, and textual genres. For this investigation they looked at the work by Labov and Waletzky (1967), and Stein and Glenn (1979), as well as work on textual recall studies (Kintsch and Dijk 1978).

While my students were very well-read in composition studies, and in writing center studies in particular, they, quite frankly, had never heard of any of these researchers from other fields—yet here they were conducting research on subjects not very far removed from their own. I deliberately laced their reading with research that had been conducted on the composing process in our own field's so-called heyday (the seventies and early eighties) to show them that by keeping a very isolated perspective they would be missing a plausible alternative language with which to explore their own field.

The results of this seminar were helpful to my tutors. They gained a new perspective on their own composing strategies. They developed new language with which to describe what was happening as they, and many of their tutees, worked on composing communicative texts. They were able to explain many of these new ideas to others in a less linguistically based language, and they felt comfortable with this newfound way of looking at their field. The introduction of the multidisciplinary world of text linguistics has been an important learning experience for all my writing center personnel, myself included. Its key success has been for us all to realize that the teaching of writing cannot simply be explained in the terms and through the ideas we adopted from earlier research. We can no longer rely on faded definitions and the recollections of practitioners. If we no longer use the definitions in good faith, if we no longer believe everything we have read and learned about composition in the seventies and early eighties, then we must both look inward and outward for some new, better, answer to our field's questions. Just with this one example, the exploration of text linguistics, my writing center personnel were able to see the relationships between text (broadly defined) and a host of new disciplines.

Conclusion

This exploration of theory outside the usual area studied by writing center personnel is just one small example of how writing center personnel can play a more active role in the composition community. We must believe we are vital to the community and, as such, that our voices need and must be heard if we are to help improve writing and writers at all levels. While we have helped define ourselves, to ourselves, by our stories of the trials and tribulations of our daily existence within the academic community, we must do more than tell stories to each other.

The field of composition is rapidly expanding, and with the expansion of this macro-community must come the expansion of the micro-communities which make up the whole. Therefore, the writing center must expand its focus and scope as the rest of the field does likewise. To expand, to reach out to other communities' ideas and theories, and to present our own important ideas and theories, requires more work on our part.

We must review what it is we have learned from our practitioner's role for the last ten years, and then move forward with a sense of pride. Harris's (1992) call to the next generation of writing center personnel is apt. She wishes for more work in our expanding field:

> [M]ore publications that are researched-based, that give a clearer, more complex sense of the theories that inform writing center pedagogy, that

explore the potential of new technologies, that unite theories of practice.
It is time, I believe, for writing center scholarship to move beyond the
practical. This does not mean that we should abandon our practical
orientation or stop telling our stories, for these features are at the core of
who we are. But it does mean that we should stretch toward an understanding of the principles that inform writing center pedagogy, asking not
just what works, but why it works. (210)

This essay has been a story in that it has outlined in a case study how a
writing center has had to move forward to come to terms with the need for a
new theory and how the exploration of this new theory has improved the
center's personnel as teachers, tutors, and theorists. Harris is correct—our
traditional stories have been important to us, yet, perhaps, they have provided
us too much insulation against the harsh world out there. We have developed
a community of writing center people who have struggled to develop what
they "feel" is an effective way to improve writers and writing in our academy.

However, we must not stop here. We must now demonstrate that our
feelings are theoretically valid, that these are not simply "ideas from the
trenches" without validity or applicability to other areas of the community,
and that we can understand and critique others' guiding principles, theories,
and philosophies. We must look for other vehicles to explain what it is we do
in the writing center and we must show others in the composition community
that our practices have strong, well-developed, theoretical groundings. We
must understand that we have important voices in the composition community, and that because we have to be heard to inform the field we should not
hide on small streets off the main road. We must exclaim our newfound
theoretical knowledge and rationale, not publicly wallow in the histories of
our budgetary or personal despair. We must wear our writing center labels
with more pride and we must become more active inside and outside the
community—we must publish our stories, our theories, our pedagogical applications across the community. This essay attempts to show one center's
journey inside and outside its community, reaching alien theoretical grounds
to discover areas of mutual importance. This journey has resulted in tutors
returning with applicable spoils, and, in attempting to apply these new theories, these tutors have begun to profess expanded definitions of "writing
center," "composition community," and "writing theory."

This next generation of writing center personnel has already learned a
valuable lesson which perhaps the previous generation did not learn: if we
wish to be treated as professors of composition, then we must do more to
profess our importance and place in a multidisciplinary, theory-rich, philoso-
phy-deep, community. This lesson, though, could only have been learned
through the earlier struggle of "mere practitioners."

References

Austin, John. 1962. *How to Do Things With Words*. London: Oxford University Press.

Beach, Richard, and Lillian S. Bridwell, eds. 1984. *New Directions in Composition Research*. New York and London: Guilford Press.

Beaugrande, Robert-Alain de. 1980. *Text, Discourse, and Process*. Norwood, NJ: Ablex.

Beaugrande, Robert-Alain de, and Wolfgang Ulrich Dressler. 1981. *Introduction to Text Linguistics*. London and New York: Longmann.

Brannon, Lil, Melinda Knight, and Vara Neverow-Turk. 1982. *Writers Writing*. Upper Montclair, NJ: Boynton/Cook.

Bruffee, Kenneth A. 1984. "Collaborative Learning and the 'Conservation of Mankind.' " *College English* 46, 635–52.

Clark, Hebert, and Eve Clark. 1977. *Language and Psychology*. New York: Harcourt, Brace and Jovanovich.

Colby, Benjamin. 1966. "Ethnographic Semantics." *Current Anthropology* 7, 3–32.

Dijk, Teun Van. 1977. "Acceptability in Context." *Acceptability in Language*. Ed. Sidney Greenbaum. The Hague: Mouton, 39–61.

Faigley, Lester. 1986. "Competing Theories of Process: A Critique and a Proposal." *College English* 48, 527–42.

Farrell, Pamela, ed. 1989. *The High School Writing Center: Establishing and Maintaining One*. Urbana, IL: National Council of Teachers of English.

Flower, Linda S. 1988. "The Construction of Purpose in Writing and Reading." *College English* 50, 528–50.

Fox, Tom. 1990. *The Social Uses of Writing: Politics and Pedagogy*. Norwood, NJ. Ablex.

Givon, Talmy. 1978. "Negation in Language: Pragmatics, Function, Ontology." *Syntax and Semantics IX: Pragmatics*. Ed. Peter Cole. New York: Academic, 69–112.

Goffman, Erving. 1978. *Frame Analysis*. New York: Harper and Row.

Grice, Paul. 1978. "Further Notes on Logic and Conservation." *Syntax and Semantics IX: Pragmatics*. Ed. Peter Cole. New York: Academic, 113–27.

Halliday, Michael, and Ruqaiya Hasan. 1976. *Cohesion in English*. London: Longman.

Harris, Jeanette. 1992. Review of *The Writing Center: New Directions*. *The Writing Center Journal* 12.2, 205–10.

Harris, Muriel. 1986. *Teaching One-to-One: The Writing Conference*. Urbana, IL: National Council of Teachers of English.

Kail, Harvey, and John Trimbur. 1987. "The Politics of Peer Tutoring." *WPA: Writing Program Administration* 11, 5–12.

Keele, Steven. 1973. *Attention and Human Performance*. Pacific Palisades: Goodyear.

Kintsch, Walter, and Teun van Dijk. 1978. "Toward a Model of Text Comprehension and Production." *Psychological Review* 85, 363–94.

Labov, William, and Joshua Waletzky. 1967. "Narrative Analysis: Oral Versions of Personal Experience." *Essays on the Verbal and the Visual Arts*. Ed. June Helm, Seattle: University of Washington Press, 12–44.

Lakoff, George. 1973. "Fuzzy Grammar and the Performance/Competence Terminology Game." *Ninth Proceedings from the Regional Meeting of the Chicago Linguistic Society,* 271–91.

Levesque, Hector, and John Mylopoulos. 1979. "A Procedural Semantics for Semantic Networks." *Associate Networks: Representation and Use of Knowledge in Computers.* Ed. Nicholas Findler. New York: Academic, 93–120.

Loftus, Geoffrey, and Elizabeth Loftus. 1976. *Human Memory: The Processing of Information.* Hillsdale, NJ: Erlbaum.

Meyer, Emily, and Louise Z. Smith. 1987. *The Practical Tutor.* New York: Oxford University Press.

North, Stephen M. 1984. "The Idea of a Writing Center." *College English* 46, 433–46.

———. 1987. *The Making of Knowledge in Composition: Portrait of an Emerging Field.* Upper Montclair, NJ: Boynton/Cook.

Odell, Lee, and Dixie Goswami, eds. 1985. *Writing in Nonacademic Settings.* New York and London: Guilford Press.

Olson, Gary A., ed. 1984. *Writing Centers: Theory and Administration.* Urbana, IL: National Council of Teachers of English.

Osgood, Charles. 1971. "Where Do Sentences Come From?" *Semantics: An Interdisciplinary Reader in Philosophy, Linguistics, and Psychology.* Eds. Danny Steinerg and Leon Jakobovits. Cambridge University Press, 497–529.

Rummelhart, David. 1977. *Introduction to Human Information Processing.* New York: Wiley.

Searle, John. 1969. *Speech Acts.* London: Cambridge.

Selzer, Jack. 1984. "Exploring Options in Composing." *College Composition and Communication* 35, 276–84.

Shannon, Claude, and Warren Weaver. 1949. *The Mathematical Theory of Communication.* Urbana, IL: University of Illinois Press.

Snow, Catherine, and Gus Meijer. 1977. "On the Secondary Nature of Syntactic Intuitions." *Acceptability in Language.* Ed. Sidney Greenbaum. The Hague: Mouton, 163–78.

Stein, Nancy, and Christine Glenn. 1979. "An Analysis of Story Comprehension in Elementary School Children." *New Directions in Discourse Processing.* Ed. Roy Freedle. Norwood, NJ: Ablex, 53–120.

Trimbur, John. 1989, October. "Consensus and Difference in Collaborative Learning." *College English* 51, 602–16.

Tulving, Endel. 1972. "Episodic and Semantic Memory." *The Organization of Memory.* Eds. Endel Tulving and Wayne Donaldson. New York: Academic, 382–404.

Wallace, Ray, and Jeanne Simpson, eds. 1991. *The Writing Center: New Directions.* New York: Garland.

Winston, Patrick. 1977. *Artificial Intelligence.* Reading, MA: Addison-Wesley.

8 Learning Disabilities and the Writing Center

Julie Neff
University of Puget Sound

Since September 1984, when Stephen North's now famous article, "The Idea of a Writing Center" appeared in *College English,* a picture of the writing conference has developed: the writer and the writing advisor sit side by side, the writer holding the pencil, the writing advisor asking probing questions about the development of the topic; or the student types text into a computer as the writing advisor fires questions designed to help the student think through the writing problem; or, in a revising session, the advisor points to a word or phrase that seems to be "wrong" for this particular paragraph as the student jots notes so she can later correct the text. In these conferences, the writing advisor tells the student to check punctuation and spelling and gives the student a handout to help with the process. After all, the writing center is not a "fix-it" shop for student papers; it is a place for writer to meet reader in order to receive a thoughtful response.

Behind these pictures of writing center conferences lie some basic assumptions: students can improve their ability to invent, organize, draft, revise, and edit based on the responses of a thoughtful reader. Even though the conference is in many ways collaborative, most of the responsibility for composing and transcribing is placed on the student writer. Recent theory and pedagogy in rhetoric and composition support these pictures of the collaborative writing conference, e.g., Bruffee, Harris, Ede, and Lunsford.

But one group of students does not and cannot fit into this pedagogical picture: students with learning disabilities. Though their particular disabilities vary, these students need a different, more specific kind of collaboration than the average student who walks through the doors of the writing center.

What Is a Learning Disability?

Although there is still some disagreement about the precise definition, learning disabilities are generally a varied group of disorders that are intrinsic to the individual.

The Learning Disabilities Act of 1968, which has only changed in small ways since it was drafted, defines a learning disability as "a disorder in one or more of the basic psychological processes involved in understanding or in using spoken or written languages." Individuals with learning disabilities are likely to experience trouble with "listening, thinking, talking, reading, writing, spelling, or arithmetic." Learning problems that are primarily due to a physical condition, like visual or hearing impairment, retardation, emotional dysfunction, or a disadvantaged situation, are not considered to result from learning disabilities. While these other problems sometimes accompany a learning disability, they are not the cause or the result of the disability. Nor are learning disabilities the result of social or economic conditions. People who have learning disabilities are born with them, or they have acquired them through a severe illness or accident, and the disability will continue to affect them over their lifetimes. Although many people overcome their learning disabilities, they do so by learning coping strategies and alternate routes for solving problems. People with learning disabilities cannot be "cured." However, with help, those with learning disabilities can learn to use their strengths to compensate for their weaknesses.

A learning disability is the result of a malfunction in the system in one or more areas. We cannot look into the brain and see the malfunction, but we can see the results in a student's performance on a discrete task. The Woodcock-Johnson Test of Cognitive Ability, one of the most widely used tests for measuring learning disabilities, uncovers discrepancies between capacity and performance. Although the requirements differ from state to state, two standard deviations between potential and performance on the Woodcock-Johnson test (or similar tests such as the WAIS-R, TOWL, or WRAT) suggest that a student is learning disabled, as does an extreme scatter of subtest scores.

Some learning disabilities are truly debilitating in that the individual is unable to cope with or overcome the problems. However, many people with learning disabilities are able to function at the highest levels in one area while having difficulty in another. In fact, many people who are learning disabled in one area are gifted in another. Dyslexic and slow to read, Albert Einstein was learning disabled, as was Thomas Edison (Lovitt 1989, 5). Although these are two of the most well-known cases, they are not exceptional ones. According to specialists at a learning disabilities clinic, Another Door to Learning, one successful businessman claimed his learning disability has contributed to his success because it allowed him to view problems from a different perspective. Often learning-disabled students who come to college score in the above-average range of standard IQ tests and have finely honed skills for compensating for and adapting to their particular disability.

What Do We Know about the Brain?

While no one yet knows the precise causes of a learning disability, the materials drafted by the National Joint Committee on Learning Disabilities presume that the disability, which manifests itself in problems with the acquisition and use of listening, speaking, reading, writing, reasoning, mathematical or spatial skills, grows out of some sort of brain dysfunction.

Although researchers know much more now than they did a decade ago, the debate over just how the brain works continues. Some scientists believe that the brain is bicameral, with the left side responsible for language and reason, and the right side responsible for nonverbal, intuitive activities—the mystical if you will (Berglund 1985, 1). Others believe that the bicameral model oversimplifies the workings of the brain and is more misleading than it is useful.[1]

Richard Berglund (1985) explains that in the last several years a new "wet model" of the brain has emerged, one that is based on the theory that the brain runs on hormones. The idea that the brain is a gland run by hormones has resulted in a new, burgeoning field of medicine known as neuroendocrinology which gives credence to the idea that the learning disability has a physiological basis.

Meantime, over the past decade, cognitive psychology has moved away from the Platonic idea that human rationality grows out of pure intelligence. Instead, researchers are seeing the brain as "a knowledge medium," a storehouse for great quantities of knowledge about the world. This view of the brain represents a paradigm shift from the Platonic view, which asserts that only by reasoning with formal rules we can come to general understanding: if worldly knowledge is more important than pure reason, we have a model of human rationality that relies on information in the brain and vast associative connections that allow the human mind to turn a fragment of information into a considerable amount of knowledge. Human cognition consists not of pure reason but is instead composed of the information stored in the brain and the brain's ability to connect those pieces of information. Worldly knowledge, according to Jeremy Campbell (1989), has become far more important than pure logic.

How Does This Theory Help Us Understand a Learning Disability?

The idea of the brain as a knowledge machine, and as an organ run by hormones, can help us understand a learning disability. The brain processes enormous amounts of information. The brains of learning-disabled persons have these same properties; but often learning-disabled persons have trouble

accessing and retrieving the information, and occasionally gathering and
storing it. This is not because they are unintelligent but because of a physiological problem. Judy Schwartz, author of the book *Another Door to Learning,* says that individuals not only have to have basic information, they have
to know they have it. The substance and assumptions are inside the learning-
disabled person's brain, but he or she may not know the information is there.
To access what is known, he or she must consciously learn how to tap the
information through self-cuing or other methods. In these circumstances, the
writing center can be helpful.

Misconceptions about Learning Disabilities

Although brain theory and research support the idea that a learning disability
has a physiological basis, many people, including educators, continue to have
a number of misconceptions about people with learning disabilities. Some see
the learning-disabled students as "special education" students who are now
being mainstreamed. Some see them as manipulative individuals looking for
an excuse for bad spelling and punctuation. Some see "learning disability" as
a euphemism for "retarded." Others claim that learning disabilities do not
actually exist.[2]

Since a learning disability has a physiological basis and is not due to low
intelligence, social situations, or economic conditions, a learning disability is
not unlike other kinds of disabilities that have a physiological basis. Renee
must use a wheelchair because she was born with an imperfect spine. This
defect, not caused by low intelligence, social situation, or economic factors,
is a physiological problem that Renee overcomes by taking a slightly different
route to accomplish her goals. Renee can reach the second floor, but she won't
use the stairs; she'll use the elevator. Similarly, the learning-disabled student
can master the material; but she may need to write the exam on a computer,
and she may also need extra time to access the information she has.

A Case Study

Although learning disabilities vary widely, it may be easier to understand how
a learning disability affects an individual by looking at a specific student with
a specific disability. When Barb was in middle school, her mother asked her
to take a roast from the refrigerator and put it in the oven at 350 degrees so it
would be ready when she got home from work. The roast was in the baking
dish, seasoned, and covered with plastic wrap. At the appropriate time, Barb
did exactly as asked. The roast was done perfectly when her mother came
home, but it was coated with melted plastic.

Why hadn't Barb removed the plastic? She had taken cooking in school and often baked cakes and cookies at home. Even though she has 20/20 vision, Barb couldn't comprehend the plastic. Because the plastic exists in space, Barb's spatial problems kept her from seeing it until her mother tied it to language by saying, "This roast is covered with melted plastic." Barb replied, "I'm sorry. I didn't notice it."

Barb has a disability that affects her ability to access and create reliable images and thus to understand things spatially. She understands and gains access to her world and spatial relationships by building and shaping images with language, which in turn gives her access to the images.

Barb needed written or oral directions to remove the plastic. As soon as she had words, Barb could grasp the situation and accomplish the task. According to Carol Stockdale of Another Door to Learning, the image was recorded, but Barb only had access to it through language. Barb often said, "Well, I know that," but, in fact, she did not know it consciously until she had the language to refine the image.

In middle school, Barb was placed in an English class that taught grammar as a discrete subject: two weeks for literature, two weeks for grammar. Barb's spoken English was excellent; her speech included sophisticated syntax and vocabulary, and she was most successful with the reading and discussion of the literature. But the spatial quality of the grammar drills confounded Barb. Because she failed to grasp the spatial task of retrieving the mechanics of written English, spatial labels like "adverb" meant nothing to her. While she could use an adverb correctly in spoken and written English, she could not "see" the term "adverb" any more than she could see the plastic wrap.

When Barb started high school, her classes were content rich; they stressed worldly knowledge. Although she continued to have difficulty with math and chemistry, she found that her writing and especially the mechanics improved as she took courses in history, literature, and art and music history. In these courses, she was learning the language that would allow her to store and retrieve the information. The more information she had the better she became at making connections, and these connections were as apparent in the class-room as in the kitchen.

Because Barb was coping well with her reading and writing in her high school classes, she did not anticipate that "driving class" would be a problem. But as Barb sat behind the wheel of the family sedan to have a practice session with her mother, her mother realized that learning to drive, a spatial task, would be much more difficult than learning art history.

Barb edged the car toward the pavement from the gravel shoulder of the road. "Turn the car a little to the left, Barb, and as you pick up speed, ease onto the pavement," her mother said patiently. Barb eased the car onto the grey cement at about 20 mph. But soon she was back on the gravel, and then a minute later she had drifted to the left side of the road. Many novice drivers drift, but Barb remained unaware of both the drift and resulting position. "Barb, you're driving on the wrong side of the road! Do you realize what could have happened?!" Barb's mother exclaimed.

"I'm sorry," Barb replied calmly; "I didn't notice." And indeed she did not notice, even though she saw. Barb had not yet used language which "uncovered" the images before her eyes to build and access the images that would allow her to drive safely.

Though she had never thought much about it before, Barb's mother realized that driving is in many ways a spatial task. According to Jeremy Campbell's theories, Barb's brain was capable of storing and connecting great amounts of information; her learning disability kept her from accessing it.

Carol Stockdale, a learning-disabilities specialist who had worked with Barb, suggested several strategies for conquering the problem. Barb walked around the car, touching it and measuring it against herself to see how big it was, all the time having a conversation with herself that translated the spatial into verbal dimensions. She went back to the country road near her home to look at the lines that marked the road and to touch the road and the gravel on the shoulder of the road and to say, "These are the lines that mark the lane, and these are the rocks that mark the side where I do not want to drive." As she found her way to all of her usual spots—the store, the school, the hardware store—she developed an internal conversation: "Turn right at the Exxon sign; turn left at the blue house on the corner."

Navigating through Space

And so Barb learned to use verbal clues to navigate through space. Understanding how to learn to drive gave Barb insight into conquering all kinds of spatial problems. Although she continued to have difficulty with mathematics and foreign language in high school, her ability to write academic papers about topics in her language-based academic courses—history, literature, and art history—continued to improve.

When Barb went to college, she needed help with kinds of structures that were new to her, and she needed specific models to understand the shapes of analytical papers particular to certain courses. She also needed these models translated into language. For Barb, looking at something was not seeing it, at least not until she had shaped and refined the image with language.

More and more confident of her ability to know the world through language, Barb was increasingly comfortable with difficult ideas, for instance, in her college philosophy class: "Plato uses serval [sic] arguments to prove the existence of the forms: the first argument occurs in the Meno when Socrates shows that learning is merely a recollection of previous knowledge of forms by questioning a slave boy about the Pythagorean theorem." Despite the misplaced letter in the word "several," and the misplaced final phrase, the sentence involves sophisticated content communicated in an equally sophisticated sentence structure. This sentence is not the work of a basic writer or a person unable to deal with the intellectual challenges of higher education. Still, because of her difficulty accessing spatial information, Barb needed help with organization, mechanics, and new kinds of writing tasks.[3]

The Role of the Writing Center

Although learning-disabled students come to the writing center with a variety of special needs, they have one thing in common: they need more specific help than other students.

Often writing center directors do not know what kind of a learning disability the student has, but because the spatial systems and language systems overlap and act reciprocally, students who are dyslexic and students who are spatially impaired may demonstrate many of the same problems with spelling, grammar, development, and organization.[4] Therefore, they will need similar kinds of assistance.

By changing the picture of the writing conference, the writing center director can ensure that learning-disabled students, no matter what the disability, are being appropriately accommodated. The writing advisors still need to be collaborators, but they also may need to help the students retrieve information and shape an image of the product. They may be called upon to demonstrate organization or to model a thesis sentence when the students cannot imagine what one might look like. The advisors may have to help the students call up detail in ways that would be inappropriate for the average learner. They may need to help with the physical production of texts. And they may need to help with correcting mechanics when the papers are in their final stages.

Paradoxically, and at the same time, the writing advisor must help the students be independent through self-cuing; creating a dependent atmosphere does not foster the students' ability to cope, does not develop the students' self-esteem, and does not help the students become better writers. The writing advisor must treat learning disabled persons as the intelligent, resourceful persons they are. Conferences without respect and understanding are seldom successful.

Prewriting

Many of the discovery techniques commonly used in the composition class and in the writing center may not be productive for students with learning disabilities because, though these students may have the information, they may have no way to access it. The picture of the eager student freewriting to discover ideas needs to be amended when one works with learning-disabled students. Freewriting is almost impossible for most because they do not know, and can't imagine, what to write. Students with language retrieval problems may not be able to call up any words at all to put on the paper. This holds true for students with either spatial impairments or language difficulties.

For learning-disabled students, freewriting leads from one generalization to another or from one specific to another. Because they do not see the relationship between the specific and the general, without intervention they are locked in a non-productive cycle, unable to succeed unless it is by accident. And if they do succeed by accident, they do not understand their success. According to Carol Stockdale at Another Door to Learning, many learning disabled students have no way of intentionally creating order.

Freewriting is also frustrating for persons who are learning disabled because it requires them to write without knowing where they are going. Just as Barb had trouble understanding the road, other learning-disabled students need to know where they are going so they will know when they get there. Unable to recognize what is relevant and what is not, they find the freewriting an exercise in futility, while other students may find it a way to create knowledge.

In the writing center, directed conversation can take the place of freewriting. Because these students have trouble accessing what they know, they are unlikely to realize they know great amounts of information. Here, the writing advisor plays an important role. Nowhere else on most campuses can writers find an individual who will ask the leading questions that can unlock trapped information.

In some cases, the writing advisor may need to ask students like Barb specific, seemingly obvious questions to help them unlock the ideas in their minds and then take notes for them as they generate ideas for their papers. In essence the writing advisor is helping them see the plastic wrap.

Here is an example of a writing conference that respects the student's intelligence and at the same time helps him gain access to what he knows, and helps him find an organizational pattern for it.

> *Writing Advisor:* Hi David, how are you? Have a seat.
>
> *David:* Not good. I have another paper to write for my Intro to Fiction class.
>
> *Writing Advisor:* Hmmm, you did well on your last paper, didn't you?
>
> *David:* Yes, but this time I don't have anything to write about.
>
> *Writing Advisor:* Now just think back to that first paper. As I recall, you didn't have a topic for that one either the first time we talked.

David: I guess you're right, but this time I really don't know what to write about.

The writing advisor knows that David has a learning disability. Understanding the brain as Jeremy Campbell explains it, as the great storehouse of knowledge, she suspects that David knows a great deal about the potential topic; she knows she will need to help David gain access to the tremendous information he does have.

Writing Advisor: What is the assignment?

David: To write a 3–4 page paper about *The Great Gatsby.*

Writing Advisor: David, I know you're worried about this paper, but I also know from the last paper we talked about how smart you are and how much you actually know. So let's just chat for a few minutes about the book without worrying about the paper.

The writing advisor turns her chair toward David and takes off her glasses. She realizes that despite David's high scores on standard I.Q. tests and good study habits many of his teachers have considered him "slow," careless, or lazy. She wants to be sure she treats him as the intelligent person he is. She begins with the obvious questions that will help him focus on the book and what he knows.

Writing Advisor: Who wrote *The Great Gatsby?*

David: F. Scott Fitzgerald. He was married to Zelda. And he also wrote *Tender Is the Night.* Some people think he stole his stories from Zelda's journals. Don't you think that's right?

Writing Advisor: I do think it's "right." I did know she had a big influence on him. . . .

David: I mean he was drunk a lot and Zelda was the one who was writing all this stuff about their life. It's not fair.

Writing Advisor: I agree. This whole idea of fairness . . . was there anything in *Gatsby* that wasn't fair?

David: Yes, I don't think Tom was fair in the way he treated Daisy. He had an affair and he lied to her. Gatsby wasn't all that good either. He made his money illegally.

Writing Advisor: Do you think that was fair?

David: I guess not, at least not for the people he took advantage of.

Writing Advisor: I wonder if a word like "honesty" or "integrity" might help get at what we're talking about.

David: "Integrity," that's it.

When the writing advisor saw David lean forward, his eyes bright, she knew it was time to write something down. She took out a piece of paper and a pencil, wrote "integrity" in the middle of the page and showed it to David. She continues to take notes so that David can work at connecting the information without worrying about the physical production of text.

> *Writing Advisor:* Tell me who has it and who doesn't.
>
> *David:* Tom doesn't and Gatsby doesn't.
>
> [The writing advisor wrote "Tom" on the left side of the page and "Gatsby" under it and connected each word to "integrity" with a line.]
>
> *Writing Advisor:* Tell me why you don't think they have integrity.

David recounted example after example and the tutor noted each one under the appropriate name. As he talked, David included other characters and decided whether each had integrity or not and gave appropriate examples. In each case the tutor noted the information David produced and drew lines around similar information.

> *Writing Advisor:* This is going to be a wonderful paper. Can you see the development taking shape? Look at the connections you've made.
>
> *David:* Yes, but I'm not sure how to start the introduction.
>
> *Writing Advisor:* Well, what kinds of things will your reader need to know in order to follow you through the paper?

By the time David had listed the kinds of things that he would include in the introduction, almost an hour had passed. The writing advisor wanted to conclude the session on a reassuring note, and she wanted David to know that he could teach himself to self-cue.

> *Writing Advisor:* David, you know so much about your topic, and you have really good ideas. All I did was ask you questions. Eventually you'll be able to ask yourself those same questions. But now, why don't you do some writing, and then we'll have another appointment, if you like, to look at transitions, mechanics, and those sorts of things. It's fun seeing the connections in your mind unfold.
>
> *David:* I think I can write a draft now. Will you be able to help me with spelling later in the week?
>
> *Writing Advisor:* Sure, I'll see you when the draft is done, and we'll look at all kinds of things.

Because the act of calling up the words and getting them onto paper is so difficult for some learning-disabled students, the student may be unable to concentrate on the ideas and instead only focuses on the production of text. The writing advisor may need to do the typing or the drafting so the student is free to concentrate on answering the fairly specific, sometimes leading, questions proposed by the writing advisor. The writing advisor will know when to do the typing by asking the student, "Would you like me to record so you can work on generating the words?"

Organization

Even after generating a page or two of material, students may still not be able to distinguish the important information from the supporting detail. Again writing advisors should understand that they must help the student over or around the problem. The advisors will probably say what they think is the most important element; once they say it, the students may be able to agree or disagree even though they cannot invent or articulate the idea on their own. The writing advisors might draw a map of the ideas and support for the student, or color-code the information to help with organization. The writing advisors should always be doing and saying at the same time. With learning-disabled students, just pointing seldom helps.

The writing advisor might need to model a thesis sentence for the student, asking simple questions like "What is your paper about?" "Rice," the student replies. "What about rice?" Students are often delighted and surprised when they come up with the single statement that will set the paper spinning.

The advisor may need to be just as explicit about the paper's development: "What is your first point going to be?" As the student responds, the advisor takes down the information, and then asks, "And what is your second point?" "And your third?" Showing students how to create an overview of the information and then teaching them how to categorize information will help the students manage the spatial qualities of organization.

Simply using a model like the five-paragraph essay to teach organization is unlikely to produce successful writing. Since structure grows out of content, the students may be successful one time with a five-paragraph essay, but when they try to apply the formula the next time, the formula may not work. They may be further hindered by being unable to let go of the formula or image.

A student like Barb may not be able to see paragraph breaks until the writing advisor says, "Notice how long this paragraph is," while at the same time pointing to the too-long paragraph. She may even need to say, "This is a paragraph." But the instant the advisor points it out, Barb will say, "Well, I know that." And after saying so, she does indeed know it.

Proofreading and Editing

Frank Smith (1982) makes the distinction between composition and transcription, between the composing of thought and the mechanics of getting the language down on paper according to certain conventions. Spelling and punctuation need to be done with the students so that they feel part of the process; most importantly, the editing must be specific and hands-on and must involve detailed explanations of what the advisor is doing. The writing advisor cannot expect the students to make the changes based on a rule or principle. The explanation must be specific, and it may need to be written as well as said: "Look at the beginning of this sentence. You have five words before your subject. How about a comma?" Students may agree that something is so, but they may be unable to hold the thought in their minds or recall it later.

Encouraging students to be independent through the use of a spell checker and grammar checker is essential, but the writing advisor may need to sit at the computer with students explaining how it works and its limitations. Telling students to put text through a spell check is seldom enough. The advisor may need to read the paper aloud to the students so they can catch errors: a final proofreading by the writing advisor is also appropriate for the learning-disabled students because these students may not be able to see the mistakes until they are pointed out to them.

Wheelchair-bound students can get to the third floor, but they may not be able to take the stairs. Their only routes are the elevator or the ramp. It's not that students with a learning disability can't get it, it's that they can't get it the same way the normal learner can.

Other Kinds of Organization That Affect Writing

Learning-disabled students sometimes have as much trouble coping with the organization of the writing and research time as they do with the organization of the text. Writing advisors can help by showing the students how to use a study planning sheet that contains small but regular accomplishments, and which will lead to the accomplishments of a larger task. It is not enough to tell students to do it; the writing advisors need to demonstrate the strategy, especially the first time. They should also ask the students to refer to the list on a regular basis; the markers of accomplishment need to be tangible.

Social Interaction

Many, but not all, learning-disabled students have trouble in social situations. A visit to the writing center may be one of these social situations. The student's behavior may be inappropriate: he interrupts another conversation, she stands too close or talks too much. Many people with learning disabilities are unable to "read" the nonverbal behavior of others. So even if the writing advisor frowns or looks away, the inappropriate behavior continues. Being explicit but positive will help the individual change this behavior: "Marty, please stop talking; I have something important to tell you." "Glad to see you, Sara. I'll sit here; you sit across from me; that will be a comfortable distance. I'll be ready to talk to you in a minute."

Despite the need for specific instructions and clear questions, the writing advisor must remain positive and encouraging. Often teachers and others misunderstand learning disabilities and accuse students of being lazy or dumb. As a result, college students with learning disabilities often have low self-esteem and may be defensive or uncertain of their own academic ability.

Writing advisors can make a major contribution to a learning-disabled student's success if they are positive, encouraging, and specific about the writing, the revision, and the writing process.

Working with these students in the writing center is sometimes difficult because it means modifying or changing the usual guidelines, and it may mean more and longer appointments, for instance, appointments that last an hour instead of a half hour, and a writing advisor may need to proofread. Writing centers may need to change the rules and policies that govern these sessions and change the training that staff receive. But the students have a right to services, and writing centers have a responsibility to help learning-disabled students succeed.[5] Writing centers have always been places that help students reach their full potential, and this philosophy should extend to students with learning disabilities.

Most learning-disabled students need more support and help rather than less. And writing centers can provide that assistance. For these students, writing center professionals need a new picture of the writing conference that includes the writing advisor's becoming more directly involved in the process and the product. With adequate help and support, students with a learning disability can produce better papers, and they can also become better writers.

Notes

1. At the October 1991 meeting of the International Conference on Learning Disabilities, the debate over the left brain-right brain model continued in the conference sessions. The debate is interesting in that writing center professionals often use the model to explain parts of the composing process.

2. The same law that defines a learning disability guarantees the rights of the learning-disabled person. It is just as illegal to discriminate against a learning-disabled person as it is to discriminate against a person of an ethnic minority or a person with a physical disability. Recently a professor at the University of California Berkeley refused to accommodate a student's request for untimed tests. The student filed suit, and the faculty member was required to pay monetary damages to the student. Faculty members and institutions can be held accountable for blatant discimination (Heyward).

3. Barb's is not an unusual case. As the diagnosis of learning disabilities has improved, students can be helped sooner and can be taught compensatory strategies that lead to success in high school as well as in college. In 1978 when statistics on learning disabilities were first kept, 2.6 percent of all freshmen reported having a disability. In 1988, it was 6 percent. In ten years of record keeping, the number had more than doubled. Still, many experts in the field believe that 6 percent is much too low and the number of learning disabled students is actually between 10 and 20 percent. Many cases have gone undetected.

4. Because problems with spelling and mechanics are the easiest to recognize and fix, many educators have believed that these are the only problems that learning-dis-

abled students have with writing. But a University of Connecticut study showed that 51 percent of the students had trouble with organization compared to 24 percent who had trouble with proofreading (McGuire, Hall, Litt).

5. In 1993, the American Disabilities Act (ADA), which makes discrimination against a learning-disabled person illegal, became law.

References

Bergland, Richard. 1985. *Fabric of Mind.* New York: Penguin.

Brinkerhoff, Loring. 1991. "Critical Issues in LD College Programming for Students with Learning Disabilities." International Conference on Learning Disabilities. Minneapolis, MN: October 11.

Campbell, Jeremy. 1989. *The Improbable Machine.* New York: Simon & Schuster.

Hammill, Donald D., James E. Leigh, Gaye McNutt, and Stephen C. Larsen. 1981. "A New Definition of Learning Disabilities." *Learning Disability Quarterly* 4.4, 336–42.

Heyward, Lawton & Associates, ed. 1992. *Association on Handicapped Student Service Programs in Postsecondary Education Disability Accommodation Digest* 1.2, 6.

Heyward, Salome. 1991. "Provision of Academic Accommodations." *Postsecondary LD Network News* 12, 7.

Levy, Nancy R., and Michael S. Rosenberg. 1990. "Strategies for Improving the Written Expression of Students with Learning Disabilities." *LD Forum* 16.1, 23–26.

Lipp, Janice. 1991. "Turning Problems into Opportunities." *Another Door to Learning Newsletter,* 1–3.

Longo, Judith. 1988. "The Learning Disabled: Challenge to Postsecondary Institutions." *Journal of Developmental Education* 11.3, 10–12.

Lovitt, Thomas. 1989. *Introduction to Learning Disabilities.* Needham Heights, MA: Allyn and Bacon.

McGuire, Joan. 1991. "Access and Eligibility." International Conference on Learning Disabilities. Minneapolis, MN: October 11.

McGuire, Joan, Debora Hall, and A. Vivienne Litt. 1991. "A Field-Based Study of the Direct Service Needs of College Students with Learning Disabilities." *Journal of College Student Development* 32, 101–108.

National Clearinghouse on Postsecondary Education for Individuals with Handicaps 8.2 (1989), 4.

Philosophy take-home exam. Smith College, 1991.

"The Rehabilitation Act of 1971." 1977, May 4. *Federal Register,* 93–112.

Schwarz, Judy. 1991. Personal interview. October 13.

Schwenn, John. 1991. "Stereotyped Football Players: Poor Students or Undiagnosed Learning Disabilities?" International Conference on Learning Disabilities. Minneapolis, MN: October 12.

Smith, Frank. 1982. *Writing and the Writers.* Hillsdale, NJ: Lawrence Erlbaum Associates.

Stockdale, Carol. 1991. Personal interview. October 13.

U.S. Congress. 1969. *Children with Specific Learning Disabilities Act of 1969.* Washington, D.C.: U.S. Government Printing Office.

Woodcock, Richard, and M. Bonner Johnson. 1989. *Woodcock-Johnson Tests of Achievement.* Allen, TX: Teaching Resources.

9 Individualized Instruction in Writing Centers: Attending to Cross-Cultural Differences

Muriel Harris
Purdue University

Among the defining characteristics of writing centers is the commitment to each student as an individual, to helping that particular writer develop his or her composing skills. Working on the generally accepted premise that there is no monolithically similar set of composing skills among writers, those of us in writing centers focus attention on the student's particular skills and particular needs. While we agree that group instruction in the classroom setting provides useful help, we also insist that attention be given to needs arising from differences among writers. When we talk about our method of working one-to-one and focusing on the individual, we assume that classroom teachers understand how different our individualized approach is from theirs. But that appears to be an inaccurate assumption. As we explain that we help each student with what he or she needs, in a way that is appropriate for him or her, this is too often interpreted by those outside the writing center merely as having the luxury of a class size of one to work with. As a corollary, they assume our responsibility to be one of informing students of the rules and guidelines they should already have known.

For those not involved in the individualized instructional mode of writing centers, it is indeed hard to conceptualize what the differences between the writing center and the classroom are and why those of us in writing centers keep insisting that writers benefit from personalized interaction with tutors. One way to help outsiders understand this function is to note some of the types of help we offer students when they come into the center, to suggest the range of different needs writers have. Thus, tutors begin to individualize by finding out what each particular student needs and how he or she will most effectively begin to acquire or improve some aspect of writing. We find, for example, that some writers—or writers at some times—profit from collaborative conversation as they plan or develop papers; that other writers need a listening ear or some assurance that a reader is able to follow their discourse; that some need answers to a few questions; that others benefit from help in understanding their assignments; that visual learners gain a better understanding from diagrams, flow charts, and other visual presentations than from oral or written explanations; and that still others are unaware that they have writing processes that are not entirely functional.

Among still other kinds of help that tutors offer is assistance in helping some students see why their papers are judged as unsatisfactory. It is on this type of tutorial interaction—working with students until they can fully comprehend why teachers tell them something is "deficient" or "wrong" in what they have written—that I want to focus here. Even this aspect of the multifaceted tutorial approach has subsections that need to be put aside—I am focusing here only on a particular group of difficulties that students have in understanding why their papers are inadequate—difficulties caused by social and cultural differences that students bring to their writing. Thus, one aspect or one subsection of the many ways of individualizing is helping students whose social and cultural values, predilections, and habits lead them to create discourse that does not look like accepted academic prose in American universities. Unfortunately, too often such students are not told that their writing follows different organizational strategies than American academic discourse or that it relies on patterns of development such discourse does not use. Instead, because underlying causes of the differences are not adequately recognized or understood by teachers, these students often receive low grades because of "writing deficiencies." As an example of how teachers can respond in this inappropriate way, the discomforting results of a study by Anna Söter indicate that the teachers she observed gave lower ratings to papers by students from other cultures and subcultures in instances when the writing did not conform to the teachers' expected norms for narrative writing. When Söter examined the student papers rated as deficient, she found that they conformed to norms for acceptable narratives in the students' cultures (mainly Arabic and Vietnamese) but not to the teachers' cultural expectations for this kind of discourse. The teachers' rationales for the lower ratings ("poor organization," etc.) indicated no awareness of cross-cultural differences.

When we look at the papers of students from other cultures, it is easy to understand why such judgments are made. The organization seems strange, or the thesis is not well defined, or it appears that the writer has not worked hard enough to make the meaning clear or that the writing is too general and needs more specifics. But there is a wealth of theory and research from the fields of sociolinguistics and contrastive rhetoric to help tutors recognize and work with the multicultural diversity which produces such writing. Fortunately, because of the tutorial setting, the tutor has the luxury of one-to-one collaborative conversation in an informal, nonevaluative atmosphere, and the necessary probing can progress appropriately. The following discussion, which dips into the growing body of scholarship on cross-cultural differences, will help us see more clearly this aspect of what it means to individualize, to tailor the tutorial to the particular student sitting next to us, to work with multicultural differences. It will also help us explain to those outside the writing center why tutorials look so different from classroom pedagogy. Our theoretical commitment to attending to individual differences turns into pedagogical reality whenever we use this background knowledge to help the particular writer with whom we are talking.

The Need for Tutorial Flexibility

For teachers who do not work in writing centers, working with individual differences may look like a random, aimless conversation—zigging and zagging from one direction to another. Even the advice we give tutors appears to reinforce the seeming lack of direction in a well-run session. "Be flexible," we say, or "Be ready to switch gears when things are headed in the wrong direction." From their vantage point, students are also likely to see tutorials as mere conversation and are apt to say, "Oh, we just talked," when asked what they accomplished in their sessions. The tutorial, because it cannot and should not have a syllabus, may even contribute to the marginalizing of writing centers. There appears to be a lack of rigor connected to this lack of predictable direction that leads some classroom teachers and administrators to think of tutoring as a form of teaching which requires less effort or thought and is therefore less likely to be effective. Coupled with the reductive view of tutorials as merely telling students once again what they didn't understand the first time in class or from their textbooks, such notions indeed trivialize the work of the writing center. But a basic principle in writing center pedagogy, the commitment to working with each particular writer, means that tutors cannot just acknowledge but must work with every student's individuality, finding out where that student is and uncovering those differences and needs indeed cuts a path that zigs, zags, and curls back on itself as we search with the student for what will help him or her become a better writer. Sometimes, as tutors plunge into a tutorial, they may have a sense of some likely possibilities to consider; at other times, though, tutors step out into uncharted waters with little insight as to where they and their student are headed. We don't always land on safe ground, and some tutorials are exercises in frustration because we drift aimlessly, but there are those other times when real progress is made and the writers leave the writing center far more in control of their writing than they had been. Those are indeed marvelous voyages to have been part of.

I've expended a lot of ink on some of the possible differences which cause students that I've seen in tutorials difficulties—problems such as those associated with being one- or multi-drafters (1989), having composing process problems (1985, 1983a, 1983b), being hobbled by confused or mistaken perceptions about writing (1979), and even suffering from problems that arise as writers mature (1981). While these sources of writing difficulties were not immediately obvious when I first tried to identify them, uncovering some of the effects of multicultural differences on writing has been a particularly slow, confusing, and often baffling process. But it has become especially urgent as more and more students with diverse ethnic and social backgrounds enter our universities and are asked to write the kinds of academic prose that we perceive as appropriate. One of my earliest recognitions of the chasms that can divide one culture from another was a tutorial with a student who had recently arrived in the United States from China. Enrolled in a composition course for ESL students, she was asked early in the semester to write a brief essay about her first day in this country. She was in our writing lab because, her instructor explained, she had misunderstood the assignment. The draft she brought in—two brief, labored paragraphs about her parents' educational background in China—did indeed seem far off the mark. We talked about the assignment, about the events of her arrival, and about what narrative writing is, but she still seemed unable to fathom what her essay should contain or what was inappropriate about the paragraphs she had brought with her. What seemed so obvious to me bewildered her, even my very pointed suggestions that she start with the events of her arrival in San Francisco or a meeting with relatives soon afterward in Seattle.

What that Chinese student could not tell me (because it was not at the conscious level of her awareness)—and what I knew nothing about and could not, therefore, discuss—was (as I later learned from other sources) her reluctance to seem rude and uneducated by leaping into her subject without providing the context of family background that is traditionally appropriate in her culture. Our tutorial had all the requisite twists and turns as I tried different approaches and sought different reasons for why we weren't making any headway, but I was not at that time sufficiently aware of cultural differences and their effects on rhetorical values of American academic writing. I have since learned to identify the difference between the cultural preference for providing extensive context before arriving at the subject (especially in terms of family matters) and the American preference for leaping directly into the topic in the first paragraph. I also know that because we cannot pigeonhole writers, I cannot immediately guess that this cultural difference is the cause of some other inappropriate essay written by a Chinese student. I still have to ask and listen and talk some more before I can assume anything about the student with whom I am sitting. But a review of some of the cross-cultural differences that contribute to variations in student writing will substantiate the need for the theoretical commitment to individualization that goes on in writing center tutorials.

Cross-Cultural Differences

When we work with ESL students, it is fairly easy for us to see that a large number of so-called "errors" in their English sentences are due not to carelessness but to the use of patterns from their first language. We recognize that Chinese students are likely to omit articles because their language does not use them or that students who speak Farsi as their first language are likely to omit pronouns or use adjectival forms for adverbs (Houghton 1980). In the same way, although it is not as easy to recognize, different rhetorical conventions arise from patterns, values, and preferences that prevail in cultures of other countries. This is not to say that Americans have a single set of rhetorical values, for as James Berlin's (1984) history of composition studies in America shows us, even here there are competing rhetorics vying for our allegiance. But composition textbooks and proficiency exam standards do privilege a set of similar culture-bound values and principles which we find ourselves encouraging students to follow. Unfortunately, students acculturated to other standards of appropriate, effective discourse mistakenly assume they are in some way deficient writers. The distinction they do not draw for themselves is that of the difference between an inadequate writer in any language and a writer acculturated to one set of standards who is trying to become proficient within another set of assumptions, standards, values, and preferences. Recognizing an instance of this and helping the student also to see what is happening can be a long and arduous tutorial (or set of tutorials), but it is particularly rewarding for both tutor and writer to travel this road together.

One place to begin seeing the effects of multicultural diversity on rhetorical values is to examine that all-time favorite of composition texts about essay writing, statements of main points, both in the introduction which announces the point or focus or topic of the paper as well as in topic sentences in paragraphs. Although Richard Braddock's (1974) award-winning research demonstrated that professional writers often don't have topic sentences in paragraphs, teachers still expect students to be able to tell them what each paragraph is about and what the point of the paper is. Moreover, it is expected that main points are usually announced at the beginning of an essay and will be fairly obvious to the reader, even when thesis statements or topic sentences are not specifically asked for. Though the economic dominance of the Japanese in American markets has led to greater public awareness of the Japanese preference for proceeding by indirection, how often is it acknowledged that the overt announcement of topics is merely a cultural preference, a convention of the discourse community American academics see themselves as part of? Even when this difference is recognized, it is not automatically the case that when teachers explain the importance of the topic sentence in class and emphasize that this is the way it's done here, students will acquiesce, no matter what their cultural inclinations are. Statements by Chinese students, as well as research on Chinese business practices, help us see just how difficult it is to leap into the conventions of another discourse community and why some writers cannot or do not easily announce the topic.

In a study done by Linda Wai Ling Young (1982), we see how the American preference for initial topic announcement can cause confusion and misconceptions when it clashes with the Chinese preference for delayed and more subtle topic announcement. For her study, Young observed a group of Chinese businessmen conducting business in English with some native English speakers. Young's interest was in identifying the discourse strategies being used, and her conclusion was that there is a strong Chinese preference for the steady unraveling and buildup of information before arriving at the important message or point. In the situation Young studied, the Chinese businessmen speaking in English followed their cultural preferences for how the conversation should progress. As a result, they understood the points being made, while the native-English speakers missed relevant information because—from their perspective—the points were buried in the flow of conversation. The native-English speakers' difficulties were compounded by another problem, says Young: the opening lines of the Chinese businessmen's discourse did not provide a preview statement which would have oriented the listener to the overall direction of the discourse. The native-English speakers, when interviewed later, saw this failure to address the main point as "beating around the bush." Yet another group of Chinese businessmen, when asked about putting the request (or main point) first, with the rationale following, gave a number of negative responses. That, they agreed, would be rude, pushy. They would lose face for acting too aggressively.

Such studies help us recognize the degree to which topic announcement is a cultural preference, but we also need to recognize how reluctant some Chinese students are to adopt the technique in class. One student captures much of this Chinese distaste for the rhetorical values stressed in American composition classes when he writes:

> I don't find the American style, where the topic sentence appears first, to be effective. It's not necessarily more persuasive nor convincing than the Chinese style, where the speaker, at the same time as he is speaking, is reasoning with the listener to allow the listener to see whether what he says makes sense or not. This Chinese style is more open-minded, less biased, not constrictive as the American style, where it immediately sets you up to a particular frame of mind. You see, with the American style, you can react immediately to what the speaker says without listening to the rest of his explanation. (Young 82–83)

In a comprehensive—and fascinating—article (1985), Carolyn Matalene notes the Chinese preference for indirection and speculates wryly about the possibility that when her Chinese students were "back in their crowded eight-to-a-room dormitories, they must have wondered about the stupidity of their teacher who had to have everything spelled out" (802). It may be equally apparent that a tutor cannot just say "write out your topic statement and put it there" to such students and expect them to comply.

Thus, given other cultures' preferences for indirection, I have to remember that when a student appears in our writing lab to get help with a paper that a teacher or peer-response group has said "needs a thesis statement" or "needs a clearer focus," I have backtracking to do if I suspect a possible cross-cultural difficulty. Do the students know the concept of the topic sentence? Do they know that this is an American preference? Are they comfortable following this convention, or are they perhaps backing off, cringing at the notion of being so "pushy"? It would seem that this is a fairly straightforward task, but—alas—it is not so. For example, I remember one student, American-born though of Chinese ancestry, who quietly but firmly resisted this notion of American abruptness in topic announcement because she could not accept such a persona in her writing, even while nodding in agreement as I explained that this is an accepted practice in American college writing and is what her teacher recommended for the revised version of her paper. (The student smiled, thanked me profusely, packed up her books, and left the writing lab, never to return.) Even using the "I" voice in a paper can be difficult. When Fan Shen (1989) writes about her identity problems in an American composition classroom, she describes her difficulties in being asked to give up a strong cultural preference for subordinating the self to "we" and to present herself as "I," a posture she saw as disrespectful, boastful, and pompous. The reluctance to use the first person pronoun is something that writing center tutors must keep in mind as a possible cause of problems when students appear to be having difficulties with assignments in narrative, with expressive writing, and with any other writing where we would assume that the "I" voice is most effective.

As Edward Hall (1977) has pointed out so well, cultural conflicts are rarely obvious—they involve the clash of principles or patterns of thinking we normally do not articulate or raise to the level of consciousness. Of necessity, then, tutorial conversation is often lengthy and convoluted because each student has to work through and make overt his or her previously unarticulated assumptions, and both student and tutor may have to ask all kinds of questions before the need for the desired rhetorical values becomes apparent. As an example of this problem, I have in a log I keep of my tutoring an entry about yet another Asian student who was told he needed to work on the organization of his paper. As we talked, the structure, focus, and development of his argument eventually became clear to me, though it was abundantly obvious to me why the teacher had the same difficulties I experienced in trying to see what the paper was about and how it was organized. Eventually, the student acknowledged that he could state his argument in the opening paragraph and could forecast the major supporting points he was going to make. He acknowledged that this is one possible format for writing in his own language, but he just couldn't see why choosing one way over another made much difference. He had been dismissing my comments and persisted in seeing himself as a poor writer with some other problem, not the one his teacher and I wanted to deal with. Only when we got to that point, when I could finally see that he placed little value in the notion of how strong the American preference is for topic announcement, could we begin to go forward. I couldn't have predicted the path our tutorial would take, nor can I now recall all the different directions our conversation took before we reached a productive line of discussion. The point is, though, that this particular student needed a particular kind of help, and my job as a tutor was to find out what was needed and to help the student recognize it.

The matter of topic announcement, though, is only one of many cultural assumptions embedded in what is taught in American composition classes. It is also one of the more obvious cultural preferences that teachers are beginning to recognize and deal with. But other cross-cultural differences are less apparent and are even more likely to be viewed as deficiencies in students' writing. The use of digression is one such difference. Mainstream American culture's inability to accept digression is obvious whenever we hear someone say, usually in impatient tones, "So, get to the point." Yet Michael Clyne's (1987) study indicates that digression in German academic discourse is a recognized functional feature, providing the opportunity to offer theory, ideology, or additional information or to enter into polemics with other authors. In an earlier (1981) study, Clyne found that a scholarly book in German, which was reviewed positively by German speakers, was described as "chaotic" and criticized for "lack of focus and cohesiveness" when read by English speakers in the English translation. A similar tolerance for digression in Hindi writing has been noted by Yamuna Kachru (1988). After studying the discourse features of Hindi, Kachru concludes that paragraphing in Hindi can include a great deal of digression, does not require unity of topic, has no need for an explicit topic statement, and can present a claim and its justification in separate paragraphs while material related to the background may be included in the same paragraph with the claim. This suggests a number of possible "writing problems" in English which may be (or may not be) the result of relying on cultural values different from those emphasized in American academic discourse.

The American rhetorical predilection for linearity in developing ideas is a cultural preference which appears to creep into the prose of speakers of other languages as they learn English. This can be seen in the patterns of some

Korean academic discourse. William Eggington's (1987) study of Korean discourse looks at rhetorical styles of Korean academics not proficient in English and Koreans who were educated in English-speaking universities and publishing in Korean. Those who had been educated in English-speaking universities had linear, general-to-specific rhetorical patterns in their writing while the non-English speakers typically had no thesis development, preferring instead to list points revolving around an unstated central theme. In addition, Eggington supports his findings by citing a study which showed that Korean students with a beginning ability to read English found discourse in Korean structure easier to read than prose in English structure and that the students had less recall of material read in the English structure. Another characteristic of Korean prose noted by Eggington, one that we might see a trace of in some writing in English, is the use of the "some people say" formula. It tends to appear when the writer is taking a somewhat controversial stand, and is used either to protect one's own position by enlisting anonymous support or to deflect any appearance of being too direct when criticizing another's position. The possibility exists, then, that in an argumentation paper or any paper in which a student is asked to take a stance, the student with such a culturally bound preference might not use sources in a way that would be seen as appropriate or adequate proof. As I think of how often students are asked in a variety of disciplines to argue for a particular side in an issue, I realize how much the "some people say" formula may look inadequate when the instructor is looking for an appropriately documented defense of an "I think that" stance.

The preference for subsuming one's own point within a group context can crop up in unexpected ways as well, as it became apparent to me when working with Li, a graduate student from Taiwan. In my tutoring log is an account of Li's difficulties with an ESL class assignment to write a letter to the editor of the campus newspaper. Li appeared in the writing lab to work on difficulties in finding a topic, and his teacher had noted that some brainstorming practice might help Li find appropriate material. Nothing worked because, as Li kept explaining so patiently, he didn't know enough about what is important to students at our university and wasn't sure what people thought about various potential topics we discussed. When I finally began to really listen to what Li was repeatedly saying, I realized that, given his cultural preference for voicing only those opinions commonly shared, he had no interest in a display of individualism, especially in a letter to the editor, a form which so often focuses on criticism. Li felt unprepared to be part of the common voice in this new culture and preferred not to speak up. "This is not the Chinese way," he eventually explained and even offered a Chinese aphorism on the point: "The peg that sticks up must be hammered down." Brainstorming was, of course, not what was needed.

Yet another cultural preference which can lead to so-called "writing problems" is that of the degree to which the reader/listener or writer/speaker is responsible for the clarity of the piece of communication. John Hinds (1987), who has suggested a typology of language based on this distinction, explains that "English speakers, by and large, charge the writer, or speaker, with the responsibility to make clear and well-organized statements. If there is a breakdown in communication, for instance, it is because the speaker/writer has not been clear enough, not because the listener/reader has not exerted enough effort in an attempt to understand" (143). Japanese, on the other hand, is cited by Hinds as an example of a language in which the reader/listener is responsible for understanding the communication. Thus while English speakers may go through draft after draft to come up with a satisfactory product, Japanese authors frequently compose exactly one draft, which becomes the finished product. In Japanese writing, explains Hinds, transitional statements may be absent or attenuated since it is the reader's responsibility to determine the relationships between any one part of the essay and the essay as a whole. This does not mean that Japanese writing neglects transitional statements altogether, but if they are present they may be more subtle and require a more active role for the reader in making use of them. As tutors, then, we must not leap to advice about revision—which seems so obvious to us—or expect Japanese students to see what to do with their papers when a reader has said, "I don't understand your point here."

Robert Kaplan (1988), elaborating on Hinds's typology, explains that the assumption in Japanese is of a high degree of knowledge shared by reader and writer. Kaplan also notes how the propositional structures of text change according to Hinds's typology. Readers in a reader-responsible language expect to supply some significant portion of the propositional structure while readers in a writer-responsible language expect the writer to provide most of the propositional structure. As an example of a writer-responsible text, Kaplan offers an overview of a typical *BBC World News* program, a scripted oral text. Here the news is introduced with a clearly identified outline of main points to be covered, the introduction is followed by a detailed exposition of each of the outlined main points in the order presented, and the text ends with a summary of the main points, again in the same order as presented. (It's hard to miss the conclusion here that prescriptive, traditional American freshman rhetoric texts must be doing a terrific job of preparing future writers of BBC news programs. Conversely, the five-paragraph essay is apparently alive and well on the BBC.)

While work in contrastive rhetoric focuses primarily on written discourse, Hinds's typology is intended to apply both to written and oral communication. Moving on to the cross-cultural discourse analysis of John Gumperz and others (1982) also moves us into oral communication. This is particularly relevant to tutors because our interaction with students is always in the form of oral conferencing. Misunderstandings and communication breakdowns can occur in the tutorial as well as in the piece of discourse the writer brings in. As Gumperz explains: "People from different cultural backgrounds may speak a variety of English characterized by certain conventions. It is when attitude and meaning are conveyed through one set of conventions and interpreted through another that breakdowns in communication may occur" (1). As an example, Gumperz offers from his work on differences between (Asian) Indian-English and England-English speakers his conclusion that among England-English speakers many reference words such as "this" and "those" pronouns, are used for the most part only when the referent has been previously specified. However, among Indian-English speakers when such reference words are used, they are not likely to refer to something already named. Rather, they would be inferred from the context, a process that can cause some confusion among England-English listeners. We can readily imagine that a student using such Indian-English conventions is likely to become frustrated if an American speaker loses track of what is being said. In a tutorial or in a paper, communication may seem to be breaking down, but it isn't necessarily the student's lack of understanding or lack of attention to clarity (in his terms) which is the cause.

Yet another source of potential confusion, as Gumperz, Aulakh, and Kaltrnan (1982) note, is the tendency among speakers of Indian English to use a common rhetorical strategy of repeating the previous speaker's words (as an act of politeness) or of using repetition to establish important points of thematic progression. Since an American or England-English speaker is likely to become impatient during such repetition, the result may be that the very information which the Indian speaker is trying to emphasize is being judged as irrelevant or redundant. Gumperz' work with discourse strategies of Indian English also reveals differences in the use of conjunctions as "butting in" devices to take turns in conversation. In Indian English, writes Gumperz, "and," "but," "yes," and "no" can be used simply to signal "I've got something to say" without necessarily connoting how one's comments tie to preceding speech. It is easy to see how someone proceeding on the basis of rhetorical principles in American- or England-English discourse might find logical difficulties, or lack of coherence, when someone uses "but" in the manner of Indian English. We can see how a tutor might react negatively if unaware of such differences, similar to the negative responses that occurred in the interview situations Gumperz studied. Gumperz also points out that Indian discourse has less metatalk, less talk about the topic. In American communication, we tend to make our communicative action explicit. "I have a request to make." "What I'm trying to say is . . ." or "The point is . . ." are phrases used to signal our audience as to the direction of our discourse.

American written discourse is also heavy with such metatalk, often seen as adding clarity and coherence to the writing. Again, Indian norms are very different, for, as Gumperz shows, Indian speakers move freely among topics while the American tendency is to tell listeners about the shift. "I'll come back to this later" is a typical American comment. The result is that American speakers/readers are likely to judge Indian discourse to be loose and illogical, lacking in structural clarity.

The influence of culture on communication is clearly extensive, and we are not likely to have any exhaustive or definitive catalogs in the near or distant future. In their 1980 work, which is really an extensive course packet for teaching a course to improve communication across cultural differences, Gumperz and Roberts conclude that individuals cannot be taught to communicate effectively across cultures, they must learn to do it for themselves:

> There is no single method which people can acquire and no set of rules which they can simply put into practice. The reason for this is that the conventions of language use operate within such a great range of situations and have to take account of so many variables. There is no neat equation between a type of interaction and the conventions which an individual might use. (3)

If so, then tutors have a particularly important task—helping students learn how to use conventions of American academic discourse by themselves. Writing center theory specifies that we do not "teach" students anything, we help them learn by themselves, and bridging cross-cultural differences, then, is one more thing we help students learn by themselves.

Guidelines in Working with Cultural Differences

What, then, are some guidelines to help tutors help writers? We cannot anticipate the great variety of cultural differences likely to surface in tutorials, but there are a few broad considerations to keep in mind when looking for possible cross-cultural problems in communication:

- *Look for patterns of thinking that seem at odds with accepted patterns in American discourse conventions.* As tutors we read papers for logic, organizational patterns, means of proving arguments, ways of persuading readers, methods of adding coherence, and other accepted patterns of effective discourse, but we need to ask ourselves and our students whether deviations from these norms are caused by an inability to achieve them or by preferences for other norms. No one claims that making this distinction is easy, but we must not automatically assume that the absence of some characteristic of discourse is due to a student's poor writing abilities.

- *Look for hidden or unarticulated assumptions*. Both tutor and student may be working on assumptions that are at cross-purposes with the writing or the conversational task at hand. Once we can articulate the nature of the problem, we need to look at what assumptions are at work. Is the paper not easily accessible to the reader? Is the student merely repeating what the tutor is saying? If so, what assumptions are being made? For example, if one problem is that the student seems disinterested or uninvolved in the tutorial because he only looks down or away, then there is an assumption that eye contact means involvement and interest. (Eye contact as an indication of active participation and interest is, by the way, a very definite cultural preference. A Turkish student once brought to our writing lab a fascinating essay on the prevailing tendency in her culture for students not to look a teacher directly in the eye.) Only when the assumptions have surfaced can we begin to address the question of whether or not there is some cross-cultural difference at work.

- *Look for tendencies to create stereotypes in our thinking*. Although we all try not to stereotype, it is an easy error to slip into, despite all the politically correct sensitizing going on. When one or two students of a particular nationality appear late for tutorials, do we lapse into assuming that all nationals in that group are not punctual, or do we try to learn whether time commitments are different in their worldview? When students from a particular culture seem to patronize tutors, do we too quickly label them as arrogant, or do we try to find whether cultural assumptions are at work?

Once we begin to recognize differences at work, we have to address the question of how and to what degree we ought to acquaint students from diverse cultural and ethnic backgrounds with the norms expected in the academic society they have entered. Helping them see whether and how they fit in with or differ from American academic communication patterns is, I believe, part of a tutor's responsibility. This does not mean that our goal is to help our students assimilate into this culture, but we must help them become acculturated to the degree that they can function successfully. Such a task is neither easy nor obvious, and tutors have to expect that they may stumble as often as they succeed. But honoring the diversity of students and being committed to working with their individual differences is both challenging and also basic to the concept of writing center theory and pedagogy.

References

Berlin, James A. 1984. *Writing Instruction in Nineteenth-Century American Colleges*. Carbondale, IL: Southern Illinois University Press.

Braddock, Richard. 1974. "The Frequency and Placement of Topic Sentences in Expository Prose." *Research in the Teaching of English* 8, 287–302.

Clyne, Michael. 1981. "Culture and Discourse Structure." *Journal of Pragmatics* 5, 61–66.

———. 1987. "Cultural Differences in the Organization of Academic Texts: English and German." *Journal of Pragmatics* 11, 211–47.

Eggington, William G. 1987. "Written Academic Discourse in Korean: Implications for Effective Communication." *Writing Across Languages: Analysis of L₂ Text.* Eds. Ulla Connor and Robert B. Kaplan. Reading, MA: Addison-Wesley, 153–68.

Gumperz, John J., Gurinder Aulakh, and Hannah Kaltman. 1982. "Thematic Structure and Progression in Discourse." *Language and Social Identity.* Ed. John J. Gumperz. Cambridge: Cambridge University Press, 22–56.

Gumperz, John J., and Celia Roberts. 1980. *Developing Awareness Skills for Interethnic Communication.* Occasional Papers No. 12. Singapore: SEAMEO Regional Language Centre.

Hall, Edward. 1957. *The Silent Language.* New York: Doubleday.

———. 1977. *Beyond Culture.* Garden City, NY: Doubleday, Anchor Press.

Harris, Muriel. 1979. "Contradictory Perceptions of Rules of Writing." *College Composition and Communication* 30, 218–20.

———. 1981. "Mending the Fragmented Free Modifier." *College Composition and Communication* 32, 175–82.

———. 1983a. "A Grab-Bag of Diagnostic Techniques." *Teaching English in the Two-Year College* 9, 111–15.

———. 1983b. "Modeling: A Process Method of Teaching." *College English* 45, 74–84.

———. 1985. "Diagnosing Writing Process Problems: A Pedagogical Application of Speaking-Aloud Protocol Analysis." *When a Writer Can't Write: Research in Writer's Block and Other Writing Process Problems.* Ed. Mike Rose. New York: Guilford Press, 166–81.

———. 1989. "Composing Behaviors of One- and Multi-Draft Writers." *College English* 51, 174–91.

Hinds, John. 1987. "Reader Versus Writer Responsibility: A New Typology." *Writing Across Languages: Analysis of L₂ Text.* Eds. Ulla Connor and Robert B. Kaplan. Reading, MA: Addison-Wesley, 141–52.

Houghton, Diane. 1980. "The Writing Problems of Iranian Students." ELT Documents 109: Study Modes and Academic Development of Overseas Students. ERIC, ED 201 186.

Kachru, Yamuna. 1988. "Writers in Hindi and English." *Writing Across Languages and Cultures: Issues in Contrastive Rhetoric.* Ed. Alan C. Purves. Newbury Park, CA: Sage, 109–37.

Kaplan, Robert B. 1988. "Contrastive Rhetoric and Second Language Learning: Notes Toward a Theory of Contrastive Rhetoric." *Writing Across Languages and Cultures: Issues in Contrastive Rhetoric.* Ed. Alan C. Purves. Newbury Park, CA: Sage, 275–304.

Matalene, Carolyn. 1985. "Contrastive Rhetoric: An American Writing Teacher in China." *College English* 47, 789–808.

Shen, Fan. 1989. "The Classroom and the Wider Culture: Identity as a Key to Learning English Composition." *College Composition and Communication* 40, 459–66.

Söter, Anna O. 1988. "The Second Language Learner and Cultural Transfer in Narration." *Writing Across Languages and Cultures: Issues in Contrastive Rhetoric.* Ed. Alan C. Purves. Newbury Park, CA: Sage, 177–205.

Young, Linda Wai Ling. 1982. "Inscrutability Revisited." *Language and Social Identity.* Ed. John J. Gumperz. Cambridge University Press, 72–84.

10 A Unique Learning Environment

Pamela Farrell-Childers
McCallie School, Chattanooga, Tennessee

From the inception of the first writing centers at colleges and universities, administrators and teachers alike have anticipated failure. After all, students shouldn't be helping each other, writing centers can't adapt to our inflexible schedules, we can't afford anything new, and writing centers don't fit our current curriculum. In contrast, college and high school writing center directors have considered a myriad of reasons for their existence. Stephen North (1984) let us think about the possibilities for this new kind of facility sprouting on campuses throughout the country. Some, like Olson (1984), have felt that it should "make room, provide space and time for students to talk about ideas, to explore meaning, and to freely engage in the trial and error of putting their thoughts into writing" (xi). As high schools have also developed writing centers, Farrell (1989) describes all levels of writing centers as creating "a low-risk environment" (21). Others put the emphasis on a "commitment to process, for laboratories can emphasize the writing process as classrooms, no matter how organized, seldom can" (Steward and Croft 1982, 5). Whether writing centers use computers or not, some centers emphasize a laboratory approach with the focus on grammar skills rather than on writing to learn or to inform. These differences, however, mirror the philosophy of the institution and the director of the writing center. Writing centers can and do work while overcoming the voices of gloom heard at the beginning of this chapter. In fact, writing centers enable students to learn through a variety of methods which apply writing theories that one often associates with classroom learning. The environment encourages the application of different theories within one facility for students of all levels of ability, and, through the writing center community, peer tutoring, and writing center activities, the facility actually enhances the curriculum.

Curriculum experts and educational theorists have considered this environment one which reflects a humanistic design or affective education (Ornstein and Hunkins 1988). Maslow's (1962) concept of self-actualization supports this design that focuses on the learners. In his description of the educator's task in affective education, Rogers (1962) explains that it is to create an educational environment to tap personal resources and encourage genuineness of behavior, empathy, and respect of self and others. In a writing center, this affective educational environment becomes a reality.

More and more writing centers are reflecting the idea of a low-risk environment. Whether peer tutors, graduate assistants, or faculty staff these facilities, a writing center differs from any classroom because it is a low-risk environment. Reigstad, Matsuhashi, and Luban (1978) describe their center as a place "to establish the student as a more independent writer and to give him or her some strategies that can be applied to the next piece of writing" (33). However, there are no grades given by the people working in the writing center; rather, tutors encourage dialogue that does not take place in classroom-teacher conferences. Though writing workshops in classes certainly help student writing and should continue, writing center interaction goes beyond what can occur in a classroom environment with its time constraints, ever-present evaluation, and peer pressure to respond in what students deem to be appropriate ways. It is a place where, as Warnock and Warnock (1984) explain, "writing is taught with a focus on meaning, not form; on process, not product; on authorial intention and audience expectation, not teacher authority or punitive measures; on holistic and human concerns, not errors and isolated skills" (16). Sonnier and Fontecchio contend, "By implementing holistic education, more students gain in that they are not only more attentive, but more personally involved with the learning process" (1989, 23).

In contrast to the classroom environment which Murray (1982) so aptly describes as a place where students should be granted Writing Rights, students enter the writing center to be heard, to be read, and to get feedback from another listener who isn't a classmate influenced by classroom decorum, standards, or competition. That reader/listener is also a more objective respondent who chooses to work or volunteer in the writing center rather than the dean's office, cafeteria, dorm, or sports facility. In fact, many writing center personnel are there to learn from one another as well as from the very people they are there to help.

This sense of camaraderie and sharing is another important part of the writing center atmosphere. Laughter is not foreign to writing centers; in fact, some of the best learning occurs once anxieties are lessened in a comfortable atmosphere conducive to learning. A classroom may be comfortable and conducive to learning also, but the presence of the teacher who grades students changes that atmosphere. In a writing center, peers encourage risk taking, play with language, question the validity of ideas, laugh at their own mistakes, and empathize with each other's frustrations. Tutors learn from each other's experiences, from experiences of students and from their own experiences; students learn from tutors, other clients, and themselves. Yes, there are students who come to the writing center because they have been "sent" as part of the requirement for a course or to "fix up" a poor paper. What seems to happen, however, is that many of these students return on their own because they have found people who will listen to their ideas and actually read their work. As Hawkins states, a writing center should "stand for an attitude toward students, toward writing, and toward teaching that puts control and responsibility for learning back in the hands of students" (1989, xiv). This expectation for individual achievement to the best of each student's ability is a "key factor which favorably influences affective results" (Ward 1989, 54).

Ideally, Levin (1989) points out, the writing center needs to be a place for all students, not just remedial or even gifted students (24). Brannon and Knoblauch think the writing center "is an alternative resource, with its distinctive advantages, available whenever writers at any level of competence, desire the focused attention of a discerning reader" (1984, 9). Perhaps the reason it is so effective as an alternative resource is the mere fact that a variety of writing theories may be applied in one place at the same time. For instance, on any given day in a writing center one may observe students working on all phases of the writing process, modeling the writing of others, and applying collaborative learning, writing-to-learn across the curriculum, and computer-assisted or interactive learning. These "holistic educational strategies meet the instructional needs of all students, visual and analytical" (Sonnier and Fontecchio 1989, 22).

Let me describe a typical hour in my writing center. At 8 a.m. three students wait outside for me to open the door; more appear as the printers and lights go on. As they are signing in, teachers of history, French, and biology slip by them and head toward computers. Four students move to the tables on the far side of the room, begin reading aloud and discussing their papers. Another teacher comes in and schedules a writing workshop on double-entry journals for her ESL class that is working on research writing. Two more students pick up SAT Verbal Skills software and begin working at a computer, taking turns responding to the prompts on the monitor. A tutor is conferencing with a student on revision techniques, and the four students on the far side are now writing lists of similarities and differences in human values in Miller's *Death of a Salesman* and Kafka's "Metamorphosis." Another teacher enters with a draft for publication and asks for feedback from me and two other colleagues. As the bell rings to end the first class of the day, three students stop by my desk to ask whether the Writers Club will meet this week since we've scheduled a student reading for next Tuesday evening. In just one hour, the writing center has involved students and faculty across the curriculum in application of several writing/language arts theories.

As students work through a piece of writing, giving feedback whenever needed during the writing process, they develop their own process. Holistic education, Sonnier and Buschner maintain, "provides fertile ground for students to attain positive results" (1989, 87). It is in the writing center that they have access to one-on-one response whenever they need it—not during the time when class meets or their instructor has office hours. In such "a humane environment," Ward (1984) contends, "the student is respected as an individual, treated with empathy, given encouragement, and expected to achieve" (53).

Kirby and Liner indicate, "The only consistently helpful and effective evaluation of student writings comes as the two of you sit down with the piece of writing, focusing directly on what's on the page" (1981, 201) and interact. Teachers don't have time to do that at every phase of the writing process with every student on every paper. Individual students determine their own needs, then use the services of the writing center; that is, they do not have to adapt to the needs of others. From brainstorming through revision, students and faculty use the writing center as a human, academic, and/or evaluative resource. Britton's (1975) evaluation of student writing nearly twenty years ago indicated that the majority (84%) of writing done by high school seniors was transactional. Although this percentage may be somewhat lower due to the increase in writing-to-learn activities, most college writing does fall into this mode as opposed to poetic and expressive writing. Therefore, our students and faculty need that critical evaluation of writing (not in the form of a grade) intended to communicate or inform. Writing center staffs offer that service as part of their regular duties.

Another important method of working in the affective area and improving writing is through modeling. Although the normal means of doing this is to follow the writing style of a good published writer, there are other ways of modeling in the writing center. For instance, writing decorum may be modeled. When students see professional educators working on pieces of writing in the writing center, they see research and writing in a natural and real environment. They see professionals checking dictionaries and thesauruses, questioning their own sentence structure and ideas, asking others' opinions on ideas expressed or ways of approaching a particular text. Such behavior sets an example for students and indicates to them that writing and learning are important and never end with academic degrees.

Although literature-based learning and whole language theory are associated with elementary and secondary education classrooms, they also apply to writing centers at all levels, and these methods encourage growth in the affective domain at all levels, too. Certainly the group using the far side of the writing center in the above scenario base their discussions and peer editing on works of literature to help them with thinking, writing, and learning. Christenbury and Kelly (1983) describe how "talking—asking and answering questions—often reveals our thoughts and feelings to us as well as to others" (1).

Whole language approaches incorporate studies within context across the curriculum and beyond academia to life experiences, rather than in isolation (Goodman 1986). Much of the work that occurs in the writing center does, in fact, involve whole language theory.

Collaborative learning, one of the controversial ideas to influence education, continues to be one of the most contagious activities in a writing center. Within affective environments, students "are able to approach problem situations with flexibility and intelligence and to work cooperatively with others" (Ornstein and Hunkins 1988, 181). Students and faculty alike ask each other questions, bounce ideas or pieces of writing off each other, coauthor texts, and share knowledge. One example of collaborative learning is two or more people using software at the computer. If they are trying to learn how to use the computer with word processing, the parties involved share a common link: they all want to get their ideas onto the screen, revised, edited, saved, and printed. In the process, faculty and students—honors students and remedial ones—all cheer success and suffer failure together. In a sense, the computer takes on the role of Whitman's poet as the great equalizer. The advantages of collaborative learning include greater achievement (Slavin 1987), greater use of reasoning strategies (Roftier and Ogan 1991), development of leadership skills (McKeachie 1986), and generation of better ideas than by individuals working alone (Slavin 1987).

With interactive learning, students may also be working collaboratively. For instance, consider the students working with the SAT preparation software. The software itself is interactive in that it directs the students, gives them choices, responds to their correct and incorrect choices, and directs them to more exercises that reinforce concepts when necessary or to more difficult problems. Interactive software or computer assisted instruction enables the computers to adapt instruction to student needs (McKeachie 1986). When students work in teams with such software, they learn from each other and from the software. The software provides learners with some form of supplementary and reference material to enable them to review, read further, get a quick overview, or get a deeper view than is obligatory (Romiszowski 1986).

Writing centers with computers may tend to focus more on the written product than on interaction among individuals; however, some have found that the computer actually enhances the interaction between writer and tutor in this low-risk atmosphere (Farrell 1989). What seems to make the environment different from a computer lab is that individuals are not working in isolation; instead, they are working in a comfortable place where people are communicating with each other verbally, on screen, and on hard copy. Students and faculty exchange ideas at the computers and critique one another's work on monitors. It is a safe place to take risks with writing and thinking.

Affective education includes "aspects of science that consider affective meanings in areas like environmental issues" (Beane 11). For instance, one physics instructor, Bob Mitchell, participated in a grassroots environmental/economic issue involving chip mills and the deforestation of Southeast Tennessee. By using the writing center as a resource, he learned computer skills, organizational skills, and writing skills. In fact, he not only developed effective business letters, but he also produced a plethora of documents for publication and modelled for students the process of carrying on a national and local grassroots movement on a political issue. After getting help on revision from staff and guest artists in the writing center, he produced an article, "Economics of Chip Mills," which was sent to Senator Al Gore and other United States government officials. When asked what he had learned in the writing center, Mitchell said, "An awareness of the importance of language in relation to purpose and audience."

Also, the writing center is indeed a center for writing in all subject areas. The three teachers who came into our writing center were writing in languages foreign to some of us: French, biology, and history. In an environment which encourages learning, the entire writing center staff and the students have an opportunity to learn from faculty and students alike. Psycholinguists and cognitive psychologists describe writing as "a highly complex act that demands analysis and synthesis of many levels of thinking" (Graves 1978, 6). By working in this low-risk environment, students have an opportunity to improve their thinking and learning through writing. Hersey (1984) contends that long-term effectiveness is important and that effectiveness has to do with students' attitudes at performing their work (the independence and initiative students demonstrate at their work). The difference between classroom work in this area and work in the writing center is again the environment without the teacher who evaluates the student. Martin (1976) found "the most dramatic changes in [students'] writing . . . came when teachers moved out of their role as examiner and into the role of adult consultant" (214).

There are, however, some other ways that this low-risk environment enhances writing, thinking, and learning. The writers meet to share works in progress, get feedback from peers and professionals, and give readings for others. These students are part of what Frank Smith (1986) calls a Writers Club, a group dedicated to writing and a love of the written word. Not only do these students have a built-in support system in writing centers, but they also have a chance to hear their own words, revise their ideas, and receive critical response from interested reader/listeners who are also writers. In some institutions, publications such as the literary magazine or writing center newsletter also play a part in the interaction of students and writing.

Since each writing center is unique, each reflects its own rich environment. For instance, some have a large percentage of returning students who have more experience in the real world to share with younger students and staff; others have more ESL students who add rich backgrounds of culture. Many ESL students find the writing center helps bridge the affective gap. Montalvo (1989) senses that affective education offers a form of "'caring' on the part of the teachers and in the students with the resulting 'pleasure and joy' that simply cannot be measured" (43).

Finally, one of the most exciting concepts associated with writing centers is the use of guest artists to focus on various aspects of writing. A few writing centers, for instance, actually build guest artists into their annual budgets. Some institutions handle this through other departments or schools; but if the guest artists are working out of the writing center, then the focus is on writing at the center. For example, artist Malcolm Childers, who creates etchings and poems to accompany them, gave presentations and readings in the writing center to show the relationship between the written word and the visual arts. Students were invited to examine closely the etchings on display and then the artist recited poems that went with several of his works. Students saw how the sounds and images of the words reinforced concepts in the art. The next period he spoke to a group of artists and reversed the emphasis. Art majors began to see the significance of writing in their work just as writers saw how important it was to consider all the senses when writing. Another time, KAL, syndicated political cartoonist for the *Baltimore Sun*, shared some of his cartoons, then discussed the difference between written and visual satire. Together, he and the students created a political cartoon which he left for display in the writing center. Again, the guest artist crossed the line between disciplines. Guest artists may include people in professions where they use writing; in other words, they present the role of writing in their careers.

More frequently, guest artists include poets, novelists, essayists, editors, or technical writers. They may lead workshops, give readings or hold individual conferences. Through these affective experiences, students "develop some organization of preferences, appreciations, and attitudes on which to act" (Beane 8–9). Students begin to feel the importance of writing not only in their lives but within the fiber of the institution when such value is given to writing in the center. The bonus of using such guest artists is an increase in writing for publication and in using the writing center. When such happenings take place, students want to be there for both the planned and spontaneous ones!

Attitudes are hard to assess, but those of us who have become part of a writing center atmosphere know that this place is full of fertile minds with "what ifs." Eisner reminds us, "There can be no affective activity without cognition" (1982, 28), but by maintaining a positive affective setting, writing centers provide rich environments where students and faculty find it easy to walk in, sit down, and get down to writing, thinking, and learning.

References

Beane, James. 1990. *Affect in the Curriculum: Toward Democracy, Dignity, and Diversity*. New York: Teachers College Press.

Brannon, Lil, and C. H. Knoblauch. 1984. "A Philosophical Perspective on Writing Centers and the Teaching of Writing." *Writing Centers: Theory and Administration*. Urbana, IL: National Council of Teachers of English, 36–47.

Britton, James et al. 1975. *The Development of Writing Abilities*. London: Macmillan Education.

Christenbury, Leila, and Patricia Kelly. 1983. *Questioning: A Path to Critical Thinking*. Urbana, IL: National Council of Teachers of English.

Eisner, Elliot W. 1982. *Cognition and Curriculum: A Basis for Deciding What to Teach*. New York: Longman.

Farrell, Pamela B. 1987. "Writer, Peer Tutor and Computer: A Unique Relationship." *The Writing Center Journal* VIII:l, 29–34.

———. 1989. *The High School Writing Center: Establishing and Maintaining One*. Urbana, IL: National Council of Teachers of English.

Goodman, Ken. 1986. *What's Whole in Whole Language*. Portsmouth, NH: Heinemann.

Graves, Donald. 1978. *Balance the Basics: Let Them Write*. New York: Ford Foundation Papers on Research about Learning, 8–9.

Hawkins, Thom. 1984. "Introduction." Ed. Gary Olson. *Writing Centers: Theory and Administration*. Urbana, IL: National Council of Teachers of English, xi–xiv.

Hersey, P. 1984. *The Situational Leader*. Escondido, CA: Center for Leadership Studies.

Kirby, Dan, and Tom Liner. 1981. *Inside Out: Developmental Strategies for Teaching Writing*. Upper Montclair, NJ: Boynton/Cook.

Levin, Amy K. 1989. "Goals and Philosophies of High School Writing Centers." Ed. Pamela B. Farrell. *The High School Writing Center: Establishing and Maintaining One*. Urbana, IL: National Council of Teachers of English, 23–30.

Martin, Nancy. 1976. "Language Across the Curriculum: A Paradox and Its Potential for Change." *Educational Review* 28, 206–19.

Maslow, Abraham H. 1962. *Toward a Psychology of Being*. New York: D. Van Nostrand.

McKeachie, Wilber J. 1986. *Teaching Tips: A Guidebook for the Beginning College Teacher*. Lexington, MA: C. C. Heath.

Montalvo, Frank F. 1989. "Bridging the Gap." Ed. Isadore L. Sonnier. *Affective Education: Methods and Techniques*. Englewood Cliffs, NJ: Educational Technology Publications, 37–44.

Murray, Donald. 1982. *Learning by Teaching*. Upper Montclair, NJ: Boynton/Cook.

North, Stephen. 1984. "The Idea of a Writing Center." *College English* 46.5, 433–46.

Olson, Gary, ed. 1984. *Writing Centers: Theory and Administration*. Urbana, IL: National Council of Teachers of English.

Ornstein, Allan C., and Francis P. Hunkins. 1988. *Curriculum: Foundations, Principles, and Issues*. Boston: Allyn and Bacon.

Reigstad, Tom, Ann Matsuhashi, and Nina Luban. 1978. "One-to-One to Write: Establishing an Individual Conference Writing Place at Your Secondary School." *English Journal* 67, 68–70.

Roftier, Jerry, and Beverly J. Ogan. 1991. *Cooperative Learning In Middle-Level Schools*. Washington, DC: National Education Association.

Rogers, Carl. 1962. "Toward Becoming a Fully Functioning Person." Ed. A. Combs. *Perceiving, Behaving, Becoming*. Washington, DC: ASCD Yearbook, 21–33.

Romiszowski, A. J. 1986. *Developing Auto-Instructional Materials*. New York: Michols Publishing.

Slavin, Robert E. 1987. *Cooperative Learning: Student Teams*. Washington, DC: National Education Association.

Smith, Frank. 1986. *Insult to Intelligence: The Bureaucratic Invasion of Our Classrooms*. New York: Morrow.

Sonnier, Isadore L., and Craig A. Buschner. 1989. "Delivering Affective Education." Ed. Isadore L. Sonnier. *Affective Education: Methods and Techniques*. Englewood Cliffs, NJ: Educational Technology Publications, 87–90.

Sonnier, Isadore L., and Giovanni Fontecchio. 1989. "Holistic Education-Affective Results=Teaching the Whole Person." Ed. Isadore L. Sonnier. *Affective Education: Methods and Teaching*. Englewood Cliffs, NJ: Educational Technology Publications, 19–27.

Steward, Joyce S., and Mary K. Croft. 1982. *The Writing Laboratory: Organization, Management, Methods*. Glenview, IL: Scott, Foresman.

Ward, Patty M. 1989. "Conditions Conducive to Affective Results." Ed. Isadore L. Sonnier. *Effective Education: Methods and Techniques*. Englewood Cliffs, NJ: Educational Technology Publications, 31–56.

Warnock, Tilly, and John Warnock. 1984. "Liberatory Writing Centers: Restoring Authority to Writers." Ed. Gary Olson. *Writing Centers: Theory and Administration*. Urbana, IL: National Council of Teachers of English, 16–23.

11 Buberian Currents in the Collaborative Center

Tom MacLennan
University of North Carolina–Wilmington

> Relation is reciprocity . . . our students teach us, our works form us . . .
> we live in the currents of universal reciprocity.
>
> —Martin Buber, *I and Thou*

Introduction

Over the past few years, a very healthy paradigm shift has occurred in our profession toward more collaboration. David Bleich (1988) writes, "Any literate act is a development of one's implication in the lives of others, and the cultivation of literacy always entails psychosocial, ethical, and political practice" (67). Writing centers have always been involved in the lives of others. Christina Murphy (1991) notes that "students learn how to develop their analytical and critical thinking skills through dialogic exchanges with the tutor" (238). During the time I have been director of The Writing Place at UNC–Wilmington, our center has stressed collaborative efforts and dialogic exchanges. We want our staff to become familiar with the truly exciting collaborative learning theory and research, and to incorporate that research into their practice as consultants. An effective tool for talking precisely about dialogic exchanges is to employ some of the language of Martin Buber. In our work with training consultants to accommodate over 6,400 student appointments a year, we find that there are five Buberian currents that complement, parallel, and help illustrate collaborative theory and practice in very concrete terminology.

Culture Clubs and Burkean Parlors

Joseph Trimmer (1988) divided the thirty-year evolution of writing centers into six whimsical "chapters" in his "Story Time: All About Writing Centers."

Trimmer notes that most centers began in 1960 as writing workshops where recalcitrant faculty helped recalcitrant students clean up their papers. The second chapter, which took place about 1965, was the writing lab, where one moved from frame to frame in some sort of programmed approach to learning about "writing." Chapter three introduced the writing clinic (circa 1970) where underpaid students would help other students clean up their "limiters," those major sins such as fused sentences, that would limit a student's grade in composition. The fourth chapter, circa 1975, introduced the writing center, where revolutionaries whispered process secrets about freewriting, drafting, and revising, and where they became confused about whether they were to help the student or the teacher. Chapter five focused on the learning center of the mid-1980s, where, amidst stylish decor and rows upon rows of computer terminals, graduate students and faculty mused over fundamental research questions. Finally, Trimmer predicts the writing centers of the 1990s might head in one of two directions. First, four of the previous five chapters might be "written off as heresy and one canonized as the story about writing centers" (34). Or centers might become comfortable "Culture Clubs" where center staff and clientele are invited to reflect on any of the foci of the previous five chapters. Implied in Trimmer's "Culture Club" is a healthy sense of reciprocal dialogue that many writing centers see as the heart of their campus mission. He underlines this by noting that reflection is critical because it creates both conversation and culture (34–5).

Lunsford (1991) also endorses the importance of reciprocal reflection in writing centers in a thought-provoking article entitled "Collaboration, Control, and the Idea of a Writing Center." Writing centers have three alternatives according to Lunsford. They can be "Storehouse Centers" (similar to the kinds of centers in Trimmer's first three chapters) because they "operate as information stations or storehouses, prescribing and handing out skills and strategies to individual learners . . . often use[ing] 'modules' or other kinds of individualized learning materials" (4). She argues that in Storehouse Centers "control resides in the tutor or center staff, the possessors of information, the currency of the Academy" (7). Lunsford's second alternative is the "Center as Garret" (4). Garret Centers are similar to the centers described in Trimmer's fourth chapter because "they see knowledge as interior, as inside the student, and the writing center's job as helping students get in touch with this knowledge, as a way to find their unique voices, their individual and unique powers" (5). Garret Centers "seem to invest power and control in the individual student knower, though [Lunsford cautions] such control is often appropriated by the tutor/teacher" (7). The kind of collaboration that Lunsford and Ede (1990) have advocated for the past six years is problematized in the first two alternatives because Storehouse Centers treat knowledge as "exterior, as information to be sought out or passed on mechanically," while Garret Centers view knowledge as "interiorized, solitary, individually derived, individually held" (5).

Lunsford identifies a third, more optimal, alternative, already brought into being on various campuses as a "Burkean Parlor," a center for collaboration (7). Such a center "place[s] control, power, and authority not in the tutor or staff, not in the individual student, but in the negotiating group" (8). Lunsford even suggests that the center adopt as a motto Hannah Arendt's statement: "For excellence, the presence of others is always required" (8). This kind of center, similar to Trimmer's "Conversational Culture Club," would operate with collaboration as its first principle, "informed by a theory of knowledge as socially constructed, or power and control as constantly negotiated and shared" (9).

The Culture Club and the Burkean Parlor are compelling views of the writing centers of the 90s; each center offers the kind of reciprocal collaboration suggested by the epigraph of this piece. As Lunsford (1991) notes, the biggest challenge in this kind of center is building a collaborative environment (6). The starting point for writing center directors is in the consultant training program, but it does not end there, it must also permeate the day-to-day center operation. Elsewhere, I have argued for a collaborative learning ethos in the writing center (MacLennan 1990). In The Writing Place at UNC-Wilmington, we stress an ethos imbued with the theory, practice, and awareness of collaboration, where effective dialogue and questions flourish within a central interactive helping principle or attitude. In developing such an ethos, I employ some of the language of Martin Buber, since his terminology illuminates collaborative learning theory and research. The five Buberian concepts that we use the most in The Writing Place are I-It, I-Thou, the narrow ridge, relation is reciprocity, and encounter.

I-It/I-Thou

Briefly stated, I-It indicates a relationship of separation; I-Thou establishes a healthy reciprocal relationship. In his introduction to Buber's *Between Man and Man* (1963), Maurice Friedman observes, "I-Thou and I-It stand in fruitful and necessary alternation with each other" (xiv). Friedman makes another important distinction in noting:

> The difference between these two relationships is not the nature of the object to which one relates, as is often thought. Not every relation with an animal or thing is an I-It. The difference, rather, is in the *relationship itself*. I-Thou is a relationship of openness, directness, mutuality, and presence. . . . I-It, in contrast, is the typical subject-object relationship in which one knows and uses other persons and things without allowing them to exist for oneself in their uniqueness. (italics mine, xiv)

In the early 60s, what Trimmer refers to above as writing workshops, clinics, and labs may have unknowingly established an I-It relationship with clientele because the primary focus was on correcting errors, programmed instruction, and fixing "limiters." If students are regarded *only* in terms of development, organization, spelling, or usage problems, an I-It relationship may have been established before the consulting session unfolded. An I-Thou relationship can be established when a consultant approaches a session with an open, supportive, and helpful frame of mind. We endorse Ronald C. Arnett's observation:

> *I* is the beginning of dialogue in community, but it is not sufficient. The *We* of communicative exchange must emerge for Buber's version of human community to be invited. This *We* embraces the *I* and the *Thou,* the me and the you, the person and the event with each being accessible to the other. (1986, 158)

In our training program, establishing the kind of accessibility Arnett describes begins with our first training session. The first thing we have prospective consultants do is to complete the *Style Delineator* developed by the Mind Styles research of Gregorc (1985). This research-based self-analysis instrument demonstrates a number of important points about how we develop and use our own mental qualities. Gregorc's key ideas are summarized as follows. First, all people perceive and order the universe in particular ways. Second, our individual "mind style" depends on how we employ what Gregorc calls the four basic mediation channels: Concrete Sequential (thorough, detailed, ordered, practical, and product oriented), Abstract Sequential (evaluative, analytical, concerned with ideas, logical, and research-oriented), Abstract Random (sensitive, aesthetic, spontaneous, colorful, nonjudgmental, and person-oriented), and Concrete Random (intuitive, experimental, creative, trouble-shooter, risk-taker, innovative, and a practical dreamer). Third, each person has the same basic mediation abilities at her/his disposal, making it possible for anyone to understand and relate to individuals and environments on common ground if we choose. Fourth, beyond the basic amount of mediation abilities, most of us function best by favoring the one or two channels which make us different and special. Fifth, what makes perfect sense to me, because of my own individual inclinations, may be totally useless to someone else. Sixth, we can either be broadminded and acknowledge and honor strengths and weaknesses in ourselves and others, or narrowminded and attend to one point of view. The former position epitomizes the I-Thou stance, while the latter leads to an I-It stance. Finally, serious self-study promotes not only our understanding of our selves, but of others, and our environment.

The primary value in having consultants complete this inventory early in their training is that the ensuing discussion *always* reveals the diversity of style preferences amongst them. Also, right from the outset of their training, it helps them realize that this diversity will be present in the clientele they work with in The Writing Place. This notion of diversity underlines another important point of Lunsford's: successful collaboration lies "not only [in] . . . reaching consensus but in valuing dissensus and diversity" (1991, 9). This point is also echoed in Buber's notion of the give-and-take necessary in effective human communication.

We have always used Gregorc's instrument because of its accessible language and because the instrument has validity and reliability; however, recent research suggests some other ways of familiarizing beginning consultants with themselves and the diverse audiences they will be collaborating with. Scharton and Neuleib (1991) note that each person working in their large writing, reading, and study skills center brings their own unique gifts to the center. They utilize those gifts through administration of the Myers-Briggs Type Indicator (184–204). Kirsten Benson (1990) reports that graduate student tutors develop an understanding of their own cognitive abilities and those of their students by reading excerpts from William Perry's *Forms of Intellectual and Ethical Development In the College Years* (24–36). Benson writes, "Perry describes college students as moving from a dualistic viewpoint, through awareness of multiplicity and relativism, and finally into commitment in relativism" (27–28). Benson also observes that while Perry's work yields insights into middle- to upper-middle class white male's ways of knowing, it does not yield significant insight into the cognitive development of women. To compensate for this absence, she uses excerpts from Mary Belenky, et al. (1986) *Women's Ways of Knowing* in her training program (29). Jean Kiedaisch and Sue Dinitz (1991) investigated the relationship between client satisfaction and several other variables, including gender. They discovered that female tutors scored significantly higher than males on client satisfaction and suggest further case studies looking closely at how gender affects sessions (94–95). Keidaisch and Dinitz cite Joyce Kinkead's case study of male and female tutors where "the two females were 'effective questioners' and consistently focused on global aspects, the two males 'told' students what to do and spent more time on the traditional talk of teaching—outlines, paragraphs, punctuation" (qtd. in Keidaisch and Dinitz 95). In light of the findings of Lunsford, Benson, Keidaisch, Dinitz, and Kinkead, we are rethinking the relationship between gender and the I-Thou relationship in consulting sessions in The Writing Place. As much as I admire and am influenced by Buber's thought, when he wrote about mankind, he usually wrote about *man*-kind. I am convinced that all of our training in the writing center must continuously be self-reflective and employ current theory and critical perspectives.

It is critical to the success of our training program that our consultants recognize that successful I-Thou collaboration begins with both a catholic sense of audience and, in Lunsford's words, recognition that "control" in a consulting session lies not just with a consultant, or with a student, but in "the negotiating group," a third alternative that is similar to what Buber referred to as the "Narrow Ridge."

The Narrow Ridge

One of the most lucid discussions of Buber's narrow ridge takes place in a work by Arnett I cited earlier:

> A metaphor for the 'narrow ridge' might be a tightrope walker attempting to keep his or her balance; as he or she leans too far to one side, adjustment must be made and balance regained. The 'narrow ridge' in human communication involves a balancing of one's concern for self and others. One must be open to the other's viewpoint and willing to alter one's position based upon appropriate and just cause, if necessary. However, as mentioned earlier, being concerned for oneself and the other does not necessarily mean a compromise or an acceptance of another's viewpoint. One *may* accept a compromise or even change to the other's viewpoint; such moves are done out of a commitment to finding the 'best' principle or solution. (36–37)

In The Writing Place, we see this kind of give-and-take interaction as being most healthy. The ideal at which we want our consultants to aim as consultant and client negotiate together is an I-Thou ethos. We see successful collaboration as the interaction of four elements: (1) maintaining a theoretical awareness, (2) giving to the session, (3) gaining from the session, (4) remaining open to mutual discovery of options. Our most memorable consultations take place on the narrow ridge, which, as Arnett points out, embodies a third alternative, where both parties assume a genuine responsibility for each other (36). Optimal contact on the narrow ridge leads to another Buberian concept, *encounter,* which I will explore later in this paper.

I see a strong parallel between Buber's narrow ridge and Lunsford's negotiating group because they articulate the kind of collaboration where power and control are shared and negotiated by both parties. Both Buber and Lunsford are concerned with preserving the equality of both parties and valuing the relation between both parties as something worthy of respect. Collaboration is a reciprocal relationship. Relation, according to Martin Buber, is reciprocity.

Relation Is Reciprocity

In staffing The Writing Place, we look for consultants who we think will value the fact that they will learn as much, sometimes more, than they will share with clientele. As Buber notes, we learn from our students and are formed by our works, and we live in currents of universal reciprocity (1970, 67). Emily Meyer and Louise Z. Smith (1987) underscore this point by noting that reciprocal questioning can lead students to examine an assignment's key question, to determine some boundaries for an acceptable response, and to pinpoint the question the student draft answers (100). After reading through the transcript in Meyer and Smith, our future consultants role-play the act of reciprocal questioning. Therefore, familiarity with Buber's tripartite definition of communication is an important part of our early training sessions. In writing about communication in *Between Man and Man,* Buber notes:

> I know three kinds. There is genuine dialogue—no matter whether spoken or silent—where each of the participants really has in mind the other or others in their present and particular being and turns to them with the intention of establishing a living mutual relation between himself and them. There is technical dialogue, which is prompted solely by the need of objective understanding. And there is monologue disguised as dialogue, in which two or more men, meeting in space, speak each with himself in strangely torturous and circuitous ways and yet imagine they have escaped the torment of being thrown back on their own resources. (19)

Arnett (1986) notes that all of these forms of communication have, indeed, their place in modern society; however, genuine dialogue is never commanded, but invited. This "relationship-centered communication that is sensitive to what happens to both self and other approaches dialogic communication" (7). The next step in our training program is showing how Buber's thought is reflected in collaborative theory and practice.

We read and discuss John Trimbur's (1985) essay, "Collaborative Learning and Teaching Writing," noting how Buber's ideas about dialogue and relationships interact with the origins, theory and current practices of collaborative learning. Our training sessions also include having consultants complete and discuss the Murray Card Activity that appears in Thomas J. Reigstad's and Donald McAndrew's *Training Tutors for Writing Conferences* (1984). Role playing in this activity pragmatically illustrates how a reciprocal relationship can be instituted at every stage of the composing process by remaining open to another's viewpoint and altering your own position when it leads to more effective collaboration. Buber would call this "negotiating on the narrow ridge."

Our instructional library contains a comprehensive selection of composition and writing center journals. We are always on the lookout for critical articles that underscore Buberian collaboration. For example, two recent "must-read" articles were Lunsford and Ede's "Rhetoric in a New Key: Women and Collaboration" (1990) and Jane Tompkins' "Pedagogy of the

Distressed" (1990). An article that will be added this semester is the Lunsford article that I have referred to throughout this piece. All of these articles effectively reinforce Buberian notions of dialogue, reciprocity, and the narrow ridge.

We introduce a final Buberian concept in our training sessions by noting two critical points made by Pamela Vermes in *Buber* (1988), an excellent introduction to the life and thought of Martin Buber. First, that relation always entails reciprocity in the life of genuine dialogue. Our consultants constantly tell us that one of the most rewarding aspects of working in The Writing Place is the feeling that they are learning more than the student writer. That kind of reciprocal relationship does not take place unless flexibility merges with active listening, questioning, and responding. Second, relation sometimes leads to encounter (40–41).

Encounter

Vermes points out that while Buber considered relation an attitude of mind, or a psychological stage, encounter was an event, something that happens (42). She goes on to state that "encounter represents the high peak of relational life, the lightning flash which suddenly illumines the way. . . . the coming together into existential communion of two I's and two Thou's" (43). One might even equate encounter with Maslow's idea of a "peak experience."

One of my own most vivid experiences with an encounter occurred several years ago. A student who I will call James had been assigned an I-Search paper by one of our English instructors and he was my last appointment on a Friday afternoon. James was a student-athlete, and, I must admit, I began stereotyping him as soon as he walked into our writing center. He said that he had no idea what topic he wanted to explore. During the early stages of our session, I found out that he had played high school football and basketball. Football was his favorite sport, but his basketball talent had brought him to our school. We spent most of the session dredging up and then rejecting various sports topics. James wasn't interested in becoming a professional athlete, coach, trainer, sports reporter or announcer. It was late in an early fall afternoon, the weekend loomed ahead of both of us, we were both tired and perhaps even a bit frustrated. My own attitude was more I-It than I-Thou, and I sensed that James probably felt the same way. I suggested another appointment early the following week.

As he was packing up to leave, and I was completing his reporting form, he casually mentioned that he was going to attend a high school football game that night. He added that while he really had enjoyed playing high school football, he hated to wear the generic, drab uniforms his team had worn for years. He compared them to Penn State's, saying that his team didn't even have a logo on their helmets. James mentioned something that had not come out during our session together. Namely, that he had been interested in drawing since his elementary school years. In high school, he had enjoyed sketching and drafting. He had even approached his coach with an idea for a helmet logo for the team but his idea had been rejected. For the next thirty minutes, our conversation moved into a general discussion of NFL teams, their respective uniforms and team logos. I also shared with James that when I was a high school student, during the pre-TV years, most teams did not even have logos on their helmets. We both seemed to realize we were on to something and we continued our conversation. An idea for his I-Search topic occurred to both of us simultaneously. How did team logos evolve in the NFL? The major part of our collaborative efforts, I might add, occurred after we had completed our formal consulting session. As Ken Macrorie (1988) writes, a topic had selected the writer (62). However, the topic was not James's idea, nor my idea, it was a collaborative idea.

Something sparked both of us that late afternoon to continue our conversation long after our consulting session had "officially" ended. My own reflections on that afternoon are that once we had worked through an early I-It relationship with James's half-hearted attempts to decide on a topic and my initial stereotyping of him, we moved gradually into a shared I-Thou relationship on the narrow ridge where we negotiated the dimensions of the problem, articulating it in a reciprocal, give-and-take basis. Our eventual discovery of the topic makes me certain that what we experienced is what Buber refers to as an encounter. Our conversation leading up to and immediately after the topic occurred to us was animated, energizing, and an hour had transpired after our consulting session officially ended.

I worked with James several other times as he shaped his paper and we both learned a lot from it. Frequently, I have regretted the fact that I did not ask him for a copy of his paper. I do remember James discovered that the Los Angeles Rams were the first team to use a logo, the result of a player painting rams horns on his practice helmet and management liking the idea. He also learned that the Cleveland Browns to this day do not have a helmet logo, although during the late 1950s the player's number appeared on the side of the helmet. James also thought that the tiger stripes that envelop the entire Cincinnati Bengals' helmet was one of the more innovative designs. I also recall he was critical of the New England Patriots' logo (a football center dressed in colonial garb ready to hike the ball), suggesting instead of that "busy" design, the Patriots could convey the same connection by merely using a three-cornered hat. His personal aesthetic favorites were the lone star of the Dallas Cowboys and the horseshoe design of the Baltimore/Indianapolis Colts because both were models of classic simplicity. James even visited the Pro Football Hall of Fame in Canton, Ohio, during Fall Break that year.

Conclusion

I have outlined what James learned during his I-Search—a legitimate question is: What did I learn and what did it tell me about Buberian currents in the writing center? I learned that the fatigue factor can move one toward an I-It relationship, because that is exactly how I felt when I first met James. That lesson translated into providing periodic scheduled breaks for consultants, no matter how busy things get in the writing center. Having my own preconceived notions about topics that would interest student-athletes punctured was another painful lesson. Like the male tutors mentioned above in Kinkead's research, I was telling when I should have been listening. I also learned the power of relation being reciprocal when James and I engaged in collaborative dialogue about a topic that mutually interested us. James also taught me a lesson in popular culture. While I had long been a football fan, I never had even remotely considered the aesthetic nature of logos, or that they could be read as semiological codes. As a matter of fact, perhaps the most important thing we both learned was, as Macrorie (1988) observes, that the search becomes exciting when it means something to you (56). The excitement of the search, I would argue, is the key indicator that a writing center consultation has moved *beyond* an I-Thou relationship to the encounter stage. I don't even consider the topic of team logos idiosyncratic anymore, as I did during the early stages of working with James. The other day, when browsing through a local bookstore, I noted Marc Okkonen's *Baseball Uniforms of the Twentieth Century,* an exhaustively researched, oversized volume of full-color detailed drawings of every uniform worn by all of the major league teams in baseball, complete with team logos.

In summary, my work with James suggested possible stages of a writing center consultation. These stages, reflected in the language of Martin Buber: I-It (depersonalization), Meeting on the Narrow Ridge (establishing a reciprocal relationship), I-Thou (a successful collaboration), and Encounter (both parties are changed as a result of the consulting session). My experience with James suggests a number of implications for further research. I am interested, for instance, in determining whether the Buberian framework is evident in other sessions with other consultants. Another area that interests me is the role gender plays in successful consultations. Also, what role does learning style play in writing center consultations? Finally, does the work of other writers/philosophers suggest alternative frameworks for writing center collaboration?

Postscript

Martin Buber's writing is prolific. Maurice Friedman's bibliography in The Library of Living Philosophers volume *The Philosophy of Martin Buber* runs 37 pages (749–86). Additionally, the thirty descriptive and critical essays in the same volume examine Buber's philosophy and its influence on aesthetics, education, theology, politics, history, natural science, psychotherapy, and several philosophical currents (41–686). Let me suggest a less daunting task by recommending three volumes which are both accessible and elucidating. Walter Kaufman's translation of Buber's *I and Thou* is one that I have returned to for over twenty years. It contains a comprehensive prologue by Kaufman and is an excellent translation. For an overview of Buber's life and thought, Pamela Vermes's brief volume *Buber* is highly recommended because it contains the most cogent explanations of the five Buberian concepts this essay has explored. Another book that explores the implications of Buber's philosophy on the field of communications is one that I have also cited throughout this piece, Ronald C. Arnett's *Communication and Community: Implications of Martin Buber's Dialogue*. This book, like so many other translations of Buber, contains an excellent foreward by Maurice Friedman, whose lucid introductions, readable translations, and comprehensive biographies have been indispensable to my understanding of how Buber's thought shapes my own life as an educator.

References

Arnett, Ronald C. 1986. *Communication and Community: Implications of Martin Buber's Dialogue*. Carbondale: Southern Illinois University Press.

Belenky, Mary Field, et al. 1986. *Women's Ways of Knowing*. New York: Basic.

Benson, Kirsten F. 1990. "Assessment and Development in Graduate Tutor Training." *Focuses* 3, 24–36.

Bleich, David. 1988. *The Double Perspective: Language, Literacy & Social Relations*. Oxford University Press.

Buber, Martin. 1963. *Between Man and Man*. Trans. Ronald Gregor Smith. Intro. Maurice Friedman. New York: Macmillan.

———. 1970. *I and Thou*. Trans. Walter Kaufman. New York: Scribner's.

Friedman, Maurice, and Paul Arthur Schlipp, eds. 1967. *The Philosophy of Martin Buber*. LaSalle, IL: Open.

Gregorc, Anthony F. 1985. *Style Delineator*. Columbia, CT: Gregorc Associates.

———. *Gregorc Style Delineator: Development, Technical and Administration Manual*. Columbia, CT: Gregorc Associates.

Kiedaisch, Jean, and Sue Dinitz. 1991. "Learning More from the Students." *The Writing Center Journal* 12, 90–100.

Lunsford, Andrea. 1991. "Collaboration, Control, and the Idea of a Writing Center." *The Writing Center Journal* 12, 3–10.

Lunsford, Andrea, and Lisa Ede. 1990. "Rhetoric in a New Key: Women and Collaboration." *Rhetoric Review* 8, 234–41.

MacLennan, Tom. 1990. "Martin Buber and a Collaborative Learning Ethos." *The Writing Lab Newsletter,* 6–8.

Macrorie, Ken. 1988. *The I-Search Paper.* Portsmouth: Boynton.

Meyer, Emily, and Louise Z. Smith. 1987. *The Practical Tutor.* New York: Oxford University Press.

Murphy, Christina. 1991. "Writing Centers in Context: Responding to Current Educational Theory." *The Writing Center: New Directions.* Ed. Ray Wallace and Jeanne Simpson. New York: Garland, 276–88.

Neuleib, Janice, and Maurice Scharton. 1991. "The Gift of Insight: Personality Type, Tutoring, and Learning." *The Writing Center: New Directions.* Eds. Ray Wallace and Jeanne Simpson. New York: Garland, 134–204.

Okkonen, Marc. 1991. *Baseball Uniforms of the Twentieth Century.* New York: Sterling.

Perry, William G. 1970. *Forms of Intellectual and Ethical Development in the College Years: A Scheme.* New York: Holt.

Reigstad, Thomas J., and Donald McAndrew. 1984. *Training Tutors for Writing Conferences.* Urbana, IL: National Council of Teachers of English.

Tompkins, Jane. 1990. "Pedagogy of the Distressed." *College English* 52, 653–60.

Trimbur, John. 1985. "Collaborative Learning and Teaching Writing." *Perspectives on Research and Scholarship in Composition.* Eds. Ben W. McClelland and Timothy R. Donovan. New York: Modern Language Association, 87–109.

Trimmer, Joseph. 1986. "Story Time: All About Writing Centers." *Focuses* 1, 27–35.

Vermes, Pamela. 1988. *Buber.* New York: Grove.

12 "The Use of Force": Medical Ethics and Center Practice

Jay Jacoby
University of North Carolina–Charlotte

Consider the following case. The paper that appears below was written by a freshman in response to the assignment, "Write about someone who means a great deal to you":

> My Grandma Connie is sixty eight years old, It is funny I never think of her in terms of age. When I look at her I do not notice the wrinkles or grey hair—she does not have much gray hair anyway, though she does possess the most calm and understanding grey eyes a grandmother could have.
>
> Once she beat my fifteen-year-old brother at arm-wrestling, disgracing him in front of his buddies.
>
> She lives by herself, now that Grandpa is gone, in a big house that he built himself some thirty odd years ago. Sometimes she will complain about why Grandpa put a window here or why he did not put a door there. Then she will get quiet like she is remembering when they were here together and first moving into their own new house with a door where a window should be.

Before typing a final copy of her paper, the student decides to bring her draft to the writing center. It is her first visit. She hands the draft to a tutor and asks, "What do you think? What should I do now?"

How legitimate would it be—considering the argument that students should "own" the texts they write—for the tutor to return the student's questions: "What do *you* think? What do *you* want to do now"? What if the student unconditionally surrenders the autonomy offered her, saying, "No fair! You're the tutor. It doesn't matter what *I* think." Do we run the risk of playing "hot potato" with authority over the text? Do we damage our credibility—and that of the writing center—if we do not offer pointed suggestions for improvement? Exactly who should control the tutorial session?

Let us now assume that the tutor chooses to be less directive. Through the use of guiding questions, the tutor wants to lead the student to examine her choices. So, the tutor asks, "Is there any part of this paper that you would have developed more if you had had the time?" (kindly implying that lack of time, rather than any other considerations, led to what the tutor perceives as an underdeveloped paper). And what if the student does *not* say, as the tutor might have hoped, "Well, I guess I don't say much in the second paragraph"? What if, instead, she says, "Well, I know I wouldn't change the *second* paragraph, the way it just makes a statement and then gets out of the way"? Is it okay to disagree with such a minimalist point of view? And would that simply be a disagreement between peers? Or does the tutor's authority, based on his or her presumed knowledge about descriptive detail, paragraph development, etc., upset any equality of opinion between tutor and client?

Finally, let us assume that the student comes to the writing center only *after* her instructor has returned the paper with a grade of "D" and a note saying, "This isn't college-level writing. Go to the writing center." Assume that another note comes to the tutor from the instructor saying, "Help this student understand writing expectations in college: introduction-thesis-development-support." What if the tutor feels that such advice is wrong, that the piece will lose something—its artlessness, its ingenuous voice—if those directions are followed? Should the tutor go against what instinct or training suggest and follow the instructor's orders? Does the tutor have any autonomy?

The discussion that follows may not offer many concrete answers to the questions raised here. It should, however, provide a fresh perspective from which to consider those questions, and a theoretical framework upon which possible solutions can be worked out. That perspective and framework draw upon work done in the field of medical ethics during the past twenty-five years. Medical ethics is the process of reasoning that health care professionals use to decide what is right, or what ought to be done, for the physical well-being of their patients and society. Entrusted with the intellectual well-being of our clients and the institutions we serve, writing center tutors can benefit from examining the ethical principles which often inform medical decision-making.

I began this chapter by "presenting a case," an activity engaged in daily by physicians. I should confess, at this point, to considerable discomfort in so clinically presenting the writer of "My Grandma Connie" as a patient to be discussed in a hospital mortality-and-morbidity session. Not long ago, however, it was common to speak of writing instruction using medical metaphors and models. Writing centers were called *labs* or *clinics*. Writers were diagnosed and remedies were prescribed. Tutors emerged from tutorials as interns did from surgery: sweating, talking a writing-center equivalent of doctor-talk; but instead of deviated septums, they dealt with bifurcated propositions, with L_1 interference rather than bowel obstructions. Tutors became the Emergency Medical Technicians of the university, specializing in "Crisis Intervention in the Writing Center" (Ware 1986), and prioritizing concerns through "Triage Tutoring" (Haynes 1988). Perhaps it was thinking along these lines that led

Richard Lanham (1979) to recommend a "paramedic method" for eliminating "lard," or wordiness, from writing (a procedure which I suppose could be thought of as a writing center equivalent of liposuction).

Of course, it should not take long for those of us employed in writing centers to recognize the limitations of medical metaphors as they apply to our work. Despite what desperate students tell us, we know that getting an "A" on a term paper, or mastering subject/verb agreement, is *not* a life-or-death situation. Despite what cynical instructors tell us, we know that student writing is not a condition, a disease to be cured. Students coming to the writing center are not patients, a word synonymous with "invalid" and "sufferer." Tutors are not physicians: they swear no oaths to Mina Shaughnessy or Ken Bruffee; their fee scale for consultation differs radically from that of a radiologist or neurosurgeon.

As Mike Rose has cogently pointed out, an "atomistic, medical model of language [and language learning] is simply not supported by more recent research in language and cognition" (1990, 210). In a recent (1991) article, Diane Stelzer Morrow has also identified the limitations of comparing medical practice to writing instruction. She cites Stephen and Susan Judy, who suggest such comparisons lead to "a pessimistic, even fatalistic, view of the student as learner," and Muriel Harris (1986), who has aptly noted that "the goal of the writing teacher is instructional, not therapeutic" (219). Writing from a unique position of being both physician and writing center tutor, Morrow does recognize, however, the potential value of thinking about what goes on in writing centers in medical terms. Such recognition is based upon certain similarities in the *relationships* between doctors and patients and tutors and clients, relationships in which, Morrow observes, "expectations are not quite so fixed as perhaps they once were" (219).

For the past several years, there has been a rising interest in ethics in the writing center, especially issues of empowerment, tutorial authority, and client autonomy. Entire sessions at professional conferences have been devoted to the subject, offering presentations with such titles as "Authority and Collaborative Learning," "Authority, Gender, and Tutors," "Notions of Authority in Peer Writing Conferences," and "Power Play: The Use and Abuse of Power Relationships in Peer Critiquing." This interest in writing center ethics is reflected by the National Writing Centers Association's awarding of two recent annual best article awards to works focusing upon ethical issues: John Trimbur's "Peer Tutoring: A Contradiction in Terms?" (1987) and Irene Lurkis Clark's "Collaboration and Ethics in Writing Center Pedagogy" (1988). While writing center professionals were turning more attention toward ethical issues involving tutor-client relationships, members of the medical community were growing more concerned about ethical issues that centered upon doctor-patient relationships. From the literature emerging out of those concerns come such titles as "Respecting Autonomy: The Struggle Over Rights and Capacities" (Katz), "Moral Problems in the Medical Worker-Patient Relationship" (McConnell), "The Refutation of Medical Paternalism" (Goldman 1983), and "Ethical Dilemmas for Nurses: Physicians' Orders versus Patients' Rights" (Mappes 1983).

Morrow has suggested that one reason for the rising interest in ethical issues—especially those involving power relationships—among doctors and writing instructors is that "both professionals are moving away from a tradition of authority to one of guide or co-learner" (228). I found these concerns converging two years ago when, as Director of Composition, I received from a first-year instructor an already graded paper on William Carlos Williams's short story, "The Use of Force." Some excerpts from that paper, which I reproduce unedited, follow:

> William Carlos Williams story, The Use of Force, kind of reminded me of the movie The Exorcist, which stares Linda Blair, as Reagan. Mathilda and Linda Blair were very much alike. They both knew something was wrong with them but were afraid to let somebody help them. Just so happens the persons trying to help them were doctors. In Reagan's case there were doctors and priests involve. . . .
>
> In both cases it seems like the doctors are fighting a never ending battle and are ready to give up. Mathilda's doctor was just as determine to examine her, as she was determined that he wasn't. In Reagan's case the doctors did give up because her problem was over their heads. That's when the priest took over.
>
> However, Mathilda's doctor finally got to examine her throat and Reagan's priest finally drove the devil out of her. Mathilda was still furious because the doctor had overpowered her, but when the priest drove the devil out of Reagan she didn't remember a thing.
>
> I don't know why I chose the Exorcist to compare with The Use of Force because The Exorcist scared the living hell out of me. I know why, because The Exorcist was a perfect example of a child in need of help but was determined not to let anyone help her. . . .

The instructor had given this paper a "D–" and sought from me some confirmation of her judgment that the paper's content and style were "not appropriate or satisfactory for a formal essay." Overwhelmed by the organizational problems and surface errors of a member of what Rose has called "America's educational underclass," this instructor also felt that her student violated rules of academic propriety by her use of colloquial diction and her decision to compare Williams's story to a sensationalistic film. She wrote to the student: "Though I would not have approved of this topic, I have to give you credit for originality. . . . If you had come for our scheduled conference, I could have helped you with your topic."

As you may recall, "The Use of Force" is a story about a doctor who suspects that his patient, a frightened young girl named Mathilda, has diphtheria. The doctor exercises his authority—granted to him by his medical knowledge—to force the child's mouth open so he can examine her throat. All of this is done at considerable cost to Mathilda: she is injured during the examination, her privacy is invaded, her trust is shattered. Nonetheless, she is found to have diphtheria, and her life is probably saved as a result of the doctor's persistence in examining her.

What is crucial to us here is the doctor's justification for compromising his patient's autonomy: "The damned little brat must be protected against her own idiocy, one says to one's self at such times. Others must be protected against her. It is a social necessity" (208). Were these the only motives, the doctor might have appeared justified, but there would not have been much of a story. Williams has the doctor reveal yet another set of motives: ". . . the worst of it was that I too had got beyond reason, I could have torn the child apart in my own fury and enjoyed it. It was a pleasure to attack her. My face was burning with it" (207–208). Later, the doctor admits that it is not so much social necessity, "But a blind fury, a feeling of adult shame, bred of a longing for muscular release" (208) that are his operatives.

Keeping the issues of "The Use of Force" in mind, let us now turn to something less dramatic, but no less serious. Do tutors have the right to compromise their clients' autonomy, their opportunities for self-determination? In the interests of "social necessity" (i.e., to maintain university standards and protect academic society from what may be thought of as student "idiocy"), can tutors act on what they perceive to be their clients' best interests (as did the doctor in "The Use of Force") and assume authority over their clients' texts? Are tutors expected to coerce the writer of "My Grandma Connie" into developing her second paragraph? Is the situation any different if tutors subtly lead her into making the choice to expand that paragraph? Must a tutor—who may be fully aware of the problems underprepared writers have in what David Bartholomae (1985) calls "inventing the university" (i.e., imagining and attempting to reproduce academic discourse)—follow an instructor's orders and convince the writer of "The Use of Force" paper that a comparison with *The Exorcist* is inappropriate? What if that tutor suspects that the instructor's rejection of the student's topic is somehow related to her annoyance about a missed conference? What about cases of L_1 or second-language interference? One tutor, faced with a Vietnamese refugee's paper, wrote that she was having problems forcing herself to point out errors: "Don't tell me I'm doing a sentimental dance around the issue. I know it. But doesn't the error of second language give the essay a quality, a sense of 'heart,' that would somehow be lost in the Americanization of the language?"

In encouraging the substitution of our discourse for the student's, we are potentially erasing at least part of that student's identity—some of his or her authenticity—in order to meet the demands of the institution. And often we do so without ever consulting honestly with the student: "Just write the paper this way; this is how it is done here!" In their perceived roles as authorities, even those tutors with the best of intentions take control of what Nancy Allen (1986) calls the "Truth of a paper" (4) and compromise whatever a writer may have intended.

Were peer tutors and others who intervene in the writing processes of others to swear an oath like the one physicians once swore to Hippocrates, that oath might draw heavily upon the ethical principle represented below:

> The dignity of the person commands us to *respect individual persons.* . . . This means that *one human being, precisely as human, does not and should not have power over another human being.* This means that individuals shall not coerce others or limit their activities or impose their will on others. Even society and its instrument, the government, must respect the freedom and privacy of individuals and can interfere only when it is necessary to protect others or for very serious and overriding social concerns.
>
> . . . A little reflection will reveal the fact that neither lawyers, clergymen, teachers, doctors, or nurses have a right to interfere with individuals or force their opinions on them, or even to act on a person's behalf without permission. . . . Specialized knowledge, even a license to practice, does not authorize professionals to control any aspect of another's life, or to limit the freedom of others. (Garrett, Baillie, and Garrett 1989, 27–28)

The principle identified here, *autonomy,* will inform nearly all the discussion that follows.

The central principle of autonomy in contemporary medical ethical theory comes as a reaction to utilitarian ethics which "locates rightness and wrongness in the *consequences* of our behavior" (Arras and Hunt 1983, 7) and has a "tendency to regard the individual as little more than a recipient of good and evil" (Miller 1983, 64). In contrast to utilitarianism, Kantian, or deontological, ethics holds that "the *principles* governing our behavior are of utmost importance" (Arras and Hunt 1983, 7). According to Bruce Miller, the primacy granted to the principle of autonomy in Kantian theory provides "firm ground to resist coercion and its less forceful, but more pervasive cousins: manipulation and undue influence. It also provides a warrant for treating a person's own choices, plans, and conception of self as generally dominant over what another believes to be in that person's best interest" (1983, 64).

Any efforts made to abrogate an individual's autonomy may be considered *paternalism,* which the OED defines as "government as by a father; the attempt to . . . regulate the life of a nation or community in the same way as a father does [for] his children." James Childress has noted, "Because the term paternalism is sex-linked, it is not wholly felicitous" (1983, 18). He would prefer the more gender-inclusive term *parentalism,* but such a term has yet to appear in the literature of medical ethics. In medical practice,

> Paternalism centers on the notion that the physician—either by virtue of his or her superior knowledge or by some impediment incidental to the patient's experience of illness—has better insight into the best interests of the patient than does the patient, or that the physician's obligations are such that he is hampered to do what is medically good, even if it is not "good" in terms of the patient's own value system. (Pelligrino and Thomasma 1988, 7)

There are essentially two forms of paternalism: *Strong* paternalism "consists in overriding the competent wishes and choices of another" and *Weak* paternalism consists of acting on behalf of someone who, for some reason, "is not afforded the full possibility of free choice" (Pellegrino and Thomasma 7).

It is fairly common to see both physicians and writing center tutors engaging in some form of weak paternalism. Such conduct is no doubt activated by the principle of *beneficence,* doing good for others. In their efforts to serve patients and students, doctors and tutors see it as their obligation to help others further their important and legitimate interests" (Beauchamp and Childress 1989, 194). And, acting upon the principle of beneficence, physicians and tutors may sometimes feel justified in abrogating their clients' autonomy. On these grounds, Bernard Gert and Charles Culver (1979) argue that it is okay to "violate a moral rule" by interfering with another person's autonomy *for that person's own good* (2).

It is difficult, however, to ascertain whether anyone acts solely, or even primarily, out of beneficence. As Childress observes, frequently "the claim to be doing good for others masks the agent's real motives, such as self-interest" (19). In the case of the doctor in "The Use of Force" it was "adult shame"—the desire not to be challenged and defeated by a child—that motivates him. He reflects, "I tried to hold myself down but I couldn't. I know how to expose a throat for inspection" (207). Similar motivations exist in the writing center, as Morrow points out: "I knew how to write and students would be coming to the writing center to learn how to write. They needed advice and I would be able to give it. . . . Medicine, like teaching, has a long tradition of the professional as authority" (223, 227). In the writing center, especially among novice tutors, there is often the irresistible urge to play—not doctor—but professor. It is, as Kay Satre and Valerie Traub have suggested, a "dynamic whereby those who have been put down by a system attempt to gain power by adopting the mode and guise of authority" (1988, 5). If the doctor knows how to expose throats, tutors know how to undangle modifiers. And, if they have read Don Murray's *Write to Learn* (1990), they know all about writing about grandmothers, and they are just waiting for a fresh client upon whom to foist that knowledge.

In addition to the difficulty of acting upon any principle that can be identified as being solely in another's best interests, there is the problem of "the absence of shared beliefs about what is good for persons and what they really need" (Childress 19). It is a problem that surfaces anytime we hand a group of writing tutors a student paper and ask for consensus about what Reigstad and McAndrew (1984) call high-order and low-order concerns (11–19). Not all tutors at my university's writing center felt that the second paragraph of "Grandma Connie" needed further work. And not all tutors were content about persuading the writer of "The Use of Force" paper into dropping the comparison with *The Exorcist*. On this matter, one tutor, Stephen Criswell, wrote:

> I think that the student had at least a germ of an idea in his/her comparison of the Williams story to the movie. . . . the student saw in both stories a child struggling against authority.
>
> It might be that the student would eventually drop *The Exorcist* part of the paper, or reduce it to a very brief mention. But the removal of that part of the paper should be the student's decision—part of his/her process. When the tutor axes that part of the paper, it seems to me that the tutor is sort of cutting off the student writer's ideas in progress. It seems like this writer still needs to work through his/her analysis of the Williams story, and that he/she is using the comparison to do that. The tutor should allow that process to happen and let the *Exorcist* part of the paper fade naturally. Telling the student to lose it seems to artificially put the writer where the tutor wants him/her.

Apparently, Stephen feels that the paternalistic intervention recommended by some of his colleagues—in part to accommodate the writing instructor's comment that the paper topic was inappropriate—would be counterproductive in this particular case.

There are those who might justify such paternalism on grounds other than beneficence. For example, they could propose grounds which the doctor in "The Use of Force" identified as "social necessity": ". . . one is justified in restricting a person's freedom in order to prevent injury or harm to other specific non-consenting individuals. . . . [or in order to] prevent impairment of institutional practices and systems that are in the public interest" by such behaviors as tax evasion, contempt of court, or other actions that "weaken public institutions" (McConnell 1982, 64–65).

Keeping such justification of paternalistic intervention in mind, it may be useful to raise the question, "With whom are writing center tutors collaborators: their student clients or the institution that employs them? Can it be both?" In medicine, physicians who still believe in upholding the Hippocratic oath seem to favor the institution since they swear "to live my life in partnership with him [who has taught me]" (McConnell 267). Frequently, in tutorial practice, though no oaths are sworn, we reveal allegiance to the institution by compromising the autonomy of student writers. That is, with little or no consultation with those writers, tutors compel them to adopt the language of academic discourse, presumably to prevent actions that "weaken public institutions," actions such as using contractions or one-sentence paragraphs, writing literary analyses in the first person, or comparing "classic" texts with those of questionable merit.

Such paternalistic practice, whether consciously intended or not, leads writing tutors to act as gatekeepers for the university. They assume postures that Mina Shaughnessy (1981) has identified as *Guarding the Tower:* "the teacher is in one way or another concentrating on protecting the academy (including himself) from the outsiders, those who do not seem to belong in the community of learners," or *Converting the Natives:* carrying "the technology of advanced literacy to the inhabitants of an underdeveloped country" (63–64). Such postures lead to a kind of mentality whereby writing center clients—by virtue of their allegedly diminished knowledge (after all, most of them are only freshmen!)—are considered as individuals whose decision-making competence can be compromised, for their own protection (we want them to pass, don't we?) and that of society.

In a discussion of medical ethics, Samuel Shuman identifies attitudes similar to those expressed above as a form of colonialism:

> Among peers, even those who attempt to influence one another's decision making, there is no colonialism; in the colonial relationship, be it benevolent or malevolent, the keepers and the kept are not peers because the latter can never freely make their own decisions. . . . Englishmen in the last century and earlier in this century justified their colonialism by arguing and even believing that they were bringing the benefits of white civilization to primitive people. In modern medical practice, one finds similar self-serving declarations, which purport to justify society's right to compromise the decision-making autonomy of patients. (75–76)

Shuman's observations apply to problems attending any collaborative effort in the writing center. Collaboration is in danger of dissolving anytime a tutor imposes his or her will upon a client, or when a client surrenders his or her will to the tutor. The latter situation is no less common in tutoring than in medicine; patients often direct their doctors to make all the decisions, to do whatever they think is best. They yield, in other words, to what has been called the "despotism of the expert" (Appelbaum, Lidz, and Meisel 1987, 28). Likewise, in the writing center, as Morrow notes, "most students begin by assuming that the tutor is in charge; most students come into the session taking a passive role" (221). Neither patient nor student demonstrates any desire to become a "knowledgeable participant" (Appelbaum, Lidz, and Meisel ix) in their respective health care or development as writers. In such situations, physicians and tutors may justify the adoption of paternalism on behalf of passive patients or students, using the argument that, "with the development . . . of his rational powers, the individual in question will accept our decision on his behalf and agree with us that we did the best thing for him" (Childress 26). But, as any browbeaten patient or student can testify, this form of acceptance is, like a forced confession, highly suspect.

There may be a way out of some of the ethical dilemmas posed here, a way that guards against the use of force no matter how benevolently intended. The solution I propose derives from the principle of *informed consent*. In medicine, this principle posits that "decisions about the medical care a person will receive, if any, are to be made in a collaborative manner between patient and physician" (Appelbaum, Lidz, and Meisel 12). Moreover, the implementation of the practice of informed consent is seen as both "a central duty of health care professionals and as a right of patients" (Appelbaum, Lidz, and Meisel 26). Garrett, Baillie, and Garrett (1989) note that the following conditions must be present in order for informed consent to take place:

> [1] The patient . . . must be competent or have decision-making capacity. . . . Decision-making capacity is the patient's ability to make choices that reflect an understanding and appreciation of the nature and consequences of one's actions and of alternative actions, and to evaluate them in relation to a person's preferences and priorities.
> [2] Competence requires not only the ability to understand the consequences of one's decisions, but freedom from coercion and such undue influence that would substantially diminish the freedom of the patient.
> [3] The health care professional . . . must have provided the necessary information and made sure that it was understood. . . . [There is] *an obligation to actually communicate and not merely an obligation to spout facts.* A recital of all the technical details and the use of technical language may not only fail to increase comprehension, but may actually destroy understanding. . . . ethics demands that the health care professional make sure the patient understands the consequences in terms of the things that are important to the patient. (28ff)

In applying the principle of informed consent in the writing center, we must foster in our clients an understanding of the nature of their actions (i.e., the decisions they make as writers), alternative actions (i.e., other decisions that could be made), and their respective consequences. Equally important, we must be sure that the decisions our clients make are *their* decisions, informed and deliberate decisions that *they* can justify on grounds that are important to them. Insuring that our clients have such understanding respects their autonomy. Clients given the opportunity for such understanding will make choices about their writing which, in ethicist Bruce Miller's terms, will preserve *Autonomy as Free Action:* choices are voluntary, rather than coerced, and intentional, i.e., the conscious object of the actor; *Autonomy as Authenticity:* choices are in keeping with a person's character, "consistent with the person's attitudes, values, dispositions, and life plans"; and *Autonomy as Effective*

Deliberator: choices are informed so a person is aware of "alternatives and the consequences of the alternatives, [has] evaluated both, and [chooses] an action based on that evaluation" (67–69).

Following a consultation with a tutor, the writer of "My Grandma Connie" should be able to acknowledge that her one-sentence paragraph violates certain conventions, calls attention to itself, and cries out for details. She should also have the opportunity to speak in support of that paragraph, or to have its potential strengths pointed out to her. In its understatement, the paragraph may communicate something significant about both the writer and her grandmother. Perhaps some of its disjointedness reveals as well a relationship between the writer and her grandfather who put doors where windows should be. Providing an elaborated narrative of the arm-wrestling incident might distract from the naive tone of the piece. In all probability the writer did not intend the effects spoken of here. For some readers, however, such effects do exist, and they work to strengthen the piece. A tutor should not immediately conclude that the paragraph is simply the result of an "instant-closure" syndrome common to inexperienced writers. Nor should a tutor, upon spotting the paragraph, immediately drag out jargon-laden handbooks, and coerce the writer to modify the paragraph to satisfy the rules of good verbal hygiene.

In a tutorial operating to support the principle of informed consent, the paragraph should be discussed along with the writer's intentions and the possible effects—*both positive and negative*—that the paragraph may have on readers. Ultimately, all decisions for revision must rest with the writer. If, upon conscious deliberation, she opts to expand the paragraph, consenting to certain expectations for college-level writing even though they compromise her original intentions, that consent is still informed rather than coerced. If she opts not to expand, it is also an informed choice. As long as the writer is aware of, and willing to take, the risk of aggravating a reader who demands paragraphs of at least three sentences, she should be able to do so and be able to explain her decision.

To allow for informed consent in the writing center, tutors may again refer to medical ethicists, this time to examine potential models for doctor-patient relationships. Drawing upon the work of Thomas Szasz and Mark Hollender (1956), Diane Morrow identifies three ways in which physicians interact with their patients: "activity-passivity" (the physician assumes responsibility for all decision making on behalf of his or her patient who willingly and absolutely defers to the physician's authority); "guidance-cooperation" (the physician essentially makes decisions which the patient carries out); and "mutual participation" (the physician and patient work together, sharing responsibility for decision making). Robert M. Veatch (1983) notes that the principle of mutual participation prevails in what he calls "The Contractual Model" of the physician-patient relationship. According to Veatch, only in such a model, which imposes obligations on both parties, "can there be a true sharing of . . . authority and responsibility, . . . a real sharing of decision making in a way that there is a realistic assurance that both patient and physician will retain their moral integrity" (50).

Morrow admits that the first two modes she cites are more prevalent in medical practice—perhaps with some justification. She then suggests that mutual participation is the model to which writing tutors should aspire. Comparing it to what Donald Murray has called "the response theory of teaching," Morrow observes, "Central to this model is a kind of balance of knowledge between the two participants: 'But as much as the teacher—the experienced writer—knows about writing, the composition teacher does *not*—and should not know the subject of the student's draft as well as the student writer' " (225). Applied in the writing center, a mutual participation/contractual model obliges clients and tutors to take active roles in the decision-making process. Clients must honestly elaborate their intentions to the best of their ability. Clients must also be prepared to explore actively any alternatives and be responsible not only for making decisions, but also for explaining them. Tutors must be sure that writers are informed of and understand the choices open to them, and that they have made those choices freely.

Under the conditions described above, the writer of the "The Use of Force" paper would first have an opportunity to explain her intentions. Perhaps in high school this student was consistently praised for relating classic texts to works that were more immediately relevant to students' lives. Perhaps her paper represented an effort to repeat her earlier writing successes. The tutor would then have an opportunity to discuss—in terms that her client would understand—expectations and protocols for academic discourse, perhaps differentiating formal and informal diction, and modes of comparison/contrast and critical literary analysis. The tutor might further discuss the importance of carefully ascertaining what the instructor expects from this assignment and the ways in which the paper may frustrate those expectations. Throughout this discussion, the tutor can draw upon her own experiences—what led her to the acquisition of such knowledge.

Imperative to this exchange would be a "mutual monitoring of information disclosure" (Appelbaum, Lidz, and Meisel 1987, viii) so both tutor and client would understand each other's motives and rationales. Equally important is that the exchange be characterized by what Robert Coles calls the "comfortable . . . give-and-take of storytelling" (18). In his *The Call of Stories: Teaching and the Moral Imagination* (1989), Coles urges both physicians and teachers to share stories with clients and to listen to clients' stories with "a minimum of conceptual static" (19). He identifies conceptual static as the abstract theoretical formulation in which professionals engage. Coles further contends that, because such static interferes with the stories clients may be trying to tell, it often gets in the way of ethical practice:

> [T]he story of some of us who become owners of a professional power and a professional vocabulary is the familiar one of moral thoughtlessness. We brandish our authority in a ceaseless effort to reassure ourselves about our importance, and we forget to look at our own warts and blemishes, so busy are we cataloging those in others. (18)

Throughout his book, Coles draws upon his own experience as a psychiatrist who gradually learned of the dangers of hastily applying theoretical constructs without ever really giving his patients the opportunity to tell their stories. Interestingly, this learning process also involved William Carlos Williams, whom Coles visited when he was in medical school, whose "doctor stories" Coles later edited, and who once told Coles, "we owe it to each other to respect our stories and learn from them" (30). Writing center tutors must also respect stories as Coles advocates; his book should stand alongside Harris's *Teaching One-to-One* (1986) and Meyer and Smith's *The Practical Tutor* (1987) as must reading for writing center professionals.

In the tutorial being considered here, both the tutor and the writer of "The Use of Force" paper should have a chance to tell their stories, to express their intentions as fully as possible. They may then be in a better position to collaborate on strategies for revising the paper. For example, perhaps discussion of *The Exorcist* would be subordinated to a more detailed analysis of Williams's story—an analysis which still originates with the similarities the student noted between the two works. Because discussion of *The Exorcist* is not eliminated, the student continues to maintain a stake in the paper, her initial response to "The Use of Force" is not rejected or devalued, and her analysis can remain meaningful to her on her own terms. The student may now be more willing to make certain accommodations—the adoption of more formal diction, for example—so as to become more credible and to present terms that are acceptable to her instructor. Naturally, all decisions about revising the paper are the student's. It is the tutor's responsibility, however, to be sure her client understands those decisions, that she can articulate reasons for the choices she makes (e.g., writing is judged differently in college than it was at my high school; I need to learn to play by a different set of rules). In such a scenario, autonomy is respected. Although it does get compromised, such compromise occurs in ways that the student can understand.

Observing that we live in an age which has undergone a "revolution in our conception of justice," Robert Veatch notes, "If the obscure phrase 'all men are created equal' means anything in the medical context where biologically it is clear that they are not equal, it means that they are equal in the legitimacy of their moral claim. They must be treated equally in what is essential to their humanity: dignity, freedom, individuality" (1983, 47). In the past two decades, attending to the legitimacy of that moral claim has caused profound changes in the field of medical ethics. They are changes that should concern any professional charged with promoting the physical, emotional, or intellectual health of others.

In addition to issues of authority and autonomy introduced here, a consideration of other medical-ethical dilemmas may also have a direct bearing on writing center practice. They include, for example, issues of confidentiality (Should doctors inform employers about the status of the employees' health? Should tutors inform instructors about all that is said in writing consultation?); issues of non-compliance (Are doctors obliged to continue treating patients who do not take prescribed medicine, continue smoking, etc.? Are tutors obliged to work with clients who repeatedly miss appointments, do not revise, do not do suggested exercises, etc.?); and issues of allocation of resources (When time and medicine is limited, should some patients be given priority over others? When tutorial assistance is limited, should some students have priority, i.e., at-risk students before all others?). Because these issues are so morally complex, and because the doctor-tutor analogy will eventually break down, encounters with medical ethical theory may not always illuminate writing center practice. Nonetheless, a working knowledge of such theory certainly can help lead to more ethically sensitive tutors and more informed decision making in the writing center.

References

Allen, Nancy J. 1986. "Who Owns the Truth in the Writing Lab?" *Writing Center Journal* 6.2, 3–9.

Appelbaum, Paul S., Charles W. Lidz, and Alan Meisel. 1987. *Informed Consent: Legal Theory and Clinical Practice*. New York: Oxford University Press.

Arras, John, and Robert Hunt, eds. 1983. *Ethical Issues in Modern Medicine*. 2nd ed. Palo Alto: Mayfield.

Bartholomae, David. 1985. "Inventing the University." *When a Writer Can't Write: Studies in Writer's Block and Other Composing-Process Problems*. Ed. Mike Rose. New York: Guilford, 134–65.

Beauchamp, Tom L., and James F. Childress. 1989. *Principles of Biomedical Ethics*. 3rd ed. New York: Oxford University Press.

Childress, James F. 1979. "Paternalism and Health Care." Robison and Pritchard, 15–27.

Clark, Irene Lurkis. 1988. "Collaboration and Ethics in Writing Center Pedagogy." *Writing Center Journal* 9.1, 3–12.

Coles, Robert. 1989. *The Call of Stories: Teaching and the Moral Imagination*. Boston: Houghton Mifflin.

Garrett, Thomas M., Harold Baillie, and Rosellen Garrett. 1989. *Health Care Ethics: Principles and Problems.* Englewood Cliffs, NJ: Prentice-Hall.

Gert, Bernard, and Charles M. Culver. 1979. "The Justification of Paternalism." Robison and Pritchard, 1–14.

Goldman, Alan. 1983. "The Refutation of Medical Paternalism." Arras and Hunt, 110–18.

Harris, Muriel. 1986. *Teaching One-to-One: The Writing Conference.* Urbana, IL: National Council of Teachers of English.

Haynes, Jane. 1988. "Triage Tutoring: The Least You Can Do." *Writing Lab Newsletter,* 12–13.

Katz, Jay. 1984. *The Silent World of Doctor and Patient.* New York: Free Press.

Lanham, Richard. 1979. *Revising Prose.* New York: Scribner's.

Mappes, E. Joy Kroeger. 1983. "Ethical Dilemmas for Nurses: Physicians' Orders Versus Patients' Rights." Arras and Hunt, 119–26.

McConnell, Terrance C. 1982. *Moral Issues in Health Care: An Introduction to Medical Ethics.* Monterey: Wadsworth.

Meyer, Emily, and Louise Z. Smith. 1987. *The Practical Tutor.* New York: Oxford University Press.

Miller, Bruce L. 1983. "Autonomy and the Refusal of Lifesaving Treatment." Arras and Hunt, 64–73.

Morrow, Diane Stelzer. 1991. "Tutoring Writing: Healing or What?" *College Composition and Communication* 42, 218–29.

Murray, Donald. 1985. *A Writer Teaches Writing.* 2nd ed. Boston: Houghton.

———. 1990. *Write to Learn.* 3rd ed. Fort Worth: Holt.

Pellegrino, Edmund D., and David C. Thomasma. 1988. *For the Patient's Good: The Restoration of Beneficence in Health Care.* New York: Oxford University Press.

Reigstad, Thomas J., and Donald A. McAndrew. 1984. *Training Tutors for Writing Conferences.* Urbana, IL: National Council of Teachers of English.

Robison, Wade, and Michael Pritchard. 1979. *Medical Responsibility: Paternalism, Informed Consent and Euthanasia.* Clifton, NJ: Humana.

Rose, Mike. 1990. *Lives on the Boundary: A Moving Account of the Struggles and Achievements of America's Educational Underclass.* New York: Penguin.

Satre, Kay, and Valerie Traub. 1988. "Non-Directive Tutoring Strategies." *Writing Lab Newsletter,* 5–6.

Shaughnessy, Mina P. 1981. "Diving In: An Introduction to Basic Writing." *College Composition and Communication* 27 (1976): 234–39. Rpt. in *The Writing Teacher's Sourcebook.* Eds. Gary Tate and Edward P. J. Corbett. New York: Oxford University Press, 62–68.

Shuman, Samuel I. 1979. "Informed Consent and the 'Victims' of Colonialism." Robinson and Pritchard, 75–99.

Szasz, Thomas, and Mark Hollender. 1956. "A Contribution to the Philosophy of Medicine: The Basic Models of the Doctor-Patient Relationship." *American Medical Association Archives of Internal Medicine* 97, 73–80.

Trimbur, John. 1987. "Peer Tutoring: A Contradiction in Terms?" *Writing Center Journal* 7.2, 21–28.

Veatch, Robert M. 1988. "Models for Ethical Medicine in a Revolutionary Age." Arras and Hunt, 47–51.

Ware, Elaine. 1986. "Crisis Intervention in the Writing Center." *Writing Lab Newsletter,* 5–8.

Williams, William Carlos. 1986. "The Use of Force." *LIT—Literature and Interpretive Techniques*. Ed. Wilfred Guerin et al. New York: Harper and Row, 205–208.

13 The Politics of Otherness: Negotiating Distance and Difference

Phyllis Lassner
Northwestern University

Cultural diversity is now a rallying point in higher education, a call for curriculum and pedagogy to reflect diverse student populations. At the vanguard of such change are faculty in composition and women's studies.[1] Marginalized themselves, they have understood only too well how dominant academic discourses, styles of relating, and power structures exclude and silence those who have not been made part of the decision-making process concerning curriculum, canonicity, and departmental, faculty, and student status. From their positions as "other" in the academy, composition and women's studies faculty have promoted student-centered, active learning as a way of democratizing higher education and encouraging students to see that they do not have to assume the role of "other" themselves.

One form of learning which promotes student empowerment is peer tutoring. Those of us who have been training students to become peer tutors have been cheered on by the practices which assume that collaborative learning will result in student writers gaining confidence and critical awareness of their composing processes. As student tutors encourage their tutees, a process of interdependence takes place. Different cognitive and composing styles and different learning and cultural experiences begin to mesh as tutees are encouraged to become their own critical readers in response to guidance from other students.

Although it seems not too long ago that peer tutoring was considered a radical innovation in higher education, this form of collaborative, one-to-one teaching is now a highly valued practice in writing centers and classes. Those of us who struggled to get peer tutoring programs off the ground relied on the testimony of Ken Bruffee, who at the first national Peer Tutoring Conference in 1984 argued that writing, anxiety-provoking for many, would become

---

I would like to thank Susan French, whose creative and critical contributions to this essay made it possible to move from theory to practice.

energizing and compelling as student peers supported each other through revising strategies. I remember him telling enrapt teachers and tutors that "tutors create conditions in which people learn to talk with each other about writing the way writers talk to each other about writing, and learn to write as those in the community of literate people write." In the years since, we have felt supported by the successful experiences we hear about at the National Peer Tutoring Conference, in *The Writing Lab Newsletter,* and from colleagues (see Trimbur).

Although sensitizing peer tutors to issues of diversity and difference is at the center of their training, my fear is that we assume unproblematic definitions of a "community of literate writers," of peerness, and of difference. As Bakhtin (1981) reminds us, "language, for the individual consciousness, lies on the borderline between oneself and the other. The word language is half someone else's" (293). The vociferous backlash even within the academy to the project of multiculturalism testifies to divergent views that not only belie any unified sense of writing community, but questions our theories and practices of who is "the other"—what is a peer?[2]

Rather than dismiss the backlash as the vestigial gasp of an anomalous conservatism, I would like to think of it as part of the social structure of diversity itself and therefore a challenge to our assumptions about peer tutoring. I wish to explore the concept and social realities of the "other" as it is constructed in the interdependent relationships between tutor and tutee. This study will negotiate definitions of peerness and difference through a method of collaboration that reveals tensions embedded in our working definitions of diversity.[3] The negotiations enacted here are between feminist theories and categories of difference I have chosen as teacher and writer, and the experiences and discussions of peer tutors in the English Composition Board (ECB) at the University of Michigan. ECB peer tutors have explored the relationship of their sense of individual differences to their sense of tutees' "otherness." Working with categories of cultural and gender differences and with diverse educational goals and experiences, they consider how they manage their sense of self as they construct the "other" with whom they hope to learn collaboratively. Reports by ECB peer tutors will follow, along with my own analysis and that of Susan French, a peer tutor who also collaborated with me on decisions about the structure and conclusions of this study.

My use of "other" reflects a history of theory beginning with Simone de Beauvoir's analysis of women's roles and developing through theories of difference such as Bakhtin's and those deriving from feminist psychology and cultural criticism.[4] Feminist theories of difference coincide with concerns about empowerment in composition by recognizing that universalizing "human nature" elides the presence of women, non-white, non-European, non-heterosexual, and other non-privileged people. Feminists, however, are not univocal about difference. In her survey and critique Linda Gordon (1991) notes that since the seventies, when distinctions between biological and cultural constructions of sexuality led to the idea of gender, debate persists about whether gender is transformative or retrograde in its social implications for women (92).[5] Understanding gender as culturally constructed led in varying degrees to men and women sharing domestic work, to women being encouraged to pursue higher education and so to enter the occupations of their choice, and to exercise some measure of sexual freedom.

While gender challenged traditional beliefs about the development of women's intellectual abilities and their destinies, it also evolved into revisionary arguments for women's unique psychology. Theories and research that recognized women's different language and "voice" (McEdwards 1985; Cameron 1990) as well as capacities for "knowing" and for ethical values (Belenky 1986; Gilligan 1982) also gave women a unique social and cultural position that threatened them in ways too reminiscent of the old biological distinctions. According to American psychoanalytic critics, women's social and emotional identification with maternal roles of nurturing endows them with an empathetic relatedness to the world outside themselves. The moral and cognitive result is that women conceptualize such abstractions as justice not as a legal construct of absolute dimensions, but as a fluid process of making ethical decisions based on the relative merits of individual cases of human welfare and conflict. French feminist theorists, influenced by the structuralist premises of psychoanalyst Jacques Lacan, developed equally distinctive characters for women. Whether they worked with or revised Lacan, these feminists called for women to write "from the body," a form of self-expression that would counter women's absence and silence in patriarchal law and language (see Marks and Courtivron 1980).

Ironically, such descriptions of women's unique psychology and enculturation replicate the universalizing gesture of the traditional assumptions they seek to revise.[6] Theorizing all women as endowed with a primary quality of nurturance not only puts them back in the kitchen, eternally excluded from public spheres of power on the grounds of their "natural" gifts, but occludes differences among women. In such an essentializing mode, where would there be room for non-pacifist or highly competitive women or for African-American or Jewish and other women whose strongly felt historical and cultural identities produce other definitions of justice and caring? As Linda Gordon (1991) summarizes the problem, "women are angered at the resultant prescription of what femaleness or female experience is when it doesn't fit them. Furthermore, since the generalizations about sisterhood and 'women's experience' came from women of dominant groups, they were not unreasonably perceived as arrogant" (94).

The peer tutors who joined our self-study suggested that only if we accept irreconcilable differences can we truly respect the integrity of students' identities and explore what kind of learning takes place between "peers." Our peer tutoring seminar on "Composition Theory and Collaborative Learning" began with discussions of cultural and gender differences with Bakhtin's definition of "the other." Bakhtin (1981) cogently combines issues of human relatedness and difference with our individual struggles to acquire literacy and to experience ourselves as part of a supportive community. We were struck by Bakhtin's warning that linguistic interchange includes the anxiety of entering foreign and possibly threatening territory: "the word does not exist in a neutral and impersonal language . . . but rather it exists in other people's mouths, in other people's contexts, serving other people's intentions: it is from there that one must take the word, and make it one's own. . . ." (1981, 293–94).

The ECB peer tutors wrote in their journals how their sense of being different from the students they were tutoring affected the tutoring process and its interchange of language. The categories of analysis developed by the tutors showed us that the "borderline" between "other people's contexts" and our own is not always clearly marked, that in fact it has to be negotiated in the process of collaborative learning because it is so often blurred. In a telling example, one peer tutor I'll call Carl claimed that being at Michigan was a rite of passage from "the time when boys and girls couldn't wait to polarize themselves from each other" to the discovery that "a number of my best friends and classmates are girls . . . and if they're like me they often enjoy the companionship of buddies of the opposite sex more than friends of their own sex. The fact that we're of different gender is as true as ever, but somewhere we came to see difference . . . differently." He then asks: "How can we get along as two kinds of people? No—how can we use it to our advantage?" He concludes that "We men can learn from women's experience and vice versa. Admittedly we're not the same, but that's no longer a sexual Mason-Dixon line, to communicate is no longer like fraternizing with the enemy. It is, rather, a chance for a second self, another side to the human experience, for those wise enough to take it."

I will explore some responses to tutoring experiences to test Carl's sense of blurred boundaries between self and other. One peer tutor wrote about meeting with a student she remembered from a previous class. This common ground, however, had to yield to a recognition of differences in order for learning to take place. I'll quote from the journal of the student I'll call Anna: "I was especially impressed with him as a peer, as he had often made intelligent comments and asked questions in class [while] I was rarely bold enough to speak in front of such a large group of people." When I first read this entry, I felt it was truly a peer tutoring situation turned upside-down. The tutor sees herself as less competent than the tutee. In her review of my draft, however,

Susan French, the peer tutor who collaborated with me in this project, observed a dynamic that goes to the heart of peer tutors' training. She noted that Anna's reflection assumed a kind of "power differential [which] is a natural, a necessary part of peer tutoring." The learning process which takes place between tutor and tutee is not static, but a constant negotiation. Our differences in learning experiences require that knowledge rests with one before it is transformed in the give and take of tutoring talk into something new that both tutor and tutee take away. This is borne out by the fact that the tutee in the above case was also impressed by Anna's feedback on sentences which did not convey what he hoped. Anna concludes: "While I find him to be verbally stronger than myself, perhaps it is I who am the stronger writer."

Anna had assumed that the good talker is the smarter and deserves to dominate the classroom discussion. Only when he discusses his writing does she see that here a different kind of articulation is required, one that transfers to learning outside the classroom. She reports:

> He asked a question about a sentence he was writing, but I was having trouble understanding because he didn't have a written copy of the paragraph in which the sentence belonged. I needed his writing to see if he made sense.

Whatever his speaking abilities were like in class, in relation to his writing, he was struggling to find an appropriate register in which to express and communicate his ideas.

In some ways, the tutor learned more than the tutee, and in others, she learned less than she should have. For the individual distinctions between speaking and writing skills were informed by another difference: gender. Although Anna never addresses this issue, studies of women's behavior in classroom discussion help us to understand how her conclusion is still shaped by her first impression (see Piliavin 1976; Gabriel and Smithson 1990). Readings showed us how women are less comfortable speaking up in various classroom settings, including the large lecture to which Anna refers. Anna's assumption that her tutee was "smarter" because he was self-assured coincides with the observations of Belenky and her colleagues (1986) that even when men are inarticulate, women assume men possess authority and, as Susan French points out, "tacitly allow them to exercise this authority." As Belenky et al. discovered, "'Women's talk,' in both *style* and *content* . . . is typically devalued by men and women alike. Women talk less in mixed groups and are interrupted more often" (17–18).

In our seminar the peer tutors used this feminist perspective to discuss their tutoring experiences and subsequently role played a variety of conversations in which to begin to understand what was meant by men's and women's talk. They saw how not only speech, but how body language and facial expression communicate hesitation or assurance, and attitudes towards oneself in relation to the other from which the other gleans messages about how to shape her or his own response. The road to empowerment in learning and writing involves discovering and discussing what peer tutors are not always able to recognize and acknowledge. These are experiences in which they become complicit in their powerlessness because they have internalized cultural signs of their inadequacies or inequalities. Through research on gender and culture, peer tutors and teachers can become conscious of responses to those experiences which are so often ignored, dismissed, or explained away. For example, Pamela Annas's (1985) work with working-class composition students offers a critique and agenda for women's self-esteem in academic settings. Recognizing class as a form of difference broadens the pedagogical implications of Gilligan's (1982) study of middle-class women's identity and moral development. In reviewing their work, ECB peer tutors recognized how empathy, what Gilligan calls a morality of caring, needs to be balanced with Annas's imperative to recognize the vulnerability in personal voices as they come to grips with the relationships of power in academic settings (see Bartholomae 1974).

Another peer tutor I'll call Dan complicates the relationship between power and difference in his journal entries:

> One of our discussions on "otherness" I found to be rather alarming. All of the females in our class felt that tutees had an affinity towards male tutors. They supported this claim by remarking how many tutees inquired into their training. . . . Oddly, none of the males remembered being asked this. It's possible that the males were asked this one time or another but did not give it a second thought.

Dan goes on to claim that he doesn't know what difference "otherness" makes in the tutoring environment: "When I tutor, I concentrate on the material." And yet he acknowledges that "when one is nervous, he or she may flirt in order to establish a rapport . . . most of the time this is harmless and nothing is meant by it. But how much would this interfere with tutoring?"

The pattern that emerges in these journal entries is the sense that this male, as the others he mentions, has trouble remembering or imagining the discomfort of the other in a learning situation where there may be more alienation than collaboration. At one level, Dan is completely comfortable and confident in his role as tutor. At another level, his confidence is a function of being blind to the power plays intrinsic to the personal interaction despite his best intentions. Dan's journal illustrates the kinds of distances between our perceptions of collaborative learning, of community, and the way others receive the verbal and non-verbal expressions of our perceptions. This distance is what I would call "otherness"—in this case formed by the way gender is part of our sense of competence and the way we relate to others and expect them to respond to us.

Susan French noted that Dan's lack of awareness about power typifies the gender differences that lead to the dangers of sexual harassment. I would argue as well that the way Dan and Anna and other tutors use language reveals the great divide between the ways we construct our social behavior and our ability to recognize the effects of our behavior on others. Anna's use of "impressed," "smarter," "verbally stronger" and Dan's deployment of statements like "I have been able to command the respect of the tutee" expose how we value or devalue ourselves and the way that this process values or devalues the other. Surely, to "command the respect" is a contradiction in terms, as was Carl's use of the phrase "use to our advantage." Both instances speak to a sense of mutuality but betray a connotation of power which favors one over the other. It is both language and event that creates what Bakhtin describes as "a dialogically agitated and tension-filled environment of alien words, value judgments and accents" (1981, 276).

Muriel Harris (1966) and others have warned us of the differences that can impede collaborative learning and how we must apprise peer tutors of the conditions of cultural and educational difference. Feminist theorists, moreover, are recognizing that cultural identities are an integral part of gender identity and that together they issue in a complex sense of difference. As the statements of these peer tutors reveal, however, not all difference is consciously perceived. Some issues are easy to recognize: ESL problems in writing, overt shyness. Sometimes, however, differences are obfuscated by the very educational practices we have learned to value. One peer tutor described such a dynamic as part of her encouraging a tutee to be independent by pressing him to express his personal views. Faced with his resistance, she reacted with symptoms of a disorder she astutely labeled "otherness stress." She recognized that when she challenged an ESL student to "please argue with me" his respect for a different style of learning endowed her with an authority he could not question and she did not accept. This may very well have been complicated, moreover, by different cultural perceptions of male and female roles in the peer tutoring relationship. In some cultures, peerness would be vexed by a woman being in the contradictory roles of nurturer, equal, and authority. When unrecognized differences in cultural learning styles clash, the result for both tutor and tutee is probably going to be a defense against the "other" which is tantamount to a defense against learning. Individual psychology functions as a cultural construction in Dan's case as well. His refusal to recognize his complicity with the sexist attitudes he deplores stems from not wanting to relinquish that feeling of "command." What he teaches and learns is that our relationship with another derives from our construction of that person according to the social, cultural, and gendered values we do not question or, as Susan French observes, "even think about."

These multidimensional issues of difference are nowhere more apparent than in peer tutoring people who are more peer-like than different. Susan French analyzes this phenomenon from her experiences tutoring students for my course called "Women Writing" in the Women's Studies Program, where despite differences in age, culture, and ideology, students agree on their collective concerns about women's voices. Her discussion follows.

> Being attached to the class, I kept abreast of issues pertinent to class and student papers which I regularly discussed with Phyllis. Students met one-on-one with me in "neutral" places like the "Mug" at the student union. Already familiar with the assignment, and at times, from previous sessions with the writer, we could dive right into the actual tutoring in a discipline that was my own. This is very different from Anna's peer-tutoring: she is highly conscious of the "otherness" and difference my peer-tutoring situation seems to mask. As a Women's Studies/Psychology major I was already personally and intellectually engaged in the material, and committed to the writers whose interests and ways of thinking often paralleled my own. Relating to the subject matter of my tutees in such a personal way has recharged my interest in tutoring and cast my work in a new light. Because the same people often came back to me, I was grateful to already have a sense of them as writers. We could pick up where we left off and discuss their writing as we both saw it progress. We did not need to work to establish a rapport—rather a writing relationship emerged as part of the process. I realized that long-term interactions are the only way to soften the power differential which is part of the first meeting of tutor and tutee. I felt much more like a tutor-friend than an extension of their professor, and from what I could observe, members of 310 perceived me in this way.
>
> The first paper challenged students to trace their history as writers—a topic I was eager to approach as a peer tutor. How natural a paper like that would be for me to write! I thought 310 students would approach it with the same confidence, but to my surprise, they expressed great anxiety. I encouraged each student I worked with to talk as much as possible, and they were often able to verbalize a response to the assignment, but they ran into problems composing. For some students, personal voice was completely separate from anything they would turn in to a professor. I remember telling Joanne, "Write that down—that's great, you can use that." Joanne's problem was not with the content, but with the process. Her spoken response was insightful and vivid, but when it came time to transfer this energy into a written form she was hitting a brick wall. Our sessions were productive because writers expressed their words in a voice they didn't think they had.
>
> I found that many of the students in this class lacked confidence in their writing. Sometimes a woman would come to me ashamed and reticent to even show me her rough draft, or would do so only after ten excuses as to why it wasn't good. Expecting terrible papers, what I most often found was the opposite. I wondered if this lack of confidence was

characteristic of women writers, especially since our voices have been invalidated and we've felt our stories weren't worth recording. How can we write about ourselves when others have standardized notions of what is scholarly, objective, and valued, separate from our own experience? As a writer I feel confident in myself, but I am still working through this collective struggle. Collaborative learning with other women helps me a great deal through this struggle because each of us joins "the other" to fill in that space of alienation. Sometimes the best gift I can give to a writer is a feeling of confidence.

Susan discovered that in various ways her tutees defied all prevailing definitions of confidence and a woman's voice, including revisionist feminist categories:

> Jane's biggest problem seemed to be confidence. She herself criticized her reliance on too much distanced analysis and not enough personal response. She wanted to present a critique of *Women's Ways of Knowing* and had trouble relating personally to Belenky's concept of silent knowers because she had never felt silenced. Her goal was to integrate theory into the personal. We discussed feminist categorization and saw a contradiction between working to destroy patriarchal structures which put people in boxes when Belenky's feminist theory does the same thing.

Susan's tutoring not only raised theoretical questions about feminist theories of difference, but enacted a critique that showed how collaborative learning depends on the integration of differences and not on "peerness." Assuming a kind of natural affinity towards writing goals between two people elides those differences which we often refuse to recognize in our efforts to legitimize collaborative learning. Susan and Jane recognized and then negotiated the distance between tutor/reader and tutee/writer by learning from and respecting their different learning styles and voices. While she encouraged Jane to add personal analysis to her theoretical discussion, Susan also engaged her in a "discussion about how women are systematically silenced in society," the result of which was a validation of Jane's preference for "distanced analysis" and a voice that defied neat dichotomies.

In contrast to Jane's penchant for academic discourse, another tutee showed how personal voice and "distanced analysis" are intertwined. Susan writes:

> Andrea, an older returning student, struck me as being self-aware; she is not inhibited by a confidence problem. Andrea works in pieces. Her process is very complicated, and she is reluctant to leave anything out—tidbits of information, theorists, perspectives. Sharing everything she learned from her research, Andrea ends up with an informative, yet cluttered and confused paper. I encouraged her to sort out her goals and outline her main ideas with the most persuasive evidence. The difficulty, however, lay in Andrea's personal involvement in her subject. As a result

of a childhood experience, having known a classmate who was brutally murdered, she was exploring the connection between pornography and sexual violence. Because talking and writing about the experience held great therapeutic value, the paper functioned beyond the assignment.

Susan continues:

> The experience was draining because of needs which went beyond writing. The role of tutor blurred into counselor, listening and supporting personal difficulty. I see meeting these personal writing needs as part of the tutoring process because without processing her feelings about her subject, Andrea cannot organize her thoughts and paragraphs. Working on mechanics for a semester while ignoring the psychology of a writer in cases like this would be like putting a bandaid over a severed arm. I see this function of listener as a necessary component of feminist writing pedagogy.

Susan questions all of her efforts to bridge the distances between herself as tutor and her tutees, refusing to take for granted the assumptions that might press her to universalize her experiences and therefore essentialize the women with whom she worked. Identifying her own needs as a "feminist writer and reader," Susan raises "an important ethical question . . . [about] projecting onto the paper what I would have written." She suggests that the feminist project of reclaiming female subjectivity may encourage "the tutor [to] lose objectivity in reader response when her own ideas about feminist writing are at the forefront of her mind." The relationship between tutor and tutee is informed here by the one between writer and subject. In both instances the integrity of the writing subject and the written subject depends on recognizing differences and distances that must be maintained if each is to survive with its own various combinations of identity. Just as differences and distances are plural here, so the integrity of identity does not imply a fixed sense of self but rather, as Susan Stanford Friedman tells us, one that is "multicontexted" (1991, 471) negotiating among historical, ideological, and psychological pressures.

Especially among those who are apparently similar, like feminist tutor and tutee, the collaborative process can become coercive if the discourse that is the dominant indicator of identity at the moment presses both parties into unquestioned allegiance. The "power differential" which so concerns Susan is activated not only by the knowledge-bearing status of the trained feminist peer tutor, but by the ideological weight of the discourse to which both tutor and tutee subscribe. Instead of inviting a fluid explorative process of knowledge-gathering, the effort to conform to a fixed definition of empowerment leads only to subjection to what Friedman calls "totalizing orthodoxies and master-disciple psychodynamics" (1991, 466). Showing how to activate multiplicity,

Friedman invokes Thomas Kavanagh's (1989) revision of poststructuralism calling for "'the elusive presence of the real, and the challenge of a voice speaking outside the various rhetorics of mastery' " (Friedman 1991, 467). So pertinent to peer tutoring, the contingencies of "real" differences, always in flux, require us to engage in a Bakhtinian dialogic among the open borders between self and other and between theory and experience.

The construction of the "other" reflects the process of relating and negotiating rather than a confrontation with a fixed, preconceived object. In this construction neither the tutor nor tutee are designated as subject or object, but rather enact a fluid process of selves relating and yet decentered by the anxieties produced by the process. In noting that these anxieties often go unnoticed, Susan French challenged me to realize that a primary risk in the learning process is in letting go of the need to feel centered, fixed, and stable in what one already knows. Instead of conceiving of decenteredness as anxiety provoking, we can theorize from the peer tutors' experience a kind of "engagement in the academy," what Friedman calls "a site of contradiction," which enables us to recognize that the constant reforming of relations in peer tutoring poses a rigorous challenge to "the ideological and institutional formations of knowledge" (1991, 471).

Notes

1. Since the list now goes back twenty years, I draw attention only to recent contributors: Pamela Annas, Patricia Bizzell, Susan McLeod, Gabriel and Smithson, Lassner.

2. I refer here not only to Bloom, D'Souza, Hirsch, but to critiques of their work that follow traditions of learning other than the predominantly left fields of composition. See Searle and Scholes.

3. I am following Susan Stanford Friedman's (1991) definition of "negotiation" here as "carr[ying] the double connotation of 'mutual discussion and arrangement'. . . . and maneuvering to clear or pass an obstacle . . . Negotiation at this post/poststructuralist point involves a commitment to self-consciously historicizing theory and theorizing history" (481–82).

4 The most influential of the American feminist psychoanalytic critics remain Chodorow and Gilligan. For a recent critique of their work, see Grosskurth. Feminist theorists of the "other" include Spivack, Lorde, and Hooks.

5. Gordon's essay includes a bibliography covering the debate over the past twenty years. Judith Butler takes the debate even further by questioning whether sex, like gender, might not also be culturally and socially constructed.

6. For problems inherent in those theories and hermeneutics which self-deceptively deconstruct dichotomous thinking with dichotomous thinking, see Ann Berthoff's most recent essay in *CCCC* (October 1991).

References

Annas, Pamela J. 1985. "Style as Politics: A Feminist Approach to the Teaching of Writing." *College English* 47, 360–71.

Bakhtin, Mikhail M. 1981. *The Dialogic Imagination*. Trans. and Ed. Michael Holquist and Caryl Emerson. Austin: University of Texas.

Bartholomae, David. 1965. "Inventing the University." *When a Writer Can't Write*. Ed. Mike Rose. New York: Guilford, 134–65.

Beauvoir, Simone de. 1974. *The Second Sex*. Trans. H. M. Parshley. New York: Vintage.

Belenky, Mary F., Blythe M. Clinchy, Nancy R. Goldberger, and Jill M. Tarule. 1986. *Women's Ways of Knowing: The Development of Self, Voice, and Mind*. New York: Basic Books.

Berthoff, Ann E. 1991. "Rhetoric as Hermeneutic." *College Composition and Communication* 42, 279–87.

Bizzell, Patricia. 1988. "Arguing about Literacy." *College English* 50, 141–53.

Bloom, Allan. 1988. *The Closing of the American Mind*. Chicago: University of Chicago Press.

Bruffee, Kenneth. 1984. "Peer Tutoring: A Conceptual Framework." Unpublished Talk, Brown University.

———. 1986. "Peer Tutoring and 'The Conversation of Mankind.'" In *Writing Centers: Theory and Administration*. Ed. Gary A. Olsen. Urbana, IL: National Council of Teachers of English, 3–15.

Butler, Judith. 1990. *Gender Trouble: Feminism and the Subversion of Identity*. New York: Routledge.

Cameron, D. J. ed. 1990. *The Feminist Critique of Language*. London: Routledge.

Chodorow, Nancy. 1978. *The Reproduction of Mothering: Psychoanalysis and the Sociology of Gender*. Berkeley: University of California Press.

Friedman, Susan Stanford. 1991. "Post/Poststructuralist Feminist Criticism: The Politics of Recuperation and Negotiation." *New Literary History* 22, 465–90.

Gabriel, Susan L., and Isaiah Smithson. 1990. *Gender in the Classroom: Power and Pedagogy*. Urbana, IL: University of Illinois Press.

Gilligan, Carol. 1982. *In a Different Voice: Psychological Theory and Women's Development*. Cambridge, MA: Harvard University Press.

Gordon, Linda. 1991. "On 'Difference.'" *Genders* 10, 91–111.

Grosskurth, Phyllis. 1991, October 24. "The New Psychology of Women." *New York Review of Books* 38, 25–32.

Harris, Muriel. 1966. *Teaching One-to-One: The Writing Conference*. Urbana, IL: National Council of Teachers of English.

Hirsch, E. D. 1987. *Cultural Literacy*. Boston: Houghton.

hooks, bell. 1990. *Yearning: Race, Gender, and Cultural Politics*. Boston: South End Press.

Kavanagh, Thomas. Ed. 1989. *The Limits of Theory*. Stanford: Stanford University Press.

Lassner, Phyllis. 1990. "Feminist Responses to Rogerian Argument." *Rhetoric Review* 8, 220–33.

Lorde, Audre. 1984. *Sister Outsider: Essays and Speeches.* Trumansberg, NY: Crossing Press.

McEdwards, Ruth. 1985. "Women's Language: A Positive View." *English Journal,* 40–43.

McLeod, Susan H. 1990. "Cultural Literacy, Curricular Reform, and Freshman Composition." *Rhetoric Review* 8, 270–79.

Marks, Elaine, and Isobelle de Courtivron. 1980. *New French Feminisms: An Anthology.* Amherst, MA: University of Massachusetts Press.

Piliavin, J. A. 1976. "On Feminine Self-Presentation in Groups." *Beyond Intellectual Sexism.* Ed. J. I. Roberts. New York: McKay, 138–59.

Scholes, Robert. 1991. "A Flock of Cultures—A Trivial Proposal." *College English* 53, 759–72.

Spivack, Guyatri. 1987. *Other Worlds.* New York: Methuen.

14 Literacy and the Technology of Writing: Examining Assumptions, Changing Practices

Joan A. Mullin
University of Toledo

Our tutor training and writing center philosophies encourage social constructionist and collaborative practices; yet the dynamics of a tutorial still position the tutor as representative of the academy and the student as outsider. These roles within a tutorial can be traced to many deeply held cultural ways of thinking. In this collection Gillam, Lassner, and especially Murphy point to the enormous body of research which addresses the various cultural traditions motivating language and action. In response, writing center practitioners train tutors to critically assess their practices, and to critique barriers relating to gender, race, and class differences that may inhibit writing center tutorials, e.g., Lassner, McLennan, in this volume. However, strongly inculcated notions of literacy also act to separate the "literate" tutor from the student. Unless we examine our definitions of literacy, we risk sustaining the gap between belief and practice which, despite our best intentions, may continue to invalidate and exclude our students' voices.

Current research in literacy suggests a theoretical blurring of the barriers traditionally connoted by the terms "literate" and "non-literate." In practice, this theoretical work manifests itself in frequent use of expressive writing, the inclusion of social critique in writing courses, or by drawing on Paulo Freire's example of using vocabulary from workers' daily lives to teach reading. Recent emphasis on "multicultural" and "multilingual" also seems to have broadened our definition of "literacy" and the qualities associated with the term. In addition, we now speak of "native literacy," "computer literacy" or even "athletic literacy," and we recognize as literate behavior the expertise and ability to convey information within a particular group. However, though "literacy" may theoretically include perspectives of "otherness," culturally, a narrower definition seems still operative in our institutions and in our tutorials.

In the past, the ability to sign legal papers and read simple text defined a literate person. Eventually, the United States Department of Education determined that to be literate meant to read and communicate at a fifth-grade level.

However, as economies grew, there also grew a need for different skills; "literacy" began to include not only the original "basics," but also the ability to "decode" and communicate more complex pieces of information. The introduction of classroom-based literacy objectives to achieve these goals implied that there was a hierarchy of particular literate practices which should be learned.

More recently, in the face of a changing student population, academe fought to define what should be expected of a literate person. Those expectations included the assumption that if students were to properly assess or interpret, they needed to have a strong, shared background from which they could draw. Given this proper background, it then followed that a literate person should be able to "interpret," "assess," and "think critically." However, it became clear from the work of Piaget, Vygotsky, and others that school alone did not provide the conditions for literate practices.

Investigating the role of literacy in society, ethnographers looked at the relationship between literacy and cultural environment. Shirley Brice Heath (1989) found that community practices in two Appalachian towns determined children's success or failure in schools, i.e., their ability to become literate according to acceptable, school-defined standards. Though E. D. Hirsch created his version of cultural literacy, feminists provided another platform from which the dominant culture was challenged; they were soon joined by a number of minority voices. Recently J. Elspeth Stuckey (1991) moved behind all these conflicts with her examination of the economic reasons for establishing "literacy." Stuckey asks whether concepts of literacy dependent on academic, text-based standards of encoding and decoding are construed to help "those in need of economic and social opportunity, or those (including ourselves) who wish to maintain their own economic and social advantage?" (viii). Heath, Hirsch, and Stuckey all acknowledge that to be literate is to claim to belong to a particular privileged group. But it is Stuckey who considers whether the object of literacy *should* be to privilege.

In an influential study of African Vai culture, Scribner and Cole were surprised to find that literacy had little importance among the Vai except for those who attended school. As Stuckey points out, the two ethnographers had assumed that literacy would give the Vai the same opportunities and status as would be given a "literate" person in Western culture (29–30). Why, she questions, should we assume that the importance granted verbal literacy in our own culture automatically confers status in other communities? And if that is a basic North American (Western) assumption, then how does this perception affect relationships between the literate (the haves) and the illiterate (the have-nots)? If literacy—knowledge about language and its cultural conventions—is thought to establish privilege, then the personal interactions between tutor and tutee may unknowingly replicate positions which disempower students by reminding them what they do not have.

Recent personal narratives like Mike Rose's *Lives on the Boundary* (1989) or Richard Rodriguez's *A Hunger of Memory* (1982) demonstrate that deeply held notions about what comprises literacy directs professional choices as well as personal interactions. These narratives point out that just as personal definitions of literacy separate one group from another, they likewise disable communication and action between groups. This particularly manifests itself in the grading system of the academy, where positive reinforcement is given to particular kinds of expression. Writing center tutors claim to be exempt from these evaluative claims of the institution.

Yet tutors do help shape student papers to conform to a particular ideologically constructed idea of "good academic writing." James Thomas Zebroski's (1990) examination of social class and writing in the classroom points to the politics of any such act of evaluation which might serve to silence the students in order to reinforce a dominant definition of literacy: "to create meaning, the reader must evaluate, and the evaluative moment—no matter how long deferred or how positively worded or how complicated or how developmental—is both inevitable and political" (82). Mike Rose's struggle against academic authority, Richard Rodriguez's inability to abandon the authority conferred on him by academe, and James Zebroski's realization that he merely functions "as an agent of the status quo" (82) mirror the positions in which tutee and tutor often find themselves.

Can instructor and tutor training, collaborative practices and social theories subvert personal, culturally constructed ideas about privileged academic literacy out of which teaching and tutoring proceed? Should they? If those who hold unexamined definitions about academic literacy teach students to be "literate," can they collaborate without dominating, or socially construct meanings without controlling outcomes? Should they?

Research has pushed tutors in our writing centers to examine many of our gender and racial stereotypes, but most of those images are likewise connected to stereotypes about literacy. Just as "diversity in race, class, and gender is often boiled down to the image of the classroom [or tutorial] as a benevolent melting pot of experiences and perspectives" (Malinowitz 1990, 153), types of literacy blend into one perspective out of which tutors operate. Instead of focusing only on how the students' abilities fail as literate practices, writing centers need "a shift from student problems, attitudes and fears as the sources of scrutiny to a serious questioning of teacher ideology" (Malinowitz 1990, 154).

Critiques of literacy definitions obligate an examination of the culture within tutors' own centers and of the operative definitions of literacy which define tutorial practices. Such critiques support current examinations of "literacy" which promote the development of multiple perspectives, contending that "true literacy means examining one's society, not simply manipulating surface features of text" (Schilb 1991, 187).

During one of our Writing Center meetings, tutors answered the question, "What does it mean to be literate?" Many respondents agreed that to be literate "is to be able to read and write about and for various discourse communities." While this seemed to be an inclusive definition, during a discussion that followed, tutors observed that students "just don't understand the idea of conventions," that it is "difficult for students to understand why [a particular professor] might want authoritative arguments first," or "how [students] might sneak their own ideas in like I do." Tutors began to question why they felt the need to give students strategies "to play the professor game. I mean, we say we 'empower writers,' but for what? or who? and *why?*"

As we examined the practices which lead students to create the kind of text the tutor-as-institutional-representative would create, we began to explore how the tutor's and student's interpretations of literacy substantiate the numbing concept that writing and reading are merely technologies. Thus, as a purveyor of technique (see Malinowitz 53), the tutor attempts to "raise" the students' literacy by supplying strategies which students lack. But students often view what we call "strategies" as technologies: if they "buy" them and "use" them, they can automatically generate an acceptable product. When literacy is viewed in this way, students become concerned with manipulation of the physical portions of text at the expense of understanding that texts are written for a particular purpose. If tutors' deeply held ideas about literacy unknowingly correspond to the idea of literacy as technology, then the student does not learn strategies as much as perform technique. Likewise, rather than examine why a particular form is being privileged over the students' particular ways of speaking and writing, both student and tutor conspire to disenfranchise the student, masking this as "empowerment," in order to create a "literate" text.

Writing center tutorials can provide students with opportunities to examine language's effects on community practices, to understand texts as collaborative, context-bound communications. But if our practices, supported by traditional concepts of literacy, remain unexamined, they will continue to encourage a formulaic, technological approach more than we might suspect. Recent conference presentations tagged as "good" tutorials those in which tutors led students toward particular interpretations. In each, the tutors knew the kind of paper usually expected, as well as the level of analysis demanded by the teacher. What follows is a scene made up from three such presentations: this "model" session proceeds with the student naming a possible symbol, the color red, in an attempt to "write about a symbol in this novel."

Tutor: So what do you think of when you think of the color red?

Student: blood, roses . . .

Tutor: Do you think of fire?

Student: Yeah, fire too.

Tutor: And how does fire tie in to this story about guilt? [The tutor, not the student, supplied the word "guilt."]

Student: Well, the sin is bad and the people thought she was a witch; they burned witches.

Tutor: Yes, they did burn witches, but once a witch was burned what did they think happened to her?

Student: After she was dead? (tutor nods) Well . . . Oh! she'd go to hell—fire!

Rather than allowing the student to pursue the connection between "witch," "sin," and "red," the tutor quickly moved the student to an "appropriate" interpretation. While the student produced an acceptable product, he also was led to rely on the tutor to set up the collaboration that would occur between the text (his ideas) and the reader (the teacher). The tutor, who *has* the knowledge, leads the student, who doesn't have it, so that a properly coded literate product results. Instead of looking at how or why a literature teacher looks at symbols so the *student* can proceed, this unbalanced collaboration reinforces the notion of literacy as technology. By examining the literate practices of that discourse community, the student could better understand what a symbol is, and how it operates in a novel. This kind of collaboration is evidenced by the following transcript from a tutorial:

Tutor: Hi, how are you? [small talk]

Tutor: What are you working on? [Student explains assignment]

Tutor: So what do you think is the purpose of this assignment?

Student: Huh?

Tutor: What is your instructor asking you to do? [Student explains assignment]

Tutor: Why do you think she wants you to do that? [Student explains assignment]

Tutor: I guess what I mean is that I was wondering why your instructor wants you to do this? Is she just seeing what you know? Finding out if you can repeat classroom information? Asking if you can use gothic architectural terminology? Asking you to write in the form of an art historian?

Student: Well, I'm supposed to imagine I'm the builder of this church. So . . . um . . . I guess I have to use the terms they used then. Oh, there weren't any buttresses yet so I don't have to explain them! . . . But how do I start?

Tutor: As you probably learned in composition, a lot of academic papers begin with an intro—stating a purpose up front. But this seems like a different assignment.

> *Student:* The teacher said this is like a narrative—a journal where I write observations. But I don't know what he wants!
>
> *Tutor:* Journal writing can be formal, informal . . . do you want to call the instructor and . . .
>
> *Student:* There was . . . wait a minute [shuffles through papers]. Here's an example from the building of St. Denis . . . it's like he wrote it for himself, but knew someone'd read it, you know? Like I could say, "Today I walked around the site of the cathedral" and then just, you know, describe what's there. It's casual, but not too much . . . it tells [the instructor] I know what a cathedral is.

In this case the tutor does not discount the student's capability to examine words and ideas, and begins to validate the student's language community. In turn, the student is not struggling to guess what it is the tutor-as-institutional-representative knows, and she can begin to think about *what* a particular assignment is asking her to do with language. The student can use her already acquired language abilities to examine another kind of community and identify its particular ways of thinking and expressing. There is no mysterious secret writing formula from which she has been kept; there is no magical acquisition of rules which will produce a text with all the required surface features. But hopefully she can discover her capacity to use her own knowledge of language to determine reasons for others' practices, and she can begin to define those practices herself.

Covino's (1991) "literacy as magic" metaphor is helpful in understanding this difference between a tutorial based on technological definitions of literacy and one based on reflectivity and critique. For those considered illiterate in the traditional sense of encoding and decoding, writing *does* seem magical. Students privilege the words and ideas of those who hold positions of shamanistic power while subordinating the words and ideas of those who don't—themselves. They hope that if they learn the right formula, as provided by a tutor, they can produce textual wonders. Students from whom an analysis of literate practices within the academic community is withheld can perceive tutors as magically manipulating surface features to produce acceptable texts.

This picture of writing center tutor and student promotes what Covino terms "false-incorrect magic," or for the purposes of this discussion, false-incorrect rhetoric. Covino (1990) points out that when a practice is reduced to such magic it

> [is] reductive
> exploits the law of motion by restriction of choices
> originates in the center of mass [academic] culture, as
>   technique
> [is] practiced as inculcation
> results in adaptation. (27)

In the first tutorial which dealt with the color red, the tutor not only reduces the category "symbol" to a specific, "red," but therein restricts the student's choice of symbol and referent. The tutor, knowing in what direction he wishes to proceed, relies on his own discipline's technique by generating the "right" questions—a process which may well seem magical to a student uninitiated in that discipline's conventions. The student, fixed on answering "correctly," is proud of his response as he discovers and then adapts the tutor's point of view.

Tutorial practice not based on manipulation, but reliant on reflection and critique, fits Covino's definition of "true- correct magic" or true-correct rhetoric for it

> [proves] generative
> enlarges the grounds for action by the creation of
>   choices
> originates on the margins of mass [academic] culture,
>   as critique
> [is] practiced as dialogue
> results in integration. (27)

In the second tutorial concerning gothic architecture, the student generates the ideas when given a series of choices and the option to produce her own choice. Through dialogue, the student must use her own language to critique and thereby discover a response; she is not encouraged to rely on a tutor's interpretation (those at the center of academic culture) but to examine and draw on her own experiences from the margins. Her resistance, rather than compliance, results in the integration of her ideas with those "others." The distinction seems very fine, and indeed, most writing center practitioners assume they promote integration instead of adaptation. Or, they recognize the adaptation, but—lacking an examination of the assumptions directing their practices—justify adaptation by claiming it was the student's choice.

However, left unexamined, writing centers often support adaptation of a dominant ideology and, therefore, a dominant "literacy." Despite our collaborative practices, we cannot undermine these technological notions and prescriptive methods. We therefore fail to see that our practices can "reproduce the status quo: the rigid hierarchy of teacher-centered classrooms is replicated in the tutor-centered writing center in which the tutor is still the seat of all authority but is simply pretending it isn't so" (Lunsford 1991, 7).

Instead of merely substantiating the separatist ideology inherent in academic literacy, tutoring can provide a space where students see writing and reading as reflective processes. Such tutorials encourage not only an acquisition of skills, but, as Rose and Rodriguez have shown us, a translation of self. While "translation" denotes change, these words hint not only at a response of subject to context, but to an actual adaptation, a change, in the context.

Tutors have the opportunity to show students that "the text is not just a message connecting two people: it is also a mediating agency for a single individual as he or she changes in response to the task of creating or comprehending symbolic verbal meaning" (Tuman 1987, 24). In creating and comprehending text, however, the onus should not be just on the student; there are two "single individual[s]" involved in writing and then reading a text. Literacy, then, involves the task of constructing as well as deconstructing ourselves (as writers), the text (as readers), and the world around us (as collaborative re-constructors of contexts).

If literacy includes this process, then the act of becoming literate in any community must entail reflection by all of its members. While this reflective analysis may involve grammatical concepts and other surface features, its use in a writing center should be to understand the purposes lodged in communicative acts. We have all worked with students who see commas as grammatical decorations whose placement is dictated by a book of rules. These students try to apply the rules from a book to the words they have written in the hope that if they do this correctly, their text will be correct, i.e., "literate." If achieving literacy involves only corrections, applications of rule and form, then "like all technologies, though it may provide certain possibilities, . . . [it] does not in and of itself make any changes in the world or in individuals" (Cooper 1991, 59).

What all writers need to know is that "learning to write is learning that *your words* are being read" by a particular group which not only separates itself with language but with ways of thinking about language (Brandt 1990, 5, emphasis added). Tutors should be providing students with opportunities to understand that "from a process perspective, literacy does not take its nature from texts. Rather, texts take their natures from the ways that they are serving the acts of writing and reading. . . . literacy [is] not the narrow ability to deal with texts but the broad ability to deal with other people as a writer or reader" (Brandt 13–14).

Unfortunately, our tutorial practices often support adaptations primarily to textual conventions, not to other people. By encouraging the student's obligation to adapt academic practices without understanding the ideological motives behind such requests, tutors, as well as teachers of composition, "repress and commonly assimilate the majority of American writers who obtain credentials in higher education, indoctrinating them into openly middle-class values of propriety, politeness, and cooperation. By taking as one of its goals the 'conventional,' composition assures that these values will maintain their continuing, if disguised or displaced, status" (Miller 1991, 7).

It is no wonder that during one of our recent meetings tutors complained that they feel "obligated to support writing practices that silence students' ideas and devalue them as learners." These tutors find themselves caught between the academy and their own theories; they object to the fact that students' "particular writing classroom and major field of study create separable and different 'standard' writing practices" (Miller 1991, 8). Miller explains what tutors in our Center experience: that students are not being "taught the agendas of these communities for including and excluding particular alternative interpretations or standards" (9). Tutors find that they must not only confront students with these "interpretations or standards," but also encourage students to positively examine their own already held literate practices. Without this comparative reflectivity, classroom writing practices and the assumptions embedded in them continue to undermine student success.

By examining their own agendas as well, tutors can stop duplicating environments that promote literacy as technology, and that separate the "haves" from the "have-nots." Seeing how this perspective determined educational practices from the very beginning of their school experiences helps tutors see the cycle of disempowerment they may continue to create in the writing center. Initially, basic readers, and later, inexperienced writers, see reading and writing as something happening *to* them not something over which they have power. Children's teachers often attune their students to the technical aspects of sound, line, and circle, stressing perfection of form and imitation. Clifford Geertz (1983) notes that children learning to read struggle trying "to make sense of the profusion of things that happen to them" (119). As a result, "children learn basic letters and sounds (and thus improve their achievement test scores), [but] they may not experience the social and personal power of print" (Dyson 1991, 118). Similarly because students have learned the rules, they may "write sentences with periods, but they may not organize those sentences to serve varied pragmatic purposes or to give voice to their daily concerns" (Dyson 1991, 110). If students believe from the start that school, like reading and writing, is happening *to* them, they will not believe they have the right, nor will they have the ability, to evaluate the system's language that is being used to shape them; they will not think of literacy as critique.

Tutors can also "happen to" students. Since our tutors come from this long tradition of language as doorkeeper technology, it is not surprising that, despite training in nondirective pedagogy, they may impose rules upon students instead of practicing reflective critique. As Covino (1991) indicates, such a reductive view of literacy is oppressive and results in mimicry. As tutors note, employing mimicry proves an efficient means of conducting a tutorial when "a student needs to get her paper in by 5:00 today!" This reductive and economically efficient practice ends up encouraging the image of a writing center as a band-aid service. In turn, the practice promotes the idea of literacy as technology. Likewise, writing center theories and stated practices may support the acknowledgement of multiple literacies, but actual practices betray an allegiance to institutional images of writing, learning, and writing centers.

There is no question that the academy's view must change along with the tutorial context, but what does that mean for a tutorial conducted right now? To teach writing in any of the current academic areas to students from many literate backgrounds, students, tutors, and teachers must engage in a critique of the way words build all communities. The difficulty involved in that process lies in understanding that words do not derive meaning merely through surface manipulation of marks on a page; the imitation of structural correctness will not, by its very correctness, make words "better" or make students "more" literate, "better" organized as human beings, or "more" creative. Engaging in reflective practices provokes changing definitions of literacy by unmasking the mystique surrounding that technological and privileging perception of reading and writing. Through critique, writers can choose to create texts which *use* surface constructions rather than produce texts which are subject *to* those technologies. When both students and tutors understand the limitations of a literacy definition which privileges and separates, they can begin to engage in a true dialogue that examines why and how texts serve different communities.

I can't say yet that I have a transcript of the perfect tutorial—one that truly resists adaptation. As tutors here know, we have more to examine—ourselves as well as our community. We have yet to engage in a wider dialogue with the composition instructors—often equally dissatisfied with their own duality. And of course, the dialogue and reflectivity must, ideally, continue throughout the academy. Nonetheless, we are beginning to open places within our tutorials where students, along with us, catch glimpses of "why" and "to what end" and "for whose benefit," along with the usual "how." It is risky at times because seeing that the gate to institutions is not as widely opened as students think can anger as well as disappoint them. But it can also give them the right and encouragement to speak out, to be heard, to change their contexts. As tutors, we can only continue to unmask our own and others' concepts about literacy. By redefining "literacy," we can work toward undermining the use of reading and writing for oppressive, reductive ends, encouraging, instead, generative processes of transformation not only of students and ourselves, but of the academy.

References

Brandt, Deborah. 1990. *Literacy as Involvement: The Acts of Writers, Readers, and Texts.* Carbondale: Southern Illinois University Press.

Cooper, Marilyn. 1991. "'We Don't Belong Here Do We?' A Response to *Lives on the Boundary* and *The Violence of Literacy.*" *Writing Center Journal* 12.1, 48–62.

Covino, William A. 1991. "Magic, Literacy and the *National Enquirer.*" *Contending with Words*. Ed. Patricia Harkin and John Schilb. New York: Modern Language Association, 23–37.

Dyson, Annie Haas. 1991, Fall. "Viewpoints: The Word and the World—Reconceptualizing Written Language Development or Do Rainbows Mean a Lot to Little Girls." *Research in the Teaching of English* 25.1, 97–120.

Geertz, Clifford. 1983. *Local Knowledge.* New York: Basic Books.

Harkin, Patty, and John Schilb, eds. 1991. *Contending with Words.* New York: Modern Language Association.

Heath, Shirley Brice. 1989. *Ways with Words.* New York: Cambridge University Press.

Lunsford, Andrea. 1991. "Collaboraton, Control, and the Idea of a Writing Center." *Writing Center Journal* 12.1, 3–10.

Malinowitz, Harriet. 1990. "The Rhetoric of Empowerment in Writing Programs." *The Right to Literacy.* Eds. Andrea Lunsford, Helene Moglen, and James Slevin. New York: Modern Language Association, 152–63.

Miller, Susan. 1991. *Textual Carnivals: The Politics of Composition.* Carbondale: Southern Illinois University Press.

Piaget, Jean. 1932. *The Language and Thought of the Child.* Trans. Marjorie Gabin New York: Harcourt Brace.

Rodriguez, Richard. 1982. *The Hunger of Memory: The Education of Richard Rodriguez: An Autobiography.* Boston: D. R. Godine.

Rose, Mike. 1989. *Lives on the Boundary: The Struggles and Achievements of America's Underprepared.* New York: Free Press.

Schilb, John. 1991. "Cultural Studies, Postmodernism and Composition." *Contending with Words.* Eds. Patricia Harkin and John Schilb. New York: Modern Language Association, 173–88.

Scribner, Sylvia, and Michael Cole. 1981. *The Psychology of Literacy.* Cambridge: Harvard University Press.

Stuckey, J. Elspeth. 1991. *The Violence of Literacy.* Portsmouth, NH: Boynton/Cook Publishers.

Tuman, Myron. 1987. *Preface to Literacy: An Enquiry into Pedagogy, Practice, and Progress.* Tuscaloosa: University of Alabama Press.

Vygotsky, L. S. 1962. *Language and Thought.* Cambridge, MA: MIT Press.

Zebrowski, James Thomas. 1990. "The English Department and Social Class: Resisting Writing." *The Right to Literacy,* eds. Andrea Lunsford, Helene Moglen, and James Slevin. New York: Modern Language Association, 81–87.

15 Tutor and Student Relations: Applying Gadamer's Notions of Translation

Mary Abascal-Hildebrand
University of San Diego

Reflective writing tutoring is not a simple activity to conduct. Gadamer (1976) suggests that the kind of understanding needed for the interpretation and translation we find in reflective tutoring "has to be acquired" (146). A tutor I will refer to as Peter is a seasoned writing center tutor; he comments about the challenge that tutors experience in their attempts to consider all that they must: "Most of the tutors I know tell horror stories about their first sessions with students" as they attempt to unify ideas about tutoring, writing, and writing assignments with ideas that signify students' lifeworlds. This kind of reflective tutoring arises from a parts-to-whole, or hermeneutic, quality available in translative tutoring. A philosophical analysis of this translation illuminates the ethical dimension inherent in the human relationships that make up tutoring; this philosophical awareness nurtures both students and tutors.

Hans-Georg Gadamer has unified philosophy and hermeneutics into a philosophical hermeneutics that expands the ethical dimension of translation.[1] Gadamer's language philosophy addresses not only the translation of speech, but also the translation of written language. Therefore, his work is appropriate for explaining that more conscious use of language is important in promoting writing tutoring as a means to learn. Tutoring that enables both tutors and students to leave a tutoring event thinking and acting differently as writers enables them to renew themselves as persons. Tutoring that affirms students' voices through their writing can enable students to renegotiate classroom relationships through their ability to address in writing what they understand, rather than what they imagine their teachers will allow them to write. This is tutoring praxis.

Gadamer (1975) defines praxis in a way that is useful for discussions about tutoring renewal. He writes about the limitations of methodological approaches to language contexts and about the need in translation to understand understanding itself. His work is based on the idea that praxis is the ethical goodwill that can be created in everyday understanding. However, he points out a paradox which concerns tutoring praxis: praxis is not easy to achieve because understanding, even when acquired, is always limited. Therefore, understanding is a never-quite-fully-accomplished activity. Gadamer's work is based on the idea that partial understanding and misunderstanding are inevitable. A tutor I will call Marie explains how she lives with the paradox while tutoring: "You want to cover a ton of territory, but it's not my nature to overload them or they won't pick up anything. So, you have to find a happy medium."

This chapter acknowledges the insights of several tutors expressed in an ethnography conducted at a theory-based writing center in a large, midwestern public university. These tutors' reflections illustrate the kind of thinking that reflective tutoring demands. Yet, while these tutors' insights portray thoughtful, reflective tutoring, some of their insights also portray frustration with the complexity in tutoring and with the challenge they find in translating for students an academic world that would rather use writing for evaluation instead of as a means to learn. This essay proposes that understanding tutoring within a philosophical hermeneutic perspective can not only engage new tutors to become reflective more readily, but it can sustain those who are already reflective tutors as they move toward higher and higher levels of understanding. It also proposes that this perspective can enable participants in writing centers to demonstrate for teachers in universities the value in using writing also to teach rather than only to test.

While interpreting and translating are not simple processes to understand and practice, tutors who are more aware of these processes can be better tutors. Another tutor, whom I will call Laurie, who has considerable writing center experience, explains her awareness of the translative dimension of tutoring ethics.

> I love it. It's all about being in balance, being able to adjust, trying to keep the balance in the discussion so students don't get upset, paying attention to how they are reacting. It's also about fairness and not being judgmental so they learn what they need to do well but not do it too soon or it'll stop their writing.

Reflective tutors interpret and translate more consciously; however, conscious translation is neither a method nor an arrangement that can be settled ahead of time between tutors and students. Rather, translation is something that happens to an interpreter in the process of using reflective judgment to simultaneously interpret and translate what she understands. When this something happens in speech, an interpreter becomes a translator. The implication is that when this something happens in a conversation, the partners become translators for one another. Their thinking lifts their conversation into a new realm—an ethical realm because they base their conversation on mutual regard for mutual understanding. Thus as Ricoeur (1984) notes, we only become aware of what we need for understanding when we are confronted with being unable to understand. Laurie explains, "Being a tutor means creating a whole new thing with each student from where you think they're coming from and from what goes back and forth. You can't assume things about students—you have to ask them." Tutors who expect that they must rethink tutoring with each student enable students to exit tutoring sessions more able to write.

Reflective tutoring is created out of an attitude toward thinking itself. This attitude is one which considers that all persons are capable of reflective action. It is the belief that they are able to think about engaging with others in ways that enable each person involved to fuse what is already known with whatever they are beginning to know. Translation arises from within this reflective process (Gadamer 1975, 1976). Translative tutors work to interpret what they believe confronts students so that they can make students' understandings more available to them. According to Laurie,

> What I have learned is that students can only write from where they really are and I think that the best way to teach writing is to use their own papers to teach it to them because whatever came out of their heads onto the paper is *something they* know about—they know how it got there.

Reflective thinking by translative tutors moves both students and tutors toward fusing new horizons wherein they make new judgments about themselves, think and act differently than before, and develop the potential to write differently.

Reflective and translative tutors are not merely reproducers of linguistic codes, or even interpreters for students of professors' writing assignments. Tutors do not merely reproduce models of writing for students that they can remove wholly from the writing center and use as templates. When tutors are more reflective concerning their potential as translators they can create more meaningful translations; they can encourage students to think of writing as a means for fusing new horizons of understanding about themselves as students and about the ideas they find in the disciplines they study. Thus, as elusive as translation may be, a translative tutoring stance can promote writing as a means to learn.

However, translation is not an easy process: "one tries to get inside the other person in order to understand his point of view . . . [but] this does not automatically mean that understanding is achieved in a conversation" (Gadamer 1975, 348). Rather, all translation is a compromise. Laurie points out the nature of this compromise for her: "[Tutoring is] that middle spot. It's not exactly a comfortable spot; you're always a little doubtful. I'm still doubtful but I'm comfortable being that way." While translation is a compromise, tutors who are aware of the reflective and translative character of compromise can be better tutors. Laurie explains: "You have to be real careful. You can't say, 'This has to be changed.' If we can lead them up to see it themselves that's the very best thing we can do." Peter illustrates this compromise in his attempt to protect the student-teacher relationship: "The downside of being a tutor between the student and the professor is that you're walking on the edge of a sword; you can't always be candid about an assignment that seems unfair—an assignment from hell."

Gadamer (1975) offers, "a compromise can be achieved in the to and fro of dialogue, so the translator will seek the best solution (to the interpretation) in the toing and froing of weighing up and considering possibilities . . . a compromise" (348). Further, his work supports the practice of writing tutoring: he contends that in the sphere of grammar and rhetoric, "language is the middle ground in which understanding and agreement . . . take place between two people" (348). Marie says of her experience in this middle ground: "I see myself as a diplomat. You've got various parties you're trying to accommodate all of them—I personally find this exciting. I'm happy with that." Acting consciously in this middle ground can be described as fulfilling a hermeneutic dimension that unifies the conversations that take place within reflective tutoring. Laurie speaks of her awareness in unifying these aspects: "My sense of self is all of these different elements combined." Another tutor I will call Jane agrees: "I am an anchor for both communities—students and teachers."

Therefore, writing center tutors need to understand the hermeneutic dimension in conversation as a unification of the part-to-whole of translation. By making this dimension available to themselves through discussions and exchanges with one another about the theory and practice of tutoring, they can learn with one another. They open their vistas on writing as they signify how they themselves engage in translation. Peter talks about his own needs as a writer in the writing center:

> We bring papers here, too. It helps because no matter how good a writer you are it never hurts to have someone else look at it. We all share writing with each other. If we have a spare minute we say, "Here, look at this," because what you think you're saying is not always what a reader thinks you're saying.

Translation becomes more clearly the process of joining a set of reciprocating parts. An awareness of this reciprocity makes it possible for both tutors and students to engage in the "play" of spoken and written thought (Gadamer 1975, 91–119).

A significant benefit of such a hermeneutic awareness is that interpretive and translative language calls for a praxis stance which requires weighing the

many and varied aspects of each tutoring context. It stipulates an acknowledgement, either definitively or tacitly, that each student's lifeworld is
uniquely composed, and, therefore, each tutoring session must be uniquely
composed. Laurie's statement that "You just can't assume things about students. You have to ask questions" points to a tutor's obligation to not impose
from without, using only general acknowledgements. With a praxis perspective, tutors are much less likely to become the "little teachers" about whom
Bruffee (1984) warns. Rather, within a praxis perspective, they relate as
participants and experience a sense of efficacy as both thinkers and writers.
This moral dimension heightens the need to reexamine tutoring within
each session so that tutors continuously renew themselves through their interactions.

Often, tutors are more conscious of methodological aspects of tutoring, and
are less conscious of how thought undergirds tutoring relationships. When
tutors understand tutoring merely as a method, they apply themselves as
mechanics, as if they believe their job is to leverage their knowledge against
students. Students usually expect that tutors are available to "fix" their writing, or at least to tell them what to do to fix it. Peter contends that this happens
more with students who come to his writing center for the first time or "if their
professors made them come to the writing center. Often it is obvious they
don't want to be here. They think our job is to tell them what to write." As
Peter points out, unless they have had experience in writing centers that stress
process, they are unaware of the relational dimension of tutoring. Students
who bring this perspective to the writing center pose a challenge to the
reflective tutor.

Likewise, university teachers are less likely to know about writing processes in a language theory context. They often misunderstand the theoretical
framework of writing centers; they imagine that their students who go to them
are likely to gain methodological rather than interpretive insights about writing. Peter laments: "I have only had a few [professors] over the years get back
to me to tell me how the tutoring made a difference. They don't often know
when they make impossible writing assignments."

In the beginning of tutoring sessions, tutors generally seek and extract
information to learn more about specific issues within assignments and
courses; students provide that information. The initial talking is more of an
information exchange than it is a creation of new meanings. An information
exchange can only initiate a tutoring event. If the event continues only as an
information exchange, it cannot become tutoring. Becoming aware of the way
in which thinking undergirds tutoring can encourage tutors, students, and
teachers to move beyond imagining tutoring as merely methodological or
technical support. Hermeneutics enables tutors and others who engage with

them to understand writing, not as a methodology, but ethically mastered "as an art" (Gadamer 1975, 345).

However, even if unconsciously, when tutors and students create conversations about the assignment and the course it reflects, they engage in a linguistic realm where they interpret and translate for one another; it is a realm in which they do not specifically plan their thoughts and actions. Their conversations center around relevant meanings that are both tacit and acknowledged, and that are based on the relationship they create by virtue of their sitting and talking together. These conversations are guided by the participants' rationality concerning one another and the writing process. This is the kind of conversation that Richard Bernstein (1983), in his work on science, hermeneutics, and praxis, portrays in examining methodology. He writes that a "true" conversation

> is not to be confused with idle chatter or a violent babble of competing voices—[it] is an extended and open dialogue which presupposes a background of intersubjective agreements and a tacit sense of relevance. There may be different emphases and stresses by participants in a conversation, and in a living conversation there is always unpredictability and novelty. (2)

When I told Laurie of Bernstein's definition of a conversation, she said, "It sounds like tutoring!" Such conversations are the essence of a process-oriented, ethical tutoring and are created rather than conducted. Gadamer (1975) writes about creating conversation.

> We say that we "conduct" a conversation, but the more fundamental a conversation is, the less its conduct lies within the will of either partner. Thus a fundamental conversation is never one that we want to conduct. Rather, it is more generally correct to say that we fall into conversation, or even that we become involved in it. (345)

In this kind of translation/conversation, each speaker must speak in ways that enable the other to grasp intended meanings. Though tutors may be students, they do not know students as particular persons, with particular lifeworlds, in particular courses, charged with particular assignments. They can only try to understand what each student brings to tutoring. Tutors use tutor language to talk with students about topics, assignments, and writing, to grasp the essence of topics and assignments, and to rethink as they write. Yet they must be aware of the need to continuously translate their language so that it is usable by students.

When students use their own language to talk about topics, assignments, and courses so that tutors can know more about the writing assignment, tutors must appropriate that language in order to conduct tutoring conversations. In turn, when tutors use the language of writing, they may use words and ideas

which are not necessarily known to students. They must also use the language
of writing in ways that students will be able to understand. Peter describes his
understanding of the challenge in translating among the various languages:

> Students worry that professors think they should know more than they
> do. I think professors come off that way because they are so interested in
> and knowledgeable about the topic that they intimidate the inexperienced
> student. Students say there are a thousand elements to write about. The
> first thing I say to them is that a paper doesn't have a thousand ele-
> ments—a good paper has one focus.

Thus, there is a third language they both must try to understand. It comprises
tutor, student, and professor/course/discipline/ academic languages. This third
language must be appropriated by both tutors and students through their
respective languages by virtue of translative interactions: "I tell them a paper
is not like a lecture, where a professor talks about this study, that study, and
another study that work around a central theme, because there is a lot that's
told in a lecture. Papers don't tell a thousand things" (Peter). This multiplicity
of languages points to the need for tutors to take a reflective, translative stance
in tutoring so that they can make available the multiple translations needed by
students.

   This multiplicity points to another dimension of difficulty inherent in
grasping the essential meanings of students and teachers: to become a living
bridge, tutors must be able to grasp the essential meanings of their *own*
tutoring lifeworld, and make the translations available, not as pairs of meanings extracted from some artificial matrix. Rather, tutors must make these
translations available through *newly constituted* meanings that are created out
of each tutoring session. Peter illustrates Gadamer's notion of the hermeneutic
(interpretive) fusion of horizons:

> There are times when you know what the professor is looking for and the
> student does not see that and you try to explain. You can't make the
> student see something—you hesitate to put words in a professor's mouth.
> So, I say, "It looks to me that this is what she's calling for."

Constituting meanings by fusing them from earlier meanings calls for a
different kind of interpretation and bridging. It calls for experiencing a translative stance as one from within which an interpretation takes place; it calls
for an interpretive stance that grasps "the other."

   Tutors who think about translation this way do not assume that what they
say or do is understood entirely by the student just the way the tutor understands. Instead, tutors who think about interpretation as translation will remember that students take tutors' interpretations, interpret them themselves
through their own lifeworlds, and come away with understandings that are
actually a blend, or a fusion of the two: "I'm better now at not telling them

what I shouldn't be telling them. It's such a hard thing to do" (Laurie). Reflective interpretation consciously considers the lifeworld of the hearer of an interpretation; thus, it becomes translation; it becomes praxis.

This essay began by pointing out that tutors do not merely reproduce or interpret, but that they interpret and translate simultaneously. Gadamer explains that understanding takes place as translation; it is not merely the result of interpretation, although interpretation is necessary for translation. Therefore, interpretation and translation take place at the same time, not in some piecemeal fashion.

Gadamer (1975) proposes that translations are always interpretations; translation is what occurs *as* the translator completes an interpretation, not *when* she does. His point can be used to describe tutoring as rooted in translation, for "every translation is at the same time an interpretation. We can even say that it is the completion of the interpretation that the translator has made of the words given" (346). As tutors interpret the words that surround the tutoring and the assignment, the words serve the translator, and the translation ultimately serves both the tutor and the student. To do this the tutor must be aware that the most suitable way to engage all of the words into a whole—a whole that includes the tutoring relationship—is to become aware of the way in which the whole is created simultaneously with its parts. This awareness of the parts and the whole requires the kind of reflective judgment noted earlier. Laurie explains: "Being in the middle, I accept [students] where they each are. To do this, I have to be fair to each of them, and fair to myself."

Such reflection is the kind that uses judgment about the words to be translated *at the same time* that it uses judgment to create the tutoring relationship for the translation of words promotes a reflective stance for the tutor *and* the student. This stance can release tutors from having to act methodologically; they can consciously translate both words *and* lifeworlds. They become better tutors when they learn that their tutoring is always about relationships, interpretations, and translations, and not about models, methods, or templates. Students benefit because they learn that thinking and talking about their writing within a tutoring relationship lifts writing out of a one-directional mode into a mode that not only allows but is built on shared thinking and expanded expression. This promotes a kind of self-conscious writing whereby students can call on what they know to support writing about topics they are exploring.

Understanding tutoring as translation encourages students' self-conscious writing, for when tutors and students come together they simultaneously interpret for themselves and for one another. As they accomplish interpretations they are translating one another's lifeworlds. They make it possible for one another to *act within* the tutoring event. Gadamer (1975) suggests that they fuse what they recognize already (the same) with their newer knowledge

(the different). In other words, they mediate a unity of sameness and difference in their language which moves them to action; tutoring is understanding
in action.

However, the act of tutoring is not achieved in writing alone, but is
achieved through speech. Tutoring language must be reflective so that it can
be recreated with each event because it is a language which tutors and students
create together again and again within *each* of their interactions.

Gadamer (1975) warns that "every conversation automatically pre-sup-
poses that the two speakers speak the same language" (347). Tutors as speakers must be aware of this presumption so that they can recreate greater
opportunities to grasp more of students' intended meanings. They can re-learn
to re-question themselves and the students they tutor, re-respond, re-attend to
signs, marks, and gestures, and re-clarify expressions. Tutors can become
interpreters and translators if they "Pay attention to how they are acting"
(Laurie).

However, while we can translate a text into speech, we can only do so by
virtue of knowing the "relationship to what is meant, to the object that is being
spoken about" (Gadamer 1975, 352). Applying this knowledge of relationships to writing tutoring, we can say that tutors can understand the writing
drafts students bring, but they can only understand them within the limits that
any written or oral text presents to a reader. That is, they are more limited by
the text until they engage in conversation with the student about the text. Their
conversation revives the intended meaning within the text and enables both
the tutor and the student to appropriate the meaning through reinterpreting it
for one another. Thus, they translate its meaning as they consider the larger
context in which the paper is being written. Even then their understanding is
limited by the text.

Gadamer (1975) explains that writing, however, presents us with the "real
hermeneutical task" because "writing involves self-alienation" (352). We do
not know that we do not understand something until we are confronted with
it. Writing is the real hermeneutic task because it requires us to account for
our not understanding in a way that is different from speech. Not understanding writing demands of a reader the most complex processes of understanding because its reading is conducted through "filters" such as time,
authorial intentionality, and the interpretive lens of the reader to imagine what
the author "means" in a text. When students bring papers to writing centers,
tutors have to step outside themselves to translate for themselves the meanings
the students apparently intend.

But Gadamer's (1976) warning can be applied to tutors: they do not have
to give up who they are in becoming more praxis-oriented tutors. He explains
that stepping aside is rather "an ecstatic self-forgetting that is experienced not

as a *loss* [emphasis in original] of self-possession, but as the free buoyancy of an elevation above oneself" (55). Thus, tutors can become themselves in tutoring: "For me, tutoring is an intellectual high" (Marie). Likewise, students do not have to give up who they are as persons in order to write; they can also step aside themselves in "an ecstatic self-forgetting" that enables them to leave behind outmoded ideas about writing. Thus, the translation required of students and tutors involves a willingness to "give over" to others' language. This giving over, self-alienation, or buoyancy is what enables tutors to promote students' higher elevations of understanding—their fusions of horizons.

As tutors and students engage in conversation that includes interpreting the assignment, along with the students' drafts, they apply their interpretive lenses and ideas about writing. This they do in the process of seeking understanding through translation of what is written and what they say to one another. They begin to use the process of understanding to understand. Yet, as students engage in a tutoring process, they often explicate their own writing as having other meanings than those which they have already written. This can be the beginning of students' awareness of the difference between writing as performance and writing as *possibility.*

In other words, the process of reading, interpreting, and translating enlarges the horizon of understanding for both the tutor and the student by virtue of their interaction. More translation is *possible* as their interaction deepens. Gadamer (1975) explains, "The horizon of understanding cannot be limited either by what the writer had originally in mind, or by the horizon of the person to whom the text was originally addressed" (356). Instead, the horizon is made possible by them.

University teachers are generally unaware of the dialectical nature of understanding. They typically assume that their assignments clearly represent what was intended. They may even assume that part of the student's task in a course is to learn enough, or even already know enough, to decipher assignments. Teachers typically also use assignments as a means for evaluating in a way that makes the writing assignment a noose for students' execution, campus style. This evaluation stance does not necessarily change when teachers refer students to writing centers. They may still expect writing center tutors to tell students what and how to write. Tutors must account for perspective and evaluative stances among teachers, but they must also account for the need to create the tutoring session around translation so that students can move from earlier ways of viewing their papers, their assignments, and their professors toward new realms of expressing what they understand.

Tutors who have become reflective, and whose reflection enables them to move their tutoring into higher and higher altitudes of understanding, are much more likely to be able to find substance in their tutoring because they understand its complexity. This reflective perspective must be encouraged because it addresses one of the frustrations tutors encounter during the complex tutoring process. But while writing centers can use hermeneutic theory to promote tutors' reflection and to enable them to explain their tutoring to themselves, centers can also use it to invite professors into their programs in myriad ways.

Teachers who understand the theoretical dimensions of writing center programs will be more able to respond to their students who go to them, and to the tutoring that goes on in them. Jane praises her experience in working as a tutor in her university's writing center project that uses theory to link tutors with students and a professor in a particular course. She sees this as an important way for everyone involved to learn about writing together. She sees it as a valuable way for teachers to consider the theory that undergirds writing center tutoring because they can see tutors in action. She says, "that is one of the reasons that I like working as a tutor linked to a particular course with a particular professor because I can get closer to where the student, the teacher, and the assignment intersect and we can work to make the assignments more appropriate to what's going on in the course." Her professor says of their writing-teaching relationship, "Jane is my teaching mirror—I look to her to learn how to think about writing assignments in my course." Another professor relates how, in his participation in this tutor-linked project, he came to a new understanding of writing: "Before I worked closely with a tutor, I thought that everyone wrote as sociologists write."

Moving students to new realms through engaging them in translating what they know into their papers can open doors into disciplines for students and promote teachers' belief in a transformative approach to writing and to writing center tutoring. Those who work in writing centers and in classrooms, both as tutors and as teachers, can use the thinking that Gadamer's philosophical hermeneutics provides to work together to shape new tutoring and classroom practice. Renewing teaching and tutoring relationships points out the potential for a praxis perspective on translative tutoring in enabling tutors, students, and teachers to powerfully renegotiate traditional forms of classroom life into those in which they can engage writing as a means to learn, and in which all who enter can become themselves.

Note

1. For a thorough discussion of Gadamer's thinking in philosophical hermeneutics, see Joel Weinsheimer's *Gadamer's Hermeneutics: A Reading of Truth and Method.* Yale University Press. 1991.

References

Bernstein, Richard J. 1983. *Beyond Objectivism and Relativism: Science, Hermeneutics, and Praxis*. Philadelphia: University of Pennsylvania Press.

Bruffee, Kenneth A. 1984. "Collaborative Learning and the 'Conversation of Mankind.' " *College English* 46, 635–52.

Gadamer, Hans-Georg. 1975. *Truth and Method*. Boston: Seabury Press.

———. 1976. *Philosophical Hermeneutics*. Translated and edited by David E. Linge. Berkeley: University of California Press.

Ricoeur, Paul. 1984. *Time and Narrative, Part I*. Chicago: University of Chicago Press.

Weinsheimer, Joel C. 1991. *Gadamer's Hermeneutics: A Reading of Truth and Method*. New Haven: Yale University Press.

Index

Editors

Joan A. Mullin is director of the Writing Center and the writing-across-the-curriculum program at the University of Toledo. Since beginning both programs in 1988, she has presented papers on writing center theory and practice, classroom pedagogy, critical hermeneutic theory, and educational philosophy at such conferences as MLA, CCCC, ECWCA, Midwest Philosophy of Education, Bergamo, and NCTE. She has published in various journals—*Composition Studies, American Journal of Pharmaceutical Education, The Sociology Teacher, The Writing Lab Newsletter*—and recently completed a guide to writing across the curriculum for the American Association of Colleges of Pharmacy. Her current work includes creating a cross-disciplinary hypertext stack for WAC instructors, and investigating the uses of visual literacy in the teaching of writing. She co-established the annual Ohio Conference on Learning Enhancement, is past chair of the East Central Writing Centers Association, and serves on the board of the National Writing Center Association, and on the editorial board of *Dialogue: A Journal for Writing Specialists.*

Ray Wallace, past president of the National Writing Centers Association, has served as writing center director and tutor-trainer at universities in Illinois, Hawaii, Tennessee, Georgia, and Louisiana. He has published widely on writing center issues, composition administration, and native and nonnative composition. Co-chair of the First National Writing Centers Conference, Wallace co-edited *The Writing Center: New Directions,* which won the NWCA 1991 Scholarship Award. He serves on the National Writing Center Board, on the editorial board of *The Writing Center Journal,* and co-edits *Dialogue: A Journal for Writing Specialists.* Wallace currently directs faculty in the humanities, sciences, and performing arts at the Louisiana Scholars College, the state's designated honors college in the liberal arts and sciences, at Northwestern State University in Natchitoches, Louisiana.

Contributors

Mary Abascal-Hildebrand is associate professor of leadership and administration at the University of San Diego, where she teaches ethics in an interdisciplinary program in American humanics and leadership, and research applications of critical hermeneutics. Her publications include "A School Board's Response to an Ethnographic Evaluation: Or, Whose Evaulation Is This, Anyway?" in *Speaking the Language of Power: Communication, Collaboration, and Advocacy* (1993) and "Understanding Education, Democracy, and Community Development in Thailand: Applying Gadamer's Theory of 'Play' in Participatory Research" in *Language and Culture: Research within a Critical Hermeneutic Tradition* (in press). She developed an interest in writing as a means to learn while participating in a theory-based writing center project at the University of Toledo, where she is also completing a Ph.D. in literary criticism.

John L. Adams is an English instructor at Loyola University in New Orleans. He directed the reading and writing lab at Morristown College. He has published articles in *The Writing Instructor, Journal of Teaching Writing,* and *Rhetoric Society Quarterly.* His books include *The Accomplished Writer,* with Katherine H. Adams, and *Teaching Advanced Composition: Why and How,* co-edited with Katherine H. Adams. He is currently working on a book concerning the University of Wisconsin's writing faculty.

Katherine H. Adams is associate professor of English at Loyola University in New Orleans. She directed the university's writing-across-the-curriculum program and four writing centers from 1987–93. She has published articles in *CCC, Rhetoric Review, Rhetoric Society Quarterly,* and other journals. Her books include *The Accomplished Writer* (with John L. Adams), *A History of Professional Writing Instruction in American Colleges,* and *Teaching Advanced Composition: Why and How,* an essay collection co-edited with John L. Adams. She is currently working on a grammar handbook and a book concerning the University of Wisconsin's writing faculty.

Pamela Farrell-Childers, Caldwell Chair of Composition at The McCallie School in Chattanooga, Tennessee, is the director of writing centers in public and private secondary schools, and has been president of NWCA, treasurer of ACE, and a poetry teacher/consultant for the Geraldine R. Dodge Foundation. Her books include *The High School Writing Center: Establishing and Maintaining One* (1989), *National Directory of Writing Centers* (1992), and *Programs and Practices: Writing Across the Secondary School Curriculum* with Anne Ruggles Gere and Art Young (1994). Her doctoral work emphasizes andragogy and lifelong learning for adults.

Sallyanne H. Fitzgerald, Ed.D., is chair of the Division of Language Arts at Chabot College in Hayward, California. She is involved in establishing a new WRAC center that will include two computer labs, funded through a Title III grant. Her current research interests are collaboration and writing center tutors. Previously at the University of Missouri-St. Louis, Sally tutored in the Writing Center, developed a tutor training program and student advisory group, and established a computer lab as part of the drop-in writing center services. She was the Director of the Center for Academic Development which housed the writing center and a board member of the Midwest Writing Centers Association where she served as associate chair and chair. Currently, Sally is an at-large member of the National Writing Centers Board and serves on the editorial board for *Writing Center Journal.* She has published a chapter in an award-winning writing center book and numerous articles, primarily in basic writing, as well as two texts for HarperCollins.

Alice M. Gillam is the founder and former director of the University of Wisconsin–Milwaukee's Writer Center, and now directs the composition program at UWM. She is completing a book, *Voices from the Center: Peer Tutoring in Theory and Practice,* and beginning work on an essay which offers a feminist view of writing program administration.

Muriel Harris is professor of English and director of the Writing Lab at Purdue University. She edits the *Writing Lab Newsletter,* has written several textbooks, including *The Prentice Hall Reference Guide to Grammar and Usage* (1994), as well as *Teaching One-to-One: The Writing Conference* (1986), and edited *Tutoring Writing: A Sourcebook for Writing Labs.* An ardent advocate of the one-to-one approach to teaching writing, she has authored book chapters and articles (appearing in journals such as *College English, College Composition and Communication, Journal of Basic Writing, Written Composition, English Journal,* and *Writing Center Journal*) on her study of individualized writing processes as well as writing center theory and pedagogy. She is currently at work coping with the mysteries of developing OWL (On-line Writing Lab), an electronic tutoring service, in her writing center.

Eric H. Hobson coordinates the writing programs and is director of the St. Louis College of Pharmacy Writing Center where he is working to develop a writing center-based writing-across-the-curriculum program to meet the needs of a professional school. The co-author of *Reading and Writing in High Schools: A Whole Language Approach,* his book *Where Theory and Practice Collide: The Writing Center* is forthcoming. In addition to publishing widely in writing center and composition journals, he serves on the Board of the National Writing Centers Association.

Jay Jacoby is professor of English at the University of North Carolina at Charlotte where he has directed its Writing Resources Center, composition program, and served as department chair. He was the 1986–87 President of the National Writing Centers Association, and currently serves on the editorial board of *The Writing Center Journal.* One of his major areas of interest is pedagogy, especially the affective dimensions of learning, and he has presented papers on this subject at several national conferences. His work has been published in *CCC, English Journal, The Writing Center Journal, Writing Lab Newsletter,* and *CEA Critic.*

Phyllis Lassner created the Peer Tutoring Program at the English Composition Board at the University of Michigan. She is now teaching in the writing program and women's studies program at Northwestern University. In addition to essays on feminist theory and composition studies, she has published two books on the Anglo-Irish writer, Elizabeth Bowen, essays on British women writers of World War II, and rediscovered and written the introduction to the reprint of the 1910 feminist novel *The Dangerous Age* by the Danish writer Karin Michaelis.

Tom MacLennan is associate professor of English at the University of North Carolina at Wilmington, where he is currently director of The UNCW Writing Place and teaches undergraduate and graduate courses in composition, literary response, and adolescent literature. He has also served as director of both the Foundations of Composition program and the Freshman Year Seminar. In addition, he was co-director of the Cape Fear Writing Project. An Executive Board member of the Southeastern Writing Center Association (SWCA) for the past four years and former editor of SWCA *Selected Papers,* his current interests include applications of mind-style theory in writing centers, writing and literature, popular culture, and English education.

Christina Murphy is director of the Writing Center and associate director of the Center for Academic Services at Texas Christian University. She is a member of the executive board of the National Writing Centers Association and is the President of the South Central Writing Centers Association and of the Texas Writing Centers Association. She also serves as chair of the National Writing Centers Association's Committee on Writing Centers and Graduate Education. Murphy is the editor of three scholarly journals: *Composition Studies, Studies in Psychoanalytic Theory,* and *English in Texas.* A member of the editorial board of *The Writing Center Journal* and of *Dialogue: A Journal for Writing Specialists,* she serves on the National Council of Teachers of English Committee to Review Affiliate Publications and is a member of the Board of Directors. Murphy has published a textbook on critical thinking skills and a study of Ann Beattie. She has contributed chapters to books on rhetoric and composition, her essays on rhetorical theory have appeared in a range of scholarly journals, and she has presented papers at many conferences in her field.

Julie Neff has attended the University of London, the University of Puget Sound, and holds a B.A. and an M.A. in English from Washington State University. She has also done graduate work in composition at the University of Washington. Neff teaches writing at the University of Puget Sound and directs The Center for Writing and Learning. She has presented papers at NCTE, CCCC, the Pacific Coast Writing Center Association Conference, and other regional conferences. She was editor of the *Washington English Journal.* Neff has also been president of the National Writing Centers Association and has contributed chapters to other books on college writing and writing centers.

Janice Witherspoon Neuleib, professor of English at Illinois State University, directs the University Center for Learning Assistance. She teaches courses in teaching literature and writing, directs the Illinois State Writing Project, directs writing assessment for the university, and writes in the fields of teacher research, composition theory, center administration, language and literacy, and learning styles. Her book with Maurice Scharton, *Inside/Out: A Guide to Writing,* translates composing theory into experiential classroom practice.

Maurice A. Scharton, associate professor of English at Illinois State University, teaches writing, language, and rhetorical theory. His essays on writing and writing assessment have appeared in *Research in the Teaching of English, College English, College Composition and Communication, Computers and Composition, The Writing Center Journal, The ADE Bulletin,* and other journals. His textbook, *Inside/Out: A Guide to Writing,* co-authored with Janice Neuleib, was published in 1993. He is presently at work on a study of motivation to write.